Edward Pollock

Historical and Industrial Guide to Petersburg, Virginia

Edward Pollock

Historical and Industrial Guide to Petersburg, Virginia

ISBN/EAN: 9783742812353

Manufactured in Europe, USA, Canada, Australia, Japa

Cover: Foto ©ninafisch / pixelio.de

Manufactured and distributed by brebook publishing software
(www.brebook.com)

Edward Pollock

Historical and Industrial Guide to Petersburg, Virginia

+ HISTORICAL +

AND

+ INDUSTRIAL +

GUIDE

TO

Petersburg, Virginia.

ILLUSTRATED.

EDWARD POLLOCK.

FOR SALE BY
T. S. BECKWITH & CO., BOOKSELLERS AND STATIONERS.
108 SYCAMORE STREET.

PREFACE.

H E compilation of this Volume has engaged my close and careful attention for the past five months. I claim for it nothing beyond fidelity to fact, so far as my best endeavors have been successful in ascertaining it.   •

In writing the "Historical Sketch" I have been greatly assisted by several friends for whose kindness I desire to express my gratitude. Many of the earlier details were supplied by Judge Drury A. Hinton, of the Supreme Court of Appeals of Virginia, and those relating to the siege of Petersburg, by Capt. W. Gordon McCabe; while the late Rev. E. S Gregory, of Lynchburg, whose widely-lamented death occurred on the 19th of the present month, most kindly placed at my disposal his "Sketch of the History of Petersburg," together with copious notes and clippings collected by him for a contemplated second edition, from which I borrowed liberally, in many places following the text. I was further aided in the arrangement of the narrative by Mr. J. Calvin Lester, to whom my best thanks are also due.

It is my earnest hope that the book may be instrumental in advancing the commercial and social interests of Petersburg and her well-beloved citizens.

EDWARD POLLOCK.

Petersburg. Va. Dec.. 31st, 1884.

BIRD'S EYE VIEW OF PETERSBURG, VA., FROM THE NORMAL SCHOOL (FLEET'S HILL).

PETERSBURG.

1884.

INTRODUCTORY.

PETERSBURG, A CITY OF VIRGINIA, lies chiefly in the County of Dinwiddie, on the south bank of the river Appomattox, twelve miles above its confluence with the James at City Point. Its suburbs extend to the eastward into Prince George County, and to the northward, across the river, into Chesterfield. It is situated on that belt of primitive fossiliferous rock which stretches from Alabama to Canada, on the fourth of the westwardly ascending terraces of Virginia, on a border of granite and sandstone forming the rocky barrier over which the waters of the upper country fall and mingle with the tide-waters of the Atlantic Slope. This situation supplies at once the two chief desiderata of a great manufacturing and commercial centre, namely, superior water-power for driving machinery, and a natural highway for the transportation of products to the sea. The meridian of Petersburg, west of Washington, is 24 minutes; its parallel, north of the Equator, is 37 degrees, 13 minutes. The present town occupies a natural amphitheatre, rising gradually from the riverfront to the south, east and west, and reaching an elevation above tidewater of about eighty feet. From the hills on the north bank of the Appomattox, a comprehensive view of the City can be obtained with its picturesque suburbs, as they spread outward and upward from the harbor until the semi-circular boundary, formed by the highest visible tier of terraces, is reached. This latter is clearly marked, being surmounted on the east by Blandford Church and Cemetery, on the south by the Reservoir and "Mount Erin," the residence of Wm. Cameron, Esq., and on the west by "East View," the summer abode of Dr. Daniel W. Lassiter. The corporate limits of the City include an area of nearly seven square miles, the greater portion of which is shaded during the summer months with luxuriant foliage. The population, according to the census of 1880, was 21,-

656, but the registration, immediately preceding the municipal election in May, 1884, of 4,916 qualified voters, would indicate a total population of about 25,000 souls.

Petersburg is distant from Richmond 23 miles; from Norfolk, 81 miles; from Lynchburg, 123 miles; from Weldon, N. C., 65 miles; and from Washington, D. C., 139 miles. Its immediate connections with these points, and the world beyond them, are as follows: The Norfolk & Western Railroad, running from the Atlantic Ocean at Norfolk to the town of Bristol, Va., on the boundary line of Tennessee; the Richmond & Petersburg Railroad, connecting this City with the Capital of the State; the Petersburg Railroad, running hence to Weldon, N. C.; and the Appomattox and James Rivers, the latter of which is also reached by a branch of the Norfolk & Western Railroad from Petersburg to City Point. The far-reaching commercial relations and general advantages enjoyed by the City will be more fully treated of in the later pages of this publication.

HISTORICAL SKETCH.

OLD FORT HENRY.

IN the year 1645, thirty-eight years after the settlement of Jamestown and during the administration of Governor Berkeley, a party was dispatched to make a permanent settlement at the head of navigation on the Appomattox River. Peace prevailed at that time between the Colonists and the Indians, having been contracted by the Governor and the friendly chief Necotowanee, the successor of the warlike Opecancanough. This cessation of hostilities was at once improved by the erection of Fort Henry at the Falls of the Appomattox, on the site of the present City. The object of this settlement, as declared by the statute, was "the prevention of the great reliefe and subsistence to the Salvages by fishing in Bristoll, *alias* Appomattocke River," and "for the defence of the inhabitants on the south side of James River." In October, 1646, Necotowanee, who is officially styled "King of the Indians," and his people, are forbidden "to come in to hunt or make any abode nearer the English plantations than the lymits of Yapin, the Black Water, and from the head of the Black Water upon a straite line to the Old Monakin Towne." But upon any occasion of a message to the Governor, or for the purposes of trade, they were permitted "to repair to fforte Henery, *alias* Appomattocke fforte, or to the house of Capt. John ffloud (Flood), and to no other place or places on the south side of the river." From this limitation as to the intercourse and trading operations of the Indians with the Colonists, and from the fact that in none of the statutes in effect at that date was this place mentioned as Peter's Point, it may safely be inferred that Major Peter Jones (after whom Peter's Point and, subsequently, Petersburg were named) had not at that time established himself as a trader at or near the Falls of the Appomattox. In the same year (1646), by an Act of the House of Burgesses, this Fort, with six hundred acres of land adjacent thereto, was granted unto Captain Abraham Wood, "whose service hath been employed at fforte Henery," and in 1653 a patent for 1,557 acres, in which was in-

cluded the first grant of 600 acres, was issued to this same gentleman, who, in the meantime, had been promoted to the rank of Major. The following is the full text of Major Wood's deed as it stands of record in the Land Office at Richmond :

To all, etc. [Whereas, etc. Now, know yee that I, the said Richard Bennett, Esq. etc. give and grant unto Major Abraham Wood, fifteen hundred, fifty-seven acres of land, lying at fforte Henery in the County of Charles City, and on the south side of Appomattocke River, bounded, viz:

from a marked tree on the back of a little swamp on Appomattocke River ;
south by east into the woods one hundred and sixty chaines, each chaine
about two poles ; thence west by south on the heads two hundred sixty-
three chaines ; and thence north by west on the river one hundred and
sixty chaines ; and thence it runneth east by north down the river to the
place we began, two hundred sixty-three chaines, including one thousand
fifty-two acres ; and from thence it runneth north by west fifteen chaines ;
thence west northwest along the river eleven chaines ; and thence west
southwest twelve chaines along the poynt ; from thence it crosseth a part
of Appomattocke River to the lower end of an island called fflea Island ;
west thirteen chaines ; from thence it runneth upon a straite line by along
the river to a poynt above the tenement of John Yonsors, including the
islands and inletts of waters, lands and rocks within the said line, being
forty-nine acres and two roods and four hundred fifty-six acres and twenty-four pearch, the residue bounded, viz : South east by south into the
woods eighty chaines, and thence on the heads southwest by west one hundred and twenty chaines ; and thence northwest by north nine chaines,
and from thence southwest by west seventy-eight chaines, and thence it
runneth north one hundred and fourteen chaines to the head line of the
one thousand fifty-two acres, including the said quantity of land ; the said
land being due unto the said Major Abraham Wood as follows, viz : Six
hundred acres, part hereof, being granted unto the said Major Abraham
Wood by Order of Assembly bearing date the first of October, 1646, and
nine hundred fifty-seven acres, the residue, by and for the transportation of
twenty persons into this Colony, etc. To have and to hold, etc. Yielding
and paying, etc. Which payment is to be made seven years after the first
grant or sealing thereof, and not before. Provided, etc. Dated the 9th
of June, 1653.

Augustin Ellsby,	Henry Newcombe,
Charles Magnory,	Will Marstone,
Symin Cooper,	Rich'd Lloyd,
George Hill,	John North,
Thos. Lynnge,	Ellin Parker,
Daniel Lyres,	Bardary Richardson,
Richard Collins,	Jonkin Leech,
Edward Hayes,	Thomas Ffield,
Jane Pryse,	Dodo. Eldridge,
Chas. Ffeatherstone,	John Joanes.

But Abraham Wood was not the earliest settler at Fort Henry ; for, by
the same Act under which the first six hundred acres of land were granted
to him in 1646, it appears that the land on which the fort stood, together
with part of the six hundred adjacent acres, had previously been owned
by one Thomas Pitt, from whom it was purchased by the House of Burgesses for the purpose, evidently, of transferring it to Wood. Thomas
Pitt may therefore be regarded as the first legal proprietor of the present
City's site.

This Major Abraham Wood was one of the most prominent persons in
the Colony. He represented the County of Henrico in the House of Burgesses at the various sessions of that august body held at James City from
October 1st, 1644, to October 5th, 1646, and the County of Charles City

A PLAN OF THE LOTS LAID OFF FOR THE TOWN OF PETERSBURG, DECR R 1738.

(COPIED AND ENGRAVED FOR "HISTORICAL AND INDUSTRIAL GUIDE TO PETERSBURG, VA. EDWARD POLLOCK, PUBLISHER.)

The above is an accurate copy of an old manuscript now in the possession of Wm. F. Spotswood, Esq., of Petersburg. It was found during the late Civil War by a Federal soldier and brought to Col. J. Albert Monroe, now of Providence, R. I., while the regiment was in the vicinity of the Taylor Mansion, before the investment of Petersburg. Col. Monroe subsequently (in September, 1874) presented it to Hon. Wm. E. Cameron, then Mayor of Petersburg, now Governor of Virginia.

from 1652 to 1654 ; and in 1656 he received the crowning honor of an appointment as one of the "Governour's Councill." In 1656 he is also found on the committee appointed to revise all the laws of the Colony, and in the same year was promoted to be Colonel of the regiment maintained jointly by the Counties of Henrico and Charles City. Subsequently he became one of the four Major Generals of the Colony.

PETER JONES,

whose memory is perpetuated in the City's name, is first heard of in 1675, when war was declared by Governor Berkeley against the Indians. Among the frontier forts to be garrisoned was the one near the Falls of the Appomattox, at Major-General Wood's " or over against him at one ffort or defensible place at ffleet's, of which Major Peter Jones be captain or chief commander." He married the daughter of Major-General Abraham Wood, and opened an establishment for trading with the Indians at a point a short distance west of what is now the junction of Old and Sycamore Streets, on the spot where stood, until recently, the foundry erected and occupied by Uriah Wells. He was one of the four gentlemen who accompanied Colonel William Byrd, the second, of Westover, on his journey to his plantation on the Roanoke River, in North Carolina, called " The Land of Eden," in the year 1733. The other members of the party were Messrs. Banister, Mumford and Mayo—names still familiar among the gentry of Virginia. It was while still absent upon this journey that Col. Byrd wrote : (See *Westover Manuscripts*, page 107) " When we got home we laid the foundation of two large cities—one at Shocco's, to be called Richmond, and the other at the foot of the Appomattox River, to be called Petersburg. These Major Mayo offered to lay out into lots without fee or reward. The truth of it is, these places, being the uppermost landing of James and Appomattox Rivers, are naturally intended for marts, where the traffic of the outer inhabitants must centre. Thus did we build not castles only, but cities in the air." " Shocco's" was the property of Col. Wm. Byrd himself, and the site of Petersburg, then called " Peter's Point," belonged to Major Peter Jones, who, according to tradition, had derived it from his father-in-law, General Abraham Wood, and who must have been a man of character and influence, as Col. Byrd mentions him in his journal as his " old friend " as well as his " fellow traveller." At this time Peter Jones must have been " well stricken in years," and died shortly afterwards, leaving a son, Abraham Jones, who secured the first charter for the City of Petersburg in 1748. The infant City, as may be seen from the Act of Incorporation, was laid out entirely on the land of Abraham Jones, and the original corporation limits embraced only a narrow strip along the river, having its eastern boundary at the trading station on Old Street and extending no farther south than what is now known as Low Street. Abraham Jones married Miss Sarah Ravenscroft, and it was their son Peter

Jones who was mentioned in the Act enlarging the boundaries of the City in 1762, which, after reciting the original incorporation of Petersburg, goes on to say, "which place has since greatly increased and become a place of considerable trade ; and whereas Peter Jones, gentleman, hath laid off twenty-eight acres of his land, adjoining the said town, into lots and streets and hath disposed of several of the said lots, the purchasers whereof have petitioned the General Assembly that the same may be added to and made part of the said town," &c. In the year 1763 this same Peter Jones, the second, built the house on West Washington Street, now occupied by Mr. Wm. E. Hinton, of the firm of Hinton & Dunn, Bankers, of this City.

RESIDENCE OF WM. E. HINTON, ESQ., WASHINGTON ST.
(BUILT BY PETER JONES, THE SECOND, IN 1763 AND ONCE KNOWN AS "FOLLY CASTLE.")

It was generally called " Folly Castle," because of the supposed extravagance of its childless owner in erecting so large a home. He died about 1775, leaving all his town property to his niece, Sarah Newsum, (daughter of his sister Lucy Jones who married Benjamin Newsum), and all his country property, including "Stirling Castle," to another niece, Martha Newsum, who subsequently married John Verell. "Stirling Castle" was pulled down and brought into Petersburg by Mr. Ashton Johnson, who had it re-erected on High Street where it is now occupied as a residence by Mr. Wm. F. Spotswood. The Sarah Newsum who inherited " Folly Castle" married Capt. Erasmus Gill, an officer in the Revolutionary

Army, and their daughter, Martha Newsum Gill, married John Hinton, from whom the present family of that name, residents of Petersburg, and Judge John Hinton, of Missouri, are descended.

But, returning for awhile to the year 1675, it will be found that at that period the country surrounding Fort Henry had already become the home of many substantial settlers. According to Bishop Meade, "settlements were, from time to time, after 1611, formed along the river up to the falls, where is now the town of Petersburg," and it is certain that the earliest records bear many a time-honored family name that also adorns the pages of our latest local directories. Among these may be mentioned such familiar patronymics as Banister, Batte, Bland, Bolling, Byrd, Eppes, Hinton, Jones, and Meade.

Among the most considerable people of the vicinity, even in these remote times, appear to have been the Bollings, whose descendants are still among the largest landed proprietors of the City, and whose family history derives special interest from its connection with the romantic story of Pocahontas. Mr. Howison states that this amiable Princess, dying at Gravesend in 1617, left a son, Thomas Rolfe, who came to Virginia and there died, leaving an only daughter, Jane Rolfe, who intermarried with Colonel Robert Bolling and became the mother of John Bolling, her only child, whose father (Colonel Robert Bolling) subsequently married Anne, daughter of John Stith, of Brunswick. The Petersburg Bollings of to-day derive their origin from this second marriage, while the descendants of John Bolling, only issue of the first marriage, are to be found scattered over the State under several honored names, for he became the father of Col. John Bolling and of five daughters who respectively married Richard Randolph, John Fleming, Dr. Wm. Gay, Thomas Eldridge and James Murray.

It was from "Appomattocke" that Capt. Henry Batte departed with his band of fourteen Englishmen and as many Indians in 1674, by command of Sir Wm. Berkeley, on the tour of western exploration which is supposed by Mr. Howison to have traversed the Alleghany range and to have penetrated as far as the great Kanawha region.

That the country between the Falls of the Appomattox and the Jamestown Settlement was becoming occupied with reasonable speed is shown by the dates of the formation of the adjacent counties, that of Surry having been laid off as early as 1652, while Prince George was carved from Charles City County in 1702, and Dinwiddie from Prince George in 1752. The Parish of Bristol, extending from the junction of the James and Appomattox Rivers, was established in 1642, with its Parish Church at Bermuda Hundred, opposite City Point, the old settlement of Sir Thomas Dale. The next place of worship erected in the Parish was probably the Ferry Chapel, which was followed in 1737 or 1738 by Blandford Church.

But this is anticipating, and it is necessary to return for a brief space to

the · :r.ts connected with "Bacon's Rebellion," and the Indian hostilities
o: .675 ⅃. In 1675, war was declared by Governor Berkeley against the
Indians, who still dwelt in large numbers, and with some show of permanent establishment, around the Appomattox Falls. Five hundred men

CITY HALL AND CLERK'S OFFICE.

were ordered to the frontier and eight forts were to be garrisoned. Among
these, as we have seen, was Fort Henry, of which Major Peter Jones, of
sacred memory, was appointed chief commander. The war flagged, as is
known, and it was not till the following year (1676) that the Indians

round Fort Henry suffered a real and heavy blow. This they received at
the hands of Nathaniel Bacon, distinguished as the first Virginia "rebel,"
who had taken the field and begun a determined warfare upon the whole
race. After sending Bland on his ill-fated expedition to Accomac, Bacon
crossed the James River at his own plantation (Curle's) and surprised the
Appomattox tribe of Indians, burning their town, killing many of their
number and dispersing the rest. Passing to the south, General Bacon destroyed many Indian towns and lodges on the banks of the Meherrin, Nottoway and Roanoke Rivers. His name at that time inspired great terror
among the redskins, who had lately been stimulated to unusual audacity
and atrocity by the feeble proceedings of Governor Berkeley. But Bacon
was not to see the results of his vigorous measures, for he died the same
year in Goochland, leaving Drummond, Hansford, and others of his fol-
lowers, to pay upon the scaffold the penalty of their singular "rebellion."
    Nothing of special importance appears to have occurred in this neigh-
borhood, for many years immediately following the events last recorded.
Peace and progress rewarded the efforts of the Colonists, and the settlement grew and flourished. In the year 1728, Col. Byrd stopped a night
at the residence of Col. Bolling, and heard the Falls, "which," he says,
"are very noisy whenever a flood happens to roll a greater stream than
ordinary over the rocks"; thus giving us a pleasing glimpse of the natural resources of water-power which are yet, and for all time, to constitute
a material element of the city's wealth and prosperity. Reference has already been made to the birth of the city in 1733, when Col. Wm. Byrd
and his travelling companions "laid the foundations" of Richmond and
Petersburg. In October, 1748, while Gooch was Governor of Virginia,
the towns of Petersburg and Blandford were established by an Act of the
General Assembly, upon lands owned and laid out by Abraham Jones and
William Poythress, respectively; and in 1752, Pocahontas, in the County
of Chesterfield, was similarly established. The Acts by which these towns
were created very wisely prohibited the building of wooden chimneys
within their corporate limits. The directors and trustees of the young
town of Pocahontas were John Bolling, Richard Eppes, Clement Reade,
Augustine Claiborne, William Kennon, John Archer, Richard Royal,
Robert Kennon, and Roger Atkinson, gentlemen. The reader who is acquainted with the present population of the City will not fail to note the
familiarity of these names. These gentlemen, however, could hardly have
consulted the oracles as to the future of their infant enterprise, for Pocahontas has never yet developed into a metropolis.
    The first mention of Dinwiddie County in the Colonial Statute-book
bears date May, 1752. Five years later (1757) Blandford Lodge, A. F.
and A. M. was chartered by the Grand Lodge of Scotland. The General
Assembly in 1762 enlarged the boundaries of the town of Petersburg and
gave explicit directions for the improvement of the added area, appointing

the following trustees to carry out the provisions of the Act : Robert
Bolling, Roger Atkinson, William Eaton, John Banister, Robert Ruffin,
Thomas Jones, Henry Walker, George Turnbull, and James Field. It was
a part of the official duty of these gentlemen " to regulate the streets of
the said town," but the irregularities still observable in the older thoroughfares would seem to indicate a considerable obliquity of vision among

ST. PAUL'S (P. E.) CHURCH, UNION STREET.

them. At this period the City seems to have been threatened with the fate
of Cincinnati, for in three separate places does the Statute-book provide
for the summary destruction of the peripatetic hog.

PETERSBURG IN THE REVOLUTIONARY WAR.

The student of American history need not be told that after the action
at Great Bridge, near Norfolk, on the 9th of December, 1775, and the

flight of Dunmore from Virginia, to which he never returned, the Colony enjoyed an absolute immunity from the British armies until the last years of the War of Independence. This immunity was first broken in 1779, when a British fleet, commanded by Admiral Sir George Collier, entered Hampton Roads and sailed up the Elizabeth River. This expedition, however, did not penetrate as far as Petersburg, but, after pillaging Portsmouth and destroying Suffolk, returned to New York. A more severe trial befell Virginia the next year, when a strong force under the command of the traitor Benedict Arnold was dispatched from New York to reduce the rebellious Colony. Arnold, with his army of 800 men, proceeded up the James River as far as Burwell's Ferry, where he left a frigate and continued the ascent to Westover and thence advanced upon Richmond. Up to the time of his departure from Westover it was not known to Governor Jefferson whether Petersburg or Richmond would be the objective point of the invasion. A general alarm was sounded, but Arnold's movements had been so sudden and the panic so complete that the invaders met with but feeble opposition, and the colonial force which responded to the Governor's summons was not only small but also undisciplined and demoralized. Mr. Jefferson's talents were better suited to times of peace than to moments of emergency and danger like the present, so, after throwing his cannon into the James River, he fled precipitately, leaving the Capital at the mercy of the enemy. After destroying the public stores together with much private property, and sending his energetic lieutenant, Simcoe, on a similar mission to Westham, Arnold retired leisurely down the river to rejoin his shipping.

A gallant demonstration on the part of the garrison of Petersburg during this campaign deserves mention. On the retreat of Arnold, some of the vessels of his fleet ventured up the Appomattox to a place known as Broadway, nine miles below Petersburg, where they were fiercely attacked by General Smallwood with three hundred militia, and driven back to City Point. "Not content with this success," says Mr. Howison, "Smallwood brought up two four-pounders and opened upon the ships at the Point ; a fire which drove them down the river to join the main fleet."

The universal demoralization which followed this bold movement of Arnold's need not be dwelt upon here. The situation was neither hopeful nor creditable, and the outlook for next year's campaign, in which Petersburg was to be more directly interested, was far from encouraging.

FREDERICK WILLIAM AUGUSTUS, BARON DE STEUBEN,

Major-General in the United States Army, and Inspector-General, was at this time in command of the forces at Petersburg. He had been a soldier in the army of Frederick the Great, and served as an aide on the King's own staff. He was also a Canon of the Church. Refusing brilliant offers made him by the King of Sardinia and the Emperor of Austria, this brave soldier set sail for America and joined the Continental Army at Valley Forge, as a volunteer, and as such participated in the battle of Monmouth. He was a veteran disciplinarian and tactician, and was possessed also of the higher qualities and accomplishments of his profession. The Baron seems to have been detained at Petersburg while on his way to the South to join the army under General Greene, and it was reserved for him to defend the City in gallant style against the invading forces of Arnold and Phillips in the following April.

On the 20th of January, 1781, Arnold reached Portsmouth in safety, although Governor Jefferson had offered a reward of five thousand guineas for his head, and was reinforced on the 26th of March, following, by General William Phillips, at the head of 2,000 men. General Phillips assumed command of the troops thus united, superseding Arnold, to the

PETERSBURG HARBOR AND POCAHONTAS BRIDGE.

great satisfaction of the soldiers, by whom the traitor was cordially despised.

On the 24th of April, 1781, the British forces, numbering 2,300 men, landed at City Point, and marched to Petersburg the next day. Baron Steuben, with only one thousand militia-men at his back, prepared to receive the invaders. He took up his position near Old Blandford Church and calmly awaited the enemy's appearance. The Royal force arrived in sight at noon on the 25th and formed its line, the left flank extending upon the plain near the town. At 2 o'clock the advance was made in two columns, and the brunt of the first onset was borne by a detachment of militia posted on the heights just beyond Blandford, under the command of Colonel Dick and Captain House, of Brunswick. This body behaved with great gallantry and disputed the ground inch by inch, performing

their manœuvres with remarkable steadiness while under fire. "The enemy," says Mr. Campbell, "were twice broken and ran like sheep, and
during two hours advanced but one mile." The main body of the Ameri-
cans posted at the Bollingbrook Warehouse, (about 200 yards east of the
Norfolk & Western Passenger Depot of today), were finally flanked by
four pieces of artillery, supported by a party of "Yagers," and compelled
to retire across the river. The retreat of the Virginians was covered by
some cannon which Steuben had posted on Archer's Hill, on the north
bank of the Appomattox. From Baker's and Archer's Hills the Baron retired, with his arms, baggage and stores, to Chesterfield Courthouse, ten
miles distant. Phillips, accompanied by Arnold, entered and took possession of Petersburg, making his headquarters at Bollingbrook, the seat of
the Bolling family, on East Hill. The loss of the Virginians, killed,
wounded and captured, was estimated at sixty men ; that of the British at
about the same number, including fourteen killed. As the conquerors
entered the town a large portion of the inhabitants made their escape.
General Phillips and the officers of his staff are said to have treated with
a good deal of courtesy their hostess, Mrs. Bolling, whom they always
addressed as "Lady Bolling." Arnold is described as "a handsome man,
who limped in his gait from a wound received at Saratoga. He was fond
of caressing children and dandling them on his knee."

The next day (April 26th) four thousand hogsheads of tobacco and the
shipping in the river were burned, and these outrages were followed by
many others of a similar character at Chesterfield Courthouse, Warwick,
Osborne's and Manchester, including the wanton destruction of many
dwellings. On arriving at Manchester, the British General learned that
the Marquis de la Fayette, who had been assigned to the responsible duty
of defending Virginia, was in command at Richmond with a small body
of Continental troops, and that the militia were flocking to his standard
in large numbers. This unwelcome news caused Phillips to change his
plans entirely. He abandoned all thought of attacking the Capital, and
marched away to Bermuda Hundred, burning mills, factories and shipping
as he went. He there re-embarked his force and set sail down the James,
but was met at Hog Island by dispatches ordering his return to Petersburg, there to await Lord Cornwallis, who was on his march from the
South. The British army reappeared at Petersburg so unexpectedly that
they surprised and captured ten Continental officers, who were engaged in
collecting boats to convey La Fayette across the Appomattox. The Marquis had not sufficient force at his command to prevent the junction of
Phillips with Cornwallis, but before the latter's arrival appeared on the
heights north of the town and opened fire with his artillery upon the invaders' headquarters. Phillips lay sick at Bollingbrook under this can-
nonade, bitterly complaining that the rebels would not suffer him to die
in peace. The fire was so heavy that it was deemed necessary to remove

him to the cellar of the house, where, however, he did not die during the bombardment, as was once believed. It appears that La Fayette did not know of the General's illness, but fired at headquarters, which he knew to be established at the Bolling mansion, in retaliation for the outrages which Phillips and Arnold had recently committed. General Phillips died on the 13th of May, and was buried in the southeast angle of the old and inner enclosure at Blandford. There, beneath a heavy shroud of ivy, reposes one whom Jefferson described as "the proudest man of the proudest nation on earth."

One week after the death of Phillips (May 20th, 1781,) Cornwallis entered Petersburg, and after remaining there three or four days, crossed the

CONFLUENCE OF THE APPOMATTOX AND JAMES RIVERS, AT CITY POINT.

James River at Westover, expecting to entrap and capture La Fayette and his force, having already written to his Government from Petersburg, "the boy cannot now escape me." How the wary young Frenchman succeeded in eluding the snares of the British commander and effecting his masterly retreat does not relate to Petersburg's part in the Revolution, which ceased with the departure of Cornwallis.

Local pride would perhaps be gratified if it could be stated that the real reason of his Lordship's hasty retirement from this vicinity was that he feared the enervating effects upon his war-worn veterans of a longer residence in so charming a spot, which he feared might become his Capua, but, unfortunately for patriotic prejudices, history has declined to pay the town this compliment, and has assigned other and more positive motives for the British movement, as stated above.

INCORPORATED.

The town, which had been "established" in 1748, and enlarged in 1762, was formally incorporated in 1784, and with it the adjacent settlements of Blandford, Pocahontas and Ravenscroft. The last named district included that triangular portion of the ancient town which lay between Sycamore, Halifax and Shore Streets. The system of government provided for by the new charter was characterized by its practical simplicity. Once a year on the first Wednesday in September, the freeholders, housekeepers, and inhabitants of the town possessing property of whatever kind amounting to the value of fifty ponnds, were to meet at the house of Wm. Durrell, or other suitable place, to elect by ballot twelve fit and able men, who on the same or the second day thereafter were to organize the municipal administration, consisting of a mayor, recorder, four aldermen and six common councilmen, whose term of official service was fixed at one year, subject to re-election. The usual powers and privileges were conferred upon this body with authority to establish laws and ordinances from time to time for the better ordering of the inhabitants of the town. A Court of Hustings was ordered to be held on the first Wednesday of each month. This appears to have been the prototype of the modern Corporation Court, except that the jurisdiction of the magistrates did not extend to penal cases, unless for breach of the municipal laws, when the penalty involved did not exceed £10 sterling or 10,000 pounds of crop tobacco. It is of early record, (1785), that this Court imposed a fine of forty shillings upon one Jacob Shafer for selling liquor on the Sabbath to "divers negroe slaves." In the same year the Court decreed that the "ordinaries," as the inns of that period were called, should serve the public at the following rates : Beefsteak, 18 pence; dinner and toddy, 3 shillings; lodging for the night, 8 pence; grog or toddy by the quart, 15 pence; córn or oats, per gallon, 1 shilling; fodder per bundle, till April next, 1½ pence; stabling, per night, 8 pence; punch per quart, 2 shillings; madeira wine, per bottle, 5 shillings; claret, 3 shillings ; port, 3 shillings; the same for Lisbon wine, and 2 shillings for beer, ale or porter.

In January, 1786, the Council respectfully rejected an application made by the Governor, Patrick Henry, for the accommodation of a number of penitentiary convicts in the city jail. The mayor's letter thanks the Governor for his "polite attention to the corporation," but "at the same time informs him that they do not choose to take charge of any criminals condemned to servitude."

In 1788 the nucleus of a fire department was formed by the organization of the Old Street Fire Company. One year later the *Virginia Gazette and Petersburg Intelligencer* made its appearance, with William Prentis, the pioneer of Petersburg journalism, as editor.

GENERAL WASHINGTON'S VISIT.

On the 14th of April, 1791, General George Washington, then serving his first term as President of the United States, arrived in Petersburg

SYCAMORE STREET, LOOKING SOUTH FROM BANK STREET.

while making a tour through the South. He was met at Osborne's, in Chesterfield County, by a detachment of the local cavalry and escorted by them to the town. Elaborate preparations had been made for the suitable reception and entertainment of this distinguished guest. Triumphal arches were erected and a grand public banquet was provided by order of the Common Hall. There was an address by the Mayor, Richard Bate, in which the All-Wise Director of human events was prayed "to prolong the life of the Father of his Country and friend of mankind to a far dis-

tant period." In his reply the President said : "The Government of the
United States, originating in the wisdom, supported by the virtue, and having no other object than the happiness of the people, reposes not on the
exertions of an individual ; yet, as far as integrity of intention may justify the belief, my agency in the administration will be consonant to your
favorable opinions, and my private wishes will always be preferred for the
prosperity of Petersburg and the particular welfare of its inhabitants."
An illumination, which formed a part of the programme for that night,
was omitted for fear of fire. The following resolution, adopted by the
Common Hall with reference to the banquet, is worthy of notice as illus-
trating that the councilmen of that day, even amid the excitement of the
festival preparations, kept a sharp eye on the municipal expense account ;
" No gentleman is to invite more than two gentlemen to dine on Friday,
and is (sic) to pay for the gentlemen they may invite."

It was reserved, however, for Petersburg's special humiliation through
all the time to come, that during this visit the hero of the "Cherry Tree
Legend " should have departed, for the only recorded time in his otherwise spotless history, from the narrow and lonely path of uncompro-
mising veracity. In referring to this deplorable event, in the *Mount Ver-
non Papers,* Mr. Everett pathetically says : " The President started from
Petersburg practicing a little artifice as to the time of his departure—of
which I recollect no other instance in his whole career—and which, involving no departure from the strictest truth, and resorted to for the best
of reasons, will not be blamed." The painful story can best be told in the
illustrious backslider's own words, taken from his diary, which are as
follows :

" *Friday,* 18th.—Having suffered very much by the dust yesterday, and
finding that parties of horse and a number of other gentlemen were intending to attend me part of the way to-day, I caused their enquiries re-
specting the time of my setting out to be answered that I should endeavor
to do it before 8 o'clock, but did it a little after 5, by which means I
avoided the inconvenience above mentioned."

The President's impression of the town will also prove interesting. He
says : " Petersburg, which is said to contain near 3,000 souls. is well situated for trade at present ; but when the James River navigation is com-
pleoted, and the cut from Elizabeth River to Pasquotank is effected, it
must decline, and that very considerably. At present it receives at the
inspections nearly a third of the tobacco exported from the whole State,
besides a considerable quantity of wheat and flour—much of the former
being manufactured at the mills near the town. Chief of the buildings
in this town are under the hill, and unpleasantly situated ; but the heights
around it are agreeable."

From this it will be seen that Washington was by no means an infallible prophet, for neither did the population of Petersburg fall off, nor was

his beloved scheme of James River navigation ever "compleated."

At the time of Washington's visit, Winfield Scott, one of the four individuals who were to succeed to his title of Lieutenant-General, was a child of five years, living in Dinwiddie County, within a few miles of Petersburg.

The cause of education was dear to the former citizens of Petersburg, as it is to her inhabitants of to-day. In December, 1794, was founded a classical school which enjoyed the dignity of being incorporated and dubbed "The Academy." This institution ranked among the first of its kind, and quickly established itself in the confidence of the State at large. Its legitimate successors are to be found in the excellent seminaries for which the modern City is justly famous.

Towards the close of the year 1795 the General Assembly adopted an Act "to amend the amendments passed for opening and extending the

THE OLD MARKET HOUSE.

navigation of the Appomattox River from Bannister's Mills as far as practicable." This legislation led to the incorporation of the Upper Appomattox Company, which forms the subject of a separate article at the conclusion of this sketch. Between the date of its establishment as a navigable stream and the opening of the Southside Railroad, the Upper Appomattox Canal was a most useful highway of trade, and the greater part of the tobacco and wheat which found its way to our market came across the levees at the head of High Street.

On the 12th of April, 1800, the good—perhaps it would be more correct to say the *bad*—people of the town were very much startled and disturbed by the mysterious falling from the sky, in considerable quantities, of a yellow powder resembling brimstone. Moral accounts were hastily balanced in nervous anticipation of some ghastly issue, but as nothing unusual followed, the phenomenon was soon forgotten and its supposed warning disregarded. At this time the population of Petersburg was estimated at 3,400—1,500 white and 1,900 colored.

At the beginning of this century the Petersburgers appear to have been magnanimously impartial in their reception and treatment of public men, for Aaron Burr, at the expiration of his Vice-Presidential term, and when he was practically ostracised by the nation on account of his duel with Hamilton, was given a grand public banquet, as he passed through the town on his way to the Southwest, where he was soon afterwards engaged in schemes of treason.

Blandford was then the most important portion of the town, and carried on a large export and import trade direct with the Old World. Among its principal enterprises was the nail factory of Roderick Haffey, the first one established in this section of the country. The hegira of its inhabitants across the valley to Petersburg was begun in 1802, the present City having by that time outgrown the sister corporations of Blandford and Pocahontas, which thenceforth maintained the more modest relation of suburbs to their successful rival. Old Blandford Church was not used as a place of worship after 1803, from which date it rapidly went to decay. The familiar lines commencing :

"Thou art crumbling to the dust, old pile," *

addressed to the ancient building, have been ascribed to the pens of several more or less distinguished authors and poets, but the preponderance of testimony favors the popular theory that they were composed by the Irish tragedian, Tyrone Power, who spent a few days here immediately before the lines were discovered, written in pencil upon the dilapidated wall.

The Petersburg Bar was very brilliant at this period, and numbered among its ornaments "Lawyer Davy Robertson," John Allison, Thomas Bolling Robertson, Winfield Scott, "Jack Baker," George Keith Taylor, Benjamin Watkins Leigh, J. A. Dunn, William Rose, and R. T. Birchett, all talented men, the last named of whom was accidentally drowned in Maryland while still very young.

---

*The following verses were found written on the wall of the old Church in 1841, with no positive clue to their authorship :

Thou art crumbling to the dust, old pile,
 Thou art hastening to thy fall,
And 'round thee in thy loneliness
 Clings the ivy to thy wall.
The worshippers are scattered now
 Who knelt before thy shrine,
And silence reigns where anthems rose,
 In days of "Auld Lang Syne."

And sadly sighs the wandering wind
 Where oft, in years gone by,
Prayers rose from many hearts to Him,
 The Highest of the High;
The tramp of many a busy foot
 That sought thy aisles, is o'er,
And many a weary heart around
 Is still for evermore.

How doth ambition's hope take wing,
 How droops the spirit now!
We hear the distant city's din;
 The dead are mute below.
The sun that shone upon their paths
 Now gilds their lonely graves;
The zephyr which once fanned their brows
 The grass above them waves.

O! could we call the many back
 Who've gathered here in vain,—
Who've careless roved where we do now,
 Who'll never meet again;
How would our very souls be stirred,
 To meet the earnest gaze
Of the lovely and the beautiful,
 The lights of other days !

                                        A Stranger.

Two local dramatists also flourished about this time, John D. Burk, historian and lawyer, who beguiled his leisure hours by writing a drama entitled "Bethlehem Gebo," and Everard Hale, of Blandford, who was inspired to the production of "Nolens Volens; or the Biter Bit." These effusions were performed on the stage of the Petersburg Theatre by the "Thespians," an amateur dramatic association.

THE BURK-COQUEBERT DUEL.

In April, 1808, occurred one of the most tragic episodes in the history of the City. It resulted in the death, under "the Code," of John Daly Burk at the hands of a young Frenchman named Felix Coquebert, whose fatal bullet cut short a career which would furnish tempting material for

RESIDENCE OF GEORGE CAMERON ESQ., SOUTH SYCAMORE STREET.

a novelist. While an undergraduate of Trinity College, Dublin, Burk had been obliged to fly for his life on account of his obnoxious political opinions and his foolhardy attempt to rescue a prisoner who was about to be executed under sentence of a court-martial. He landed in Boston in 1796 and made an unsuccessful venture there as a journalist, after which he removed to Virginia and settled in Petersburg. Here he embarked upon a semi-political and literary career, and his famous History of Virginia was abruptly closed at the account of the Revolution by his sad death. His slayer, Coquebert, had been for many years a resident of the town, where his polished grace of manner and gentlemanly bearing had earned for him a high place in popular favor. On Saturday, April 9th,

Burk and the young Frenchman were dining together at Powell's, the fashionable tavern of the day. The conversation turned upon European politics, and Burk vigorously denounced the French Government for its insolence in dealing with his adopted country.

"What will cavillers against the Administration say now?" he exclaimed, "What will they say to the letter of General Armstrong in answer to the arrogant note of Mons. Champagny? I am in hopes that when they read the honest, manly and luminous remarks of an American citizen, in repudiation of the pretentions of the French rascals, they will have honesty and modesty enough to withdraw their accusations and be silent, for the French are a nation of scoundrels."

Coquebert enquired whether these observations were intended to apply to him, and was haughtily informed that as he had chosen to intrude upon the conversation, he might take the above remarks as he pleased. In eighteen hundred and eight, there could be but one sequel to such an altercation in Virginia. On the following day Coquebert sent a challenge, which was promptly accepted by the hot-blooded Irishman. They fought at sunrise on the ensuing Monday in a ravine near Fleet's Hill, which now forms a portion of the Normal School grounds. The seconds were Richard Thweatt for Burk, and a Mr. McNae for Coquebert. The weapons chosen were regulation duelling pistols, and the distance ten paces. At the first fire Burk fell dead, shot through the heart. Coquebert and McNae fled from Petersburg, where they were never seen again. Burk's funeral was the occasion of one of the largest civic and military processions the town had ever witnessed. He was buried at Cedar Grove, near Mount Airy.

Another noteworthy duel had been fought near Petersburg in November, 1795, between John Jeffreys and a gentleman named Johnson, in which the former was killed.

THE WAR OF 1812.

Nothing of general interest again occurs in the history of the town until the breaking out of the war with Great Britain, when Petersburg was called upon to furnish her quota of troops for the invasion of Canada. On October 12th, 1812, the "Petersburg Volunteers," one hundred and three strong, were organized, with the following commissioned and non-commissioned officers: Richard McRae, captain; William Tisdale and Henry Gary, lieutenants; Shirley Tisdale, ensign; James Stevens, Robert B. Cook, Samuel Stevens and John Henderson, sergeants; and N. B. Spotswood, John Perry, Joseph Scott, Thomas G. Scott, Joseph C. Noble and G. T. Clough, corporals. Before starting for the front, the corps was presented with a handsome stand of colors by the ladies of the town. This command served under General (afterwards President) William H. Harrison, and received its baptism of fire on May 5th, 1813, at the battle of Fort Meigs, where five of the brave fellows were slain. The part borne by the City in this war was conspicuous and honorable, and earned for her the proud title of the COCKADE CITY, —a *soubriquet* which she still nobly justifies—conferred by President Madison himself. The following testimonial from the Commander-in-Chief will always be read by our citizens with pride and interest :

TABB STREET PRESBYTERIAN CHURCH AND MANSE.

HEADQUARTERS, DETROIT, 17th October, 1813.

GENERAL ORDERS.

The term of service for which the Petersburg Volunteers engaged having expired, they are permitted to commence their march to Virginia as soon as they can be transported to the south side of the lake.

In granting a discharge to this *patriotic and gallant corps,* the general feels at a loss for words adequate to convey his sense of their exalted merits. Almost exclusively composed of individuals who had been nursed in the lap of ease, they have for twelve months borne the hardships and privations of military life in the midst of an inhospitable wilderness, with a cheerfulness and alacrity which has never been surpassed. Their conduct in the field has been excelled by no other corps ; and while in camp

they have set an example of subordination and respect for military authority to the whole army. The General requests Captain McRae, his
subalterns, non-commissioned officers and privates to accept his warmest
thanks, and bids them an affectionate farewell.

By command   ' ROBERT BUTLER,
                                    Acting Assistant Adjutant-General.

Captain McRae died in May, 1854, under unfortunate and suspicious
circumstances. His body was found in the Potomac River, near the
mouth of Aquia Creek, with wounds about the head, which suggested
violence. His remains were brought to Petersburg and interred with
military honors in Blandford Cemetery, where a granite shaft, surmounted by a bronze eagle, and inscribed with his company's glorious record,
marks his last resting place. The mystery of his death was never clear-
ed up.

Mr. Reuben Clements, the last survivor of the gallant band who fought
at Fort Meigs, died in Petersburg on the 6th of October, 1881, at the advanced age of 90 years.

THE GREAT FIRE.

The history of Petersburg, like that of nearly every American town,
furnishes the record of a great conflagration. On July 16th, 1815, an old
wooden stable, between Bollingbrook and Back (now Lombard) Streets,
was found to be on fire, and a few hours later two-thirds of the town was
reduced to ashes. From Back Street to the river the flames had swept
everything before them, including the west side of Sycamore Street. Five
hundred houses were destroyed and not a dozen substantial business buildings were left standing. The loss was estimated at nearly $3,000,000,
and several human lives were sacrificed. After the fire the citizens acted
with admirable spirit, and an appeal to the other towns of the Commonwealth and the country at large, on behalf of the homeless sufferers, met
with a generous response. Rebuilding was promptly begun, and a much
improved Petersburg speedily arose from the *debris* under the busy hands
of a thousand workmen. The streets in several instances were straight-
ened and paved, the new houses were constructed of more substantial and
less combustible material, and the citizens were shortly enabled to recog-
nize in what they had at first regarded as a dire disaster, something nearly
akin to a smoke-veiled blessing.

THE ANDERSON SEMINARY.

In 1819 there died in Petersburg a worthy Scotchman named David
Anderson, who had bequeathed to the town, by his will, dated June 16th,
1812, a sum of money, the income of which, amounting to about $600,
was to be applied to the rudimentary education of the poor children of
the town. To this annuity was added $200, obtained by the City from the

Literary Fund each year. Under the present common school system the
largest seminary in the City still bears the name of the generous Scot who
first promoted the cause of learning among the poor of Petersburg.

THE ADAMS-BOISSEAU DUEL.

In 1820 the City's annals are darkened for the third time by the record
of a hostile meeting, having a fatal termination, under the barbarous and

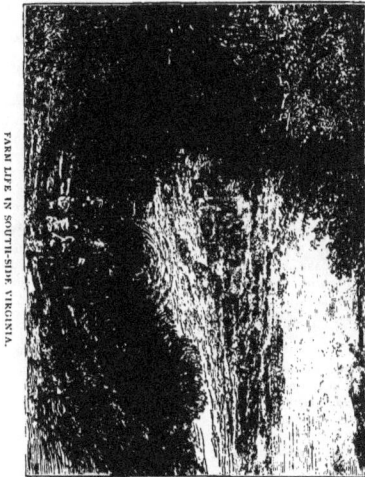

FARM LIFE IN SOUTH-SIDE VIRGINIA.

now, fortunately, almost obsolete "Code of Honor." On this occasion
two of the most energetic and thrifty business men in the community,
Adams and Boisseau by name, were rival claimants for the affections of
Miss Helen Pennington, a famous beauty and the acknowledged belle of
her day. The immediate cause of the challenge was an assault made by
Boisseau upon Adams with a whip, but the reason for this assault has
never been explained. The rivals, as was usual in such cases, referred

their quarrel to the arbitrament of an ounce of lead, and, for once "satisfaction" was meted out to *both* appellants with grim impartiality. Adams at the time of the attack was in feeble health, and as his assailant was assisted by a friend named Strong, his punishment was severe. He swore, however, to be revenged or die in the attempt. His challenge was at once accepted by Boisseau, and the meeting took place in due course. A sheltered spot in the rear of Blandford Church had been selected, and thither the duellists proceeded in carriages, accompanied by their seconds, and followed at a distance by Boisseau's aged father. Agreeably to the deadly purpose of the combatants, the usual ten paces were reduced to seven, and the principals were placed back to back. At the word "fire," Adams wheeled and shot his antagonist through the body, and the latter, although mortally stricken, succeeded in discharging his pistol and inflicting a fatal wound upon his rival. After this effort Boisseau fell dead, and Adams expired on the following morning—and thus it happened that the fair Helen lost both her lovers by one cruel blow. This tragic affair caused the most intense excitement, and the seconds, against whom the popular wrath was directed, only saved themselves from summary vengeance by a hasty flight into North Carolina.

LA FAYETTE'S VISIT.

The most notable event of the year 1824 was the visit of the Marquis de La Fayette. In consequence of the conspicuous part he had played in the history of the town during the Revolution, the Marquis had always been an object of affectionate interest to its inhabitants, and the reception accorded "the hero of two worlds" was a perfect ovation. A troop of horse met him far beyond the corporation limits and his arrival was attended with all the "pomp and circumstance" of a triumphal entry. The evidences of happiness and prosperity which now met him on all sides must have contrasted vividly with the recollections of his former visit, when he had overlooked the conquered town from behind the trunnions of his field pieces, planted on the heights of Chesterfield. Some such retrospect now engaged the veteran's mind, for, in replying to the Mayor's address of welcome, he said: "I have had in former times to lament the necessity, in the course of military operations, to disturb the repose of the good town of Petersburg while it had become *a British headquarter*, but in this very circumstance found new opportunities to witness her patriotism." After being formally presented to the Common Hall, the Marquis and his suite were entertained at a magnificent banquet, and Niblo's tavern resounded until a late hour with eloquent and enthusiastic orations in praise of "our honored guest." Next day the Marquis was escorted to the Poplar Lawn, where four hundred children of Anderson School chanted their welcome. After receiving this graceful tribute of love and veneration, the noble Frenchman bade our town a last farewell and pursued his journey—

"a man," in the language of a local reporter, "than whom his superior does not dwell beneath the vaulted roof of Heaven." A fatal quarrel on the day of La Fayette's reception, during which Raleigh Rosser was killed by Robert Finn, disturbed to some extent the harmony of the rejoicings, Finn eventually escaped the gallows, thanks to a flaw in his indictment.

THE FIRE OF 1826.

On the 15th of July in this year a vast throng of worshippers assembled in Old Blandford Church to do honor to the memory of Thomas Jefferson, who had died eleven days previously. The venerable "Parson" Andrew Syme, Rector of St. Paul's, had just ascended the pulpit

BOLLINGBROOK HOTEL ; M. A. PETTIT, PROPRIETOR.

and given out a hymn when the fire-bells of the town sounded the alarm. The congregation, which, including the military, numbered about two thousand, rushed panic-stricken from the sacred edifice. By a curious and suggestive coincidence, this was the anniversary of the conflagration of 1815, and the horrors of that time seemed about to be repeated. The fire had broken out in the same quarter as before, but as the later buildings were of brick, the flames did not make such rapid headway, and after several houses in the line of the fire had been blown up with gunpowder, —the most effective extinguisher known at that time, before the powerful modern steam fire-engines were invented—the career of the destructive-element was checked, and the commemoration services, which had been interrupted at Blandford, were concluded at the theatre.

THE MECHANICS' ASSOCIATION.

On the evening preceding La Fayette's visit, the representative mechanics of the town met at the shop of M. D. l'Anson, on Bank Street, for the purpose of uniting upon some plan to testify their appreciation of the distinguished visitor's presence, but when the news came that he would arrive on the morrow, the design was abandoned for want of time to complete the necessary arrangements. The meeting, however, was not without its useful and permanent results, for it led to the organization of a mutual improvement society, which was duly incorporated on February 2nd, 1826, under the name and style of the Petersburg Benevolent Mechanic Association. For the past sixty years this most excellent confraternity has exercised a useful and beneficent influence upon the community, and a brief sketch of its origin, objects and attainments will be given hereafter under a separate heading.

THE PETERSBURG RAILROAD COMPANY,

one of the earliest corporations of its kind in the country, secured its charter on February 10th, 1830. For the purposes of the present narrative and to avoid a hiatus in the chronological arrangement of events, it is sufficient to merely record here the fact of the Company's incorporation ; but the history of this and other railroads having direct influence upon the City's interests will be treated at some length in a special article devoted to that subject.

NAT TURNER'S INSURRECTION.

In the year 1830 occurred one of those startling incidents which are calculated to terrify the stoutest hearts and to leave an indelible impression upon the minds and nerves of a whole community. About forty miles from the town, in the neighboring county of Southampton, there had been brooding, unsuspected, a most insidious and powerful enemy to society, which suddenly revealed its existence under circumstances of unparalleled horror and atrocity. Under cover of the night, and without a note of warning, the negro insurrection, under Nat Turner, which was intended to involve the whole slave population of the South, broke out near the village of Jerusalem. Turner inaugurated his fiendish work by the butchery of his master's family and the white residents of the adjoining plantations. The news of this horrible disaster spread like wild-fire from end to end of Virginia, and the districts in which the presence of a preponderating slave population would seem to justify the fears of midnight massacres, were thrown into a state of almost helpless panic. In Petersburg the most intense excitement prevailed, and the citizens hastily prepared to render such succor as could be spared to the scattered white population of the rural districts, in the event of a general uprising on the part of the slaves. The volunteer companies were kept under arms, for, in the absence of rapid and reliable means of communication, the wildest rumors were circulated and believed. The usually careless and happy life of the strolling darkey troubadour was not an enviable one at this time, for he ran the risk of being mistaken for a bloodthirsty conspirator and dealt with accordingly. Universal terror was caused on one occa-

VIEW IN CENTRAL PARK. (POPLAR LAWN.)

sion by some thoughtless fellow blowing a horn in the street at night. A salvo of artillery from the British batteries in the stormy days of the Revolution, could hardly have created such consternation as did this silly blast, in which timid ears distinguished the savage yells of Turner's sable host. But fortunately the insurgents were neither well armed nor well disciplined, and the insurrection was suddenly crushed when one of the miscreants was killed with a charge of squirrel shot, by a planter whose premises were attacked. A few weeks later, Nat Turner, the desperate author of the riot, was captured, and in due course tried, convicted and hanged.

Petersburg and its vicinity have always been conspicuously blessed in their freedom from malignant epidemic diseases, but by some mysterious agency the cholera germ found its way here in the year 1832, and created no little alarm among our citizens. Rarely had this scourge appeared on the Atlantic slope, and the people were naturally very much affrighted at its presence. But the temperate climate and pure air of Virginia are not conducive to the establishment or spread of infectious diseases, and the unwelcome visitor disappeared after exacting but few victims. The second and last visitation of cholera occurred in 1847, when its ravages were even less fatal than in 1832.

INDUSTRIAL PROGRESS.

In the same year (1832) the Merchants' Manufacturing Company was incorporated, to manipulate cotton, flax, wool and hemp, with a capital stock of not less than $40,000, nor more than $80,000, and the charter was to endure for twenty years. The Petersburg Fire and Marine Insurance Company followed in 1834, with a capital of $100,000, with the right to increase it to $300,000. By an Act of 1835, the Petersburg militia were attached to the Fifteenth Brigade, State troops. The Petersburg Navigation Company was organized to establish a line of packets (the packet of that day was a small sailing vessel, sloop or schooner rigged) to ply between Petersburg and New York, or other Northern ports in the United States, with stock of from $40,000 to $100,000; and almost simultaneously the Petersburg Savings Institution was incorporated under the auspices of J. E. Lemoine, D. Lyon, C. F. Osborne, J. Y. Stockdell, John Dunn, N. M. Moore, A. G. McIlwaine, John Bragg, B. C. Wheary, Benjamin Jones, Joseph Bragg, A. S. Holderby, H. P. Heath, John C. Hobson, James Macfarland, Jr., T. N. Lee, Robert Leslie, Lewis Mabry, M. Thrift, Edwin James, D'Arcy Paul, Samuel Winfree, and Andrew Kevan. In 1839 the Petersburg Exchange was incorporated, and in the same year the Petersburg Towing Company was chartered, to navigate the Appomattox and James Rivers. The incorporators of the Petersburg Exchange were Leslie & Bryden, L. E. Stainback, Son & Co., Dunn, McIlwaine & Brownly, David Dunlop, T. N. Lee, and D'Arcy Paul. A handsome structure, still known as the Exchange Building, was erected on Bank Street, but the Exchange system was not popular with the merchants of the day, and, after a brief life, the enterprise languished. It was revived in 1858, but only for a very short time, after which it was finally suspended. The Exchange Building was occupied just before the civil war by the Bank of the City of Petersburg.

The career of the old Petersburg Academy had been brought to a close in 1835, when the Legislature authorized the trustees to transfer all its property, real and personal, to the Anderson Seminary. In 1838 its place was taken and worthily supplied by the Petersburg Classical Institute. It was at this excellent school that the middle-aged Petersburger of today obtained his knowledge of Pike's Arithmetic and the Latin Grammar, and its memory is often recalled with pious veneration—not unmixed, it may be, with an occasional twinge of something more substantial than that mere mental faculty which retains the knowledge of past events. The old building, once occupied by the Institute and presided over by Principal Saunders, is now used as a Public High School.

JEWISH SYNAGOGUE, UNION STREET.

It will be seen that the decade immediately following the exciting events of 1832 had passed by in unbroken tranquility. Abundant capital had sought investment and numerous enterprises had been successfully embarked. As an inevitable consequence, the town had improved during that period beyond precedent. The question which most agitated the public mind in 1842 was that of the water supply. For twenty years the lower part of the town had been supplied by the Aqueduct Company with a limited quantity of spring water, but this was no longer adequate to the demands of the increasing population, nor was it compatible with the ex-

istence of an efficient Fire Department. The Common Hall was authorized to levy a tax and proceed to lay pipes from the Basin of the Upper
Appomattox Company, whence it was thought a sufficient supply of water
could be obtained ; but a much more elaborate and satisfactory plan was
afterwards adopted, which has, except only in rare seasons of protracted
drought, always assured to the town a plentiful service of pure and wholesome water. Reservoirs were constructed on the elevated land near the
southern boundary of the city, below which flows the limpid source of
supply—"Lieutenant Run." These reservoirs were not completed, however, until 1856. Henry D. Bird was the engineer in charge and super-
intended their construction, which resulted mainly from the energetic la-
bors, in that behalf, of the Hon. R. Kidder Meade, for many years a
member of Congress from this district, and a gentleman who had acquired a strong hold upon the popular affections.

The name of Powell, it seems, was still the right one to conjure with in
connection with the hotel business, for in 1843 the Powell's Hotel Company was incorporated with a considerable capital, subscribed by A. G.
McIlwaine, D'Arcy Paul, George W. Bolling, William Talley, and William
Brownly. Old Powell's Tavern had been destroyed by fire a short time
previously. The hotel, like the ancient hostelry it succeeded, stood upon
the site now occupied by the Iron Front Building.

THE SUICIDE OF ANTOMATTI.

One event of the year 1844 was attended by circumstances of such
tragic interest that the story will be told in detail. Francis Antomatti, a
handsome young Italian, kept a fruit and confectionery store on Sycamore
Street. His gentle manners and excellent reputation had borne their legitimate harvest, and he had won the general favor of the community. At
this time a little colony of French and Italians resided within our city's
limits. Camillo Pucci, a wandering Corsican harpist, had dropped into
the town several years before, with no visible property save his harp, and
no prospect of a career other than that precarious one dependent upon his
power, as a musician, to excite the sympathies and command the charity
of his audience. But a certain Miss Quinechet, the daughter of a repu-
table French family, saw, heard, and straightway loved the humble troubadour, whom she married in spite of the strong opposition of her pa-
rents. The issue of this union was a daughter, Zenobia, who figures as
the heroine of this romantic story. Contemporaneous authorities credit
this young lady with many conspicuous and fascinating graces, and these
were not likely to escape the notice of the susceptible confectioner, Antomatti. Other bonds of sympathy already existed between Antomatti, the
Italian, and Pucci, the Corsican. Strangers, both, in a strange land, their
natural affinities had ripened into warm friendship, and the young Italian
was received into the Corsican's family circle on terms of the closest in-

timacy. As time rolled on, he learned to love the fair Zenobia, and it was generally thought that his passion was reciprocated, for the handsome pair were betrothed and expected to be married. Matters went on smoothly for a while, and Antomatti was devoted in his attentions to his sweetheart, in whose charming society his evenings were mostly spent. Gradually, however, the usually buoyant spirits of the young confectioner showed signs of strong but unaccountable depression, which were attributed by some to rumored embarrassment in his business affairs, while others suspected that a rival had supplanted him in his charmer's affection. How-

CUSTOM HOUSE AND POST OFFICE.

ever this may have been, poor Antomatti was desperately unhappy, and decided upon putting an end to his wretched existence. Selecting the venerable ruin of Blandford Church as the scene of the intended tragedy, he calmly proceeded thither on July 29th, and seeking the solitude of the north transept, deliberately placed the muzzle of a loaded pistol to his temple and inflicted upon himself a mortal wound. The old harpist, unable to find him at his store and probably suspecting that his prospective son-in-law had become the victim of self-inflicted violence, made his way to Blandford, where the ghastly truth lay revealed. Antomatti still lived, and for forty-eight hours his sufferings were intense. Ten minutes before his death he called for a mirror, and after glancing at the reflection of his distorted features, pronounced his case hopeless, turned his face to the wall and quietly expired.

POPLAR LAWN,

recently renamed Central Park, was purchased by the City in 1844 for $15,000. The New Market (Centre) was established in 1845. The lot upon part of which it stands cost the City $5,000. Other portions were sold not long afterwards for sufficient to defray the cost of the whole original purchase. In the same year the City extended its boundaries so as to include thirty acres of land in Prince George County, lying east of Blandford Cemetery.

THE MEXICAN WAR.

Petersburg furnished two companies of gallant fellows to swell the volunteer force which represented the power of the United States in the war with Mexico, and which utterly crushed the military establishment of that unfortunate Republic in two short campaigns. One was commanded by Captain (afterwards Colonel) Fletcher H. Archer, and the other by Captain William N. Robinson. Captain Archer's company was organized on the 3rd of December, 1846, and on the 14th of the same month was mustered into the service of the United States at Richmond. Captain Robinson's company was organized about a month later. The aggregate enrollment of the two companies was about one hundred and seventy men. Captain Archer's company was the first to leave. On the afternoon of Saturday, the 2nd of January, 1847, the day before it was to set out for the rendezvous at Old Point, the ladies of the town, through their chosen orator, Judge James H. Gholson, presented the command with a handsome flag, and the Captain was given a sword by his fellow-members of the Petersburg Bar. Lieutenants Franklin Pegram, D. A. Weisiger and P. A. Patterson were also presented with swords by the admiring citizens. On the following morning, about 7 o'clock, the volunteers, escorted by all the military companies of the town, were at the depot of the City Point Railroad. The scene is thus described by William R. Drinkard, the editor of the *Republican:* "Captain Archer arranged his men in double ranks, the front rank facing the rear in open order, through which the military and citizens, commanded by Captain Hugh A. Garland, passed, shaking hands with every man of the volunteers amid a torrent of scalding tears, asking God to bless them in such terms as tumultuous hearts and almost palsied tongues would allow. It was a moment of deep and painful interest—one at which strong men could weep with impunity—one at which the sobs and shrieks of women could be heard—all knowing the cause and sympathizing with the gentle sufferers. The old and better-tried Canada volunteer, looking back to the past and forward to the future, could but weep. The very servants who had waited upon and been acquainted with these young men, went through the corps crying 'Good bye, master ; God bless you master.' A farewell salute was fired and then long and loud cheers announced that the last moment had arrived. A last embrace, a kiss, another 'good-bye,' and amid the waving of hats and handkerchiefs, the bitter tears and agonizing sobs of friends, the volunteers said 'farewell.'" On January 20th, this company set sail from

FIRST BAPTIST CHURCH, WASHINGTON STREET.

Old Point on board the barque "Mayflower," and after a short delay on the island of Cuba, proceeded to Mexico and ascended the Rio Grande to Camargo, where it was temporarily stationed. Captain Robinson's company followed about a month later, taking the same route and stopping at the same station. From Camargo the Petersburg volunteers advanced to Monterey, and thence, *via* Saltillo, to Buena Vista, which place was not reached, however, until after the battle. Our two companies formed a part of the "Army of Occupation," under General Zachary Taylor, holding the lines in the neighborhood of Buena Vista and Saltillo until the close of the war. Several members of the command being on detached service, participated in more than one engagement, and many fell victims to the malignant fevers peculiar to that climate. After an absence of eighteen months the two companies returned to Virginia and were mustered out of service in August, 1848, at Old Point, whence they reached home shortly afterwards and were given a royal reception by their friends and the towns-people generally. A great feast was spread in Centre Warehouse, and the returned volunteers were made the happy subjects of eloquent speeches and innumerable toasts expressive of unbounded appreciation and cordial welcome.

The present gas-works were constructed in 1848. Seven years previously the Petersburg Gas Light Company had been incorporated with Thomas Wallace, Henry White, Dugger, Jones & Co., Joseph Orr, James Macfarland, Robert Ritchie, Robert Leslie and Daniel Foster as its incorporators. At first a capital of $15,000 to $50,000 was authorized, in shares of $50 each ; afterwards, in 1849, the company was permitted to increase its stock to a sum not less than $60,000 nor more than $120,000. The Common Hall, according to the terms of its contract with the Company, could have taken the enterprise into its own hands at any time within ten years after its inception, but the venture was too experimental to be regarded at the time as a safe investment, and the cautious, practical men then having charge of the municipal government were afraid to take even an ordinary business risk with the people's money. The growth and development of the City have greatly enhanced the value of the Company's stock, although for the first ten years it paid no dividend.

About 1848 it was found necessary to make a large addition to Blandford Cemetery. The tide of emigration in that direction has always been steady, if slow, and it is estimated that nearly thirty thousand people lie buried within the present enclosure.

The death is recorded, on February 10th, 1849, at Mobile, Alabama, in the seventy-seventh year of his age, of Col. Wm. R. Johnson, of Oakland, Chesterfield County, and a former resident, for many years, of this City. His success in horse-racing, then the favorite amusement of all classes, had gained for him the *soubriquet* of "The Napoleon of the Turf." He was a gentleman of remarkable power and influence, and was even reckoned the most popular man that ever lived in Petersburg. Many of his victories were achieved on the New Market race course in Prince George County, about a mile and a half from the City, which was, under the management of Thomas Branch, and afterwards of O. P. Hare, the centre of the racing interest of Southside Virginia.

THE NEW CHARTER OF 1850.

By an Act of March 16th, 1850, the "town" of Petersburg was promoted to the dignity of a City. At first the Mayor was elected, as of old, by the Council; but this was afterwards changed to the people's vote. The new charter was put to the popular vote on the 5th of November, and adopted by the following majority: For ratifying the Act, 151; against it, 109; for electing the Mayor by the people, 208; for electing the Mayor by the Council, 59. John Dodson was the first Mayor elected by the voice of the people. The provisions of the act are very lengthy and labored, but do not differ from the ordinary details of municipal charters. Qualified voters were described as "freeholders of lots within the said city, whether improved or not, and whether said freeholders reside therein or not, and the housekeepers and also the inhabitants of the said city who shall have resided therein for the next preceding one twelve months, such housekeepers or inhabitants possessing in their own right, within the same, movable or immovable property to the value of $150;

VIEW IN WEST-END PARK.

and such freeholders, housekeepers and inhabitants being citizens of the United States." In April, 1852, the charter was amended so as to make the following officers eligible by the popular vote : Collector of Taxes, Chamberlain, Gauger, Keeper of the Powder Magazine, Keeper of the Hay Scales, Clerk of the Market and Commissioner of Streets. The duties of these functionaries are prescribed very exactly in the act, and the City Council was made a "Returning Board" to determine the results of elections.

Intense excitement was aroused by the killing, in the spring of 1853, of Joel H. Sturdivant, the city jailor, by a man named Saddler, who was imprisoned on the charge of kidnapping. Saddler was of good family, and being desperately anxious to avoid the shame and scandal of conviction, he procured in some way a pistol, shot Mr. Sturdivant dead, and wounded "Old George," an assistant about the jail. The tragedy happened on a Sunday morning, while people were at church. As soon as the dark news was bruited, the town turned out in pursuit, *en masse*. The pursuers soon closed on the fugitive, and he, seeing that capture was inevitable, shot and killed himself in their presence with one of the charges yet remaining in his pistol. A shallow pit was dug, into which the dead body, still warm, was tumbled.

The Petersburg and Jerusalem Plank Road Company was chartered by the Legislature in 1853. The road to Jerusalem—the county town of Southampton County—is still called, much to the amusement of strangers, the Plank Road, although not a vestige of its original plank surface remains. In the same year a charter was obtained for the Petersburg Library Association by A. D. Banks, John B. Stevens, Thos. S. Gholson and W. L. Watkins. For a long time this was the only public circulating library in the City, and its shelves furnished nearly all the mental pabulum enjoyed by a whole generation. The handsome Library Building on the corner of Sycamore and Bollingbrook Streets was destroyed by fire in 1878, and a large number of the books were consumed or ruined. The building was not restored as a library, and the property passed into private hands. In 1855 the United States acquired possession of the lot on the corner of Union and Tabb Streets and erected thereon the present beautiful and substantial structure used as a Custom House and Post Office. The fine grey granite of which it is built was taken from the Whitworth quarries in Dinwiddie County, near the City.

COX'S SNOW.

On the 18th of January, 1857, the heaviest fall of snow ever witnessed in this latitude blocked all the roads so that travel was almost impossible, and brought the ordinary occupations of out-door life to a stand-still. Fences and hedges disappeared. This condition of affairs, in which an inhabitant of the great Northwest would have felt thoroughly at home, caused much inconvenience and even suffering to a community accustomed to mild winters and a light snow-fall. Dr. Joseph E. Cox, of Dinwiddie, while out driving with his friend, Mr. Traylor, was overtaken by the storm and fatally frozen before he could reach shelter. His companion was severely frost-bitten, but survived his injuries, and in time recovered. The Doctor was a most estimable citizen and the impression produced by his sad death was so profound that the storm has ever since been referred to as "Cox's Snow." Indeed, among the classes who felt its severity the most, it became an epoch from which succeeding time was measured, and it was almost as common, a quarter of a century ago, to hear of certain events having occurred "since Cox's Snow," as it became in later years to be reminded of that Elysian period which existed, in the language of the colored brethren, "fo' de wah."

THE SCHOONER "KEZIAH."

"On Sunday last, at an early hour, it was discovered that Gilbert and Sarah, two slaves of Thomas W. Eppes, had decamped." These are the

opening lines of a three-column "local" in the *Southside Democrat* of
Tuesday, June 1st, 1858. Certain strange movements on board the
schooner "Keziah," of Brandywine, Delaware, Wm. D. Bayliss, master,
then lying at the wharf, had aroused the suspicions of Officer Butts, and
the vessel was quietly watched. During the day she was observed to
weigh anchor and drop down the river. A telegram was sent to the In-
spector at Norfolk, asking him to intercept the schooner before she reached Hampton Roads, and, in the meantime, the Petersburg authorities set
out in pursuit on board the steamer "W. W. Townes" from City Point,
and sighted the chase about twenty miles below, off Hood's Landing. A
few minutes later the steamer was alongside and the officers informed the

"CENTRE HILL," ESTATE OF THE LATE ROBERT B. BOLLING, ESQ.

schooner's master that they had come to search for runaway slaves. Bayliss feigned astonishment and offered to render all the assistance in his
power. In the cabin, under a pile of miscellaneous articles, was found
Sarah, clad in male attire, and a further search discovered not only Gilbert, but also John Bull, Joe Mayo and William, all fugitive servants of
well known Petersburg families, whose flight had not as yet been suspected. On the discovery of Sarah, the master appeared very much surprised
and professed utter ignorance of her having been on board, but when the
other four were brought to light, he acknowledged the charge of kidnapping and surrendered himself a prisoner. The steamer took her prize in
tow and proceeded up the river. A telegram from City Point announced

the importance of the capture, and when the "W. W. Townes" and her charge reached the wharf at Petersburg, a large and excited crowd had gathered to witness the debarkation of the prisoners. At that time "kidnappers," as those who aided the flight of slaves were called, were the objects of universal hatred, and the officers had some difficulty in protecting Bayliss from violence. The prisoner was tried on the 10th of June, in the Circuit Court. Richard G. Pegram conducted the case for the Commonwealth, and the prisoner was defended, under orders from the court, by John F. May and W. T. Joynes. The laws of Virginia, in 1858, punished kidnapping with great severity. The evidence against Bayliss was so conclusive that his counsel's only plea was one for mercy. He was found guilty and sentenced to forty years' imprisonment in the penitentiary. The schooner's mate, Joseph J. Simpkins, who seemed to have had little or no share in the kidnapping transactions, was released. The "Keziah," according to law, was confiscated and sold at auction, when the firm of Pannill & Carter became her purchasers for $325. Bayliss remained an inmate of the State penitentiary until released by the Federal soldiers when they entered Richmond in 1865.

IN THE WAR BETWEEN THE STATES.

The record of the next two years, when read in the light of subsequent events, points to the rapid approach of the greatest crisis in the history of the City, and of the United States, namely, the bitter and protracted struggle between the Federal Government and the Southern Confederacy, which, for four long years, distracted the country and shocked the world with its horrors. It would, of course, be entirely incompatible with the objects and range of the present brief narrative to enter, even cursorily upon the vast political questions which resulted in this cruel and unnatural war. The subject is, or should be, familiar to every student of modern history, and it would therefore be superfluous to occupy these pages with any of its events other than those which directly affected the City of Petersburg and her inhabitants.

Referring to this exciting period of the City's history, the Rev. E. S. Gregory, in his *Sketch of the History of Petersburg*, published in 1878, writes as follows:

"No community in the South, not actually destroyed by the war, sacrificed more for the Confederate cause than Petersburg. When it began, the town was in the full bloom of prosperity, improvement and extension. She had a large trade directly with Europe, and every day added to her growth and wealth. Throughout the whole Union her culture, her cordiality and her enterprise were known and commended of all men. Her merchants of that day were princes of their profession, exceeded by none for their integrity, their foresight and their boldness to improve the legitimate opportunities of investment. It is said on good authority that the

improvement of the city during the twelve years just preceding the war
was perhaps more rapid and more substantial than that of any other city
in the South.

"All this and more her people dedicated with enthusiasm to the cause of
Virginia and the Confederate States, although they were opposed to secession, and had elected Mr. Thos. Branch as a Union man to the State
Convention over Mr. Thos. Wallace, Disunion, who received not more than
225 votes in the town. Yet the march of events swept them along, and
when the Ordinance of Secession was adopted on April 17th, 1861, the

RESIDENCE OF JOHN McGILL, ESQ., MARKET STREET.

news was received in no part of the State with more jubilation than in
Petersburg. War was already on the country, and the volunteers of Petersburg took the field with gay yet earnest alacrity, abundantly sustained
during the trials and perils which so soon ensued.

⁎   ⁎   ⁎   ⁎   "On every field of action on which they appeared, the soldiers of Petersburg acquitted themselves with gallantry worthy the fame
of the fair Cockade ; their battle-flags were studded with inscriptions of
victory ; and when at last the surrender took place at Appomattox Courthouse, the command to which the Petersburg companies were mostly attached, and of which a Petersburger was General, was the best and most
solidly organized of all which laid down their arms.

"The following is believed to be a substantially correct list of the companies contributed by the City to the Confederate Army, with the names
of the captains in their order by whom they were severally commanded :

"*Infantry.*—City Guard, 12th Regiment, commanded by Colonel D. A.
Weisiger ; Captains John P. May* and Charles E. Waddell.

"Petersburg Riflemen, 12th Regiment, Captains Daniel Dodson, R. R.
Banks and John R. Patterson.

" 'A ' Grays, 12th Regiment. Captains John Lyon, Robert Bowden and
Thos. P. Pollard.

" ' B ' Grays, 12th Regiment, Captains Thomas H. Bond, L. L. Marks
and S. G. White.

"La Fayette Guards, 12th Regiment, Captains Wm. H. Jarvis and J. E.
Tyler.

"Cockade Rifles, 3rd Regiment, Colonel Roger A. Pryor ; Captains Jos.
V. Scott,* Thomas Pannill and Antrobus Bond.

"Archer Rifles, 12th Regiment, Captains F. H. Archer, J. R. Lewellyn,
D. W. Paul,* and Douglas Chappell.

"Ragland Guard, 41st Regiment, Colonel J. P. Minetree ; Captains J. R.
Maney and John Weddell.

"McRae Rifles, 41st Regiment, Captains J. S. Gilliam, Sr., John Camp*
and H. M. Mingea.*

" Confederate Cadets, 41st Regiment, Captains J. B. Laurens, V. Weddell,* J. H. Meacham and James Smith.

"Confederate Guard, 9th Regiment, Captain F. M. Wright,

"*Artillery.*—Petersburg Artillery, Captains J. N. Nicholls and Edward
Graham.

"Lee Guard Artillery, Captains Jas. R. Branch and R. G. Pegram.

"Heavy Artillery, Captains G. V. Rambaut and B. J. Black.

"*Cavalry*—There were three companies of cavalry organized in the City.
The first of these was first commanded by C. Fisher, and had a number
of other captains, among whom were Junius Goodwyn, R. D. McIlwaine,
Wm. Jeter,* Jos. Jordan, Captains Proctor and Yeamans Griscom. It is
related of the latter, that in one of the actions around Petersburg his
command engaged that of his own brother, who was on the other side.
The third company was commanded by Captain E. A. Goodwyn.

" The names marked with an asterisk are those of officers who were
killed or mortally wounded during the war. It would be impossible to
follow these commands through their various experiences of battle. They
were among the first that rallied at Norfolk, and they presented a straight
but fearfully reduced front at Appomattox. If in any engagement they
fell below the highest standard of gallant duty, there is no record of its
name or date."

Petersburg was spared the actual presence of the enemy until a year or
so before the close of hostilities, but the inhabitants felt their full share
of absorbing anxiety as to the final result. The news of every battle,
whether a victory or a defeat, was read through the tears shed for a hus-
band or father, brother or son, who had bravely fallen in the fight.

The local forces of Petersburg were called out on the 5th of May, 1864, together with the companies from the adjoining counties, so that when General Butler threatened the town from below, about nine hundred troops were in the lines. These included a company from Nottoway, one from Chesterfield, one from Prince George and one from Dinwiddie.

THE NINTH OF JUNE.

A portion of the troops above enumerated had been sent to other points, and the remainder were still on the lines, guarding the City, when, about 9 o'clock on the morning of the 9th of June, Colonel Fletcher H.

MASONIC HALL., TABB STREET.

Archer, who was in command of the local forces, was informed by Col. Harrison, of General Wise's command, of the approach of the enemy, 1,800 to 2,000 strong, under General Kautz. At that time there were with Col. Archer at Rives' farm, about two miles east of the City, the skeletons of six companies, five of which were made up mainly of Petersburg men, and the sixth being from Prince George County. These companies were respectively commanded by the following officers : Captains Wolff, Alfriend, Rogers, R. F. Jarvis, W. H. Jarvis, and Lieut. Botts, and numbered in all about one hundred and twenty-five men. The personnel of this small force comprised aged and infirm men, some convalescent or furloughed soldiers from the regular army, a few foreign residents of the

City and others exempt from military service. Arrangements were made,
however, for the reception of the enemy, and the defenders were disposed
in the trenches. Captain James E. Wolff, with his company, was placed
on the extreme left, and Captain W. H. Jarvis on the extreme right. Between 10 and 11 o'clock the enemy made their appearance, and then their
demonstration, first with a reconnoitering party, on the Confederate line.
They were promptly met with a volley which unhorsed their leader within
fifty feet of the Confederate front, and were repulsed with the loss of
several horses killed and several men wounded and captured. Colonel
Archer was reinforced at this crisis by General Colston with a squad of
six men and one gun from Sturdivant's Battery. The Federal force now
dismounted and made a regular attack, which was successful, after a sharp
fight of an hour and a half, in turning the Confederate left at the position
occupied by a portion of Captain Wolff's company, under the command of
Lieut. G. V. Scott. From the point so gained the enemy had an enfilad-
ing fire on the Confederate ranks, and their "16-shooters" began to do
some terrible work. But the gallant defenders—patriarchs, invalids and
youths—stood their ground with the grim resolution of able-bodied veterans, for they were fighting within sight of their homes! "We fought
them," says Anthony M. Keiley, who took part in the battle, "till we were
so surrounded that the two nearest men to me were shot in the back while
facing the line of original approach; till our camp in rear of the works
was full of the foe; till the noblest blood of the City stained the clay of
the breastworks, as they gave out their lives, gun in hand and face forward, on the spot where their officers placed them." Wolff's company was
literally cut to pieces—being almost annihilated by its losses in killed,
wounded and captured. Captain Wolff was made prisoner and sent to
Point Lookout, where he was detained for several months.

With Wolff's defeat and capture, the stubborn fight of the 9th of June
was practically at an end, for the rest of the command, finding it impossible to hold the position any longer against such odds, retired from the
lines, the movement being by the right flank. The delay caused by this
obstinate defence enabled the cavalry of Dearing and the batteries of
Graham and Sturdivant to be brought to the front, and the City was saved
for the time being, but only at the cost of eleven precious lives from
among her brave defenders, whose original numbers had been reduced
one-half. Their gallantry on this occasion elicited the admiration of
friend and foe alike, and General Wise, who was in command of the City,
issued a general order thanking Archer and his men, on behalf of General
Beauregard himself, for their bravery and devotion. Many were captured
and taken to Northern prisons, among them the Hon. Timothy Rives, ex-
member of Congress and an ardent Union man.

During an action on the 16th of June, in which a portion of this Citizens'
corps was engaged, two others fell. The names of the killed on the 9th

and 16th of June are inscribed on a memorial tablet in Old Blandford Church.

The 9th of June is justly regarded as the proudest and most sacred day in the annals of the City, and the anniversary is still celebrated with sol-

IRON FRONT BUILDING, SYCAMORE STREET.

emn exercises, under the auspices of the ladies of the Memorial Association.

THE SIEGE OF PETERSBURG.

The beginning of the end had come. It was at Petersburg that the last determined stand of the Southern Confederacy was made, and the interest

of the last ten months of the war centred chiefly within the radius reached
by the sound of our Court House bell.   The City sustained a siege which
is without a parallel in the history of any place or of any time, when such
features are considered as the enormous disproportion in numbers and resources between the besiegers and the besieged ; the cruel earnestness of
the incessant fighting within and without the trenches ; and the peculiar
nature of the issue at stake.   The attack made upon the City on the 9th
of June was, as has been shown, unsuccessful.   On the 12th of the same
month, after the second battle of Cold Harbor, General Grant crossed the
James River and took up his position at City Point, while General Butler,
with the Army of the James, occupied Bermuda Hundred, on the north
bank of the Appomattox.   Almost simultaneously General Lee crossed
the Chickahominy and placed himself in position to protect Richmond
from attack on the north and east sides of the river, with a total force of
seventy thousand men.   Grant's army numbered a hundred thousand,
with all the world to recruit from.   The second attack, made on June
16th, by the corps of Generals Smith, Hancock and Burnside, was also
repulsed, and in the engagements that immediately followed between the
Army of Northern Virginia and the Army of the Potomac, the latter con-
fess to a loss of 10,268 men.   General Grant, the Federal commander-in-
chief, had expected to capture Petersburg by a *coup-de-main*, and was dis-
appointed beyond measure at the vigorous and sustained resistance, which
baffled his repeated assaults, and against which his vastly superior numer-
ical strength had proved powerless.   The 19th and 20th of June were employed by both armies in strengthening their respective positions and in
constructing the redoubts and parapets which still form conspicuous
features in the suburban landscape.   The siege had now fairly begun, and
the Federal lines were extended from time to time, till at last they stretch-
ed from the Appomattox, across the Petersburg & Weldon Railroad, as
far as Fort Fisher to the left, and thence back to Fort Bross, on the Black
Water Swamp, a continuous system of earth-works more than twenty-
three miles in length.   When active hostilities were resumed on the 21st,
an unsuccessful attempt, which cost them 3,000 men, was made by the
Federals to seize the Weldon Railroad, while a strong body of cavalry at
the same time tore up the tracks of the connecting railroads, and thus put
the besieged to great straits for stores and rations.   The following day,
however. a brilliant attack was made on the enemy's flank by General Mahone, who returned to the main lines at night-fall with 1,742 prisoners,
besides a vast quantity of small-arms, four guns and eight standards.
Again, on the 28th, a splendid victory was gained by the Confederates over
General Wilson, to whom had been assigned the duty of capturing or destroying the railroads in the vicinity.   And his defeat cannot be wondered
at, when, among those who rushed to the rescue of the threatened communications were such men as W. H. F. Lee, Fitz Lee, Hampton, Ma-

hone, Pegram, Lomax and Wickham. Wilson, with the utterly demoralized remnant of his cavalry, retreated across the Nottoway, leaving behind him, in the hands of the Confederates, a thousand prisoners, besides his killed and wounded, his trains, thirteen pieces of artillery and large quantities of ordnance stores and small-arms.

Grant made several other futile attempts to cut Lee's communications and destroy the Confederate arteries of supply, while at the same time he was vigorously pushing forward the completion of his extensive works

WASHINGTON STREET M. E. CHURCH.

and arming them with heavy artillery, in order that the bulk of his army might be available for such active operations as circumstances should render advisable. But it is not within the scope of this sketch to relate in detail the many exciting events which marked the ten months' siege. Thirteen pitched battles were fought around the works, besides innumerable skirmishes and other minor engagements involving the safety of the City and the lives of its gallant defenders. These latter, in fact, were of daily occurrence, while the boom of artillery and the shriek of shot and

shell, as they sped through the air on their errand of death and destruction, were sounds as familiar to the ears of the besieged as is now the
peaceful tone of the Court House bell, as it records the passing hours.

The battle of the 30th of July, however, deserves a more extended notice. It has passed into history as the "*Battle of the Crater,*" and its
horrors were unsurpassed by any other event of this long and bloody
war.

"In all the thirty miles of massive entrenchments that environed the
beleaguered City," says Gregory, "there stood no soldiers more heroic or
more faithful than her own sons, who were doing battle in the sight of
their own roof-trees for the honor and safety of their homes. Among
those killed by the Crater explosion were two officers and twenty men of
Pegram's Petersburg Battery. In the fight that followed General Mahone
won, as he deserved, enduring glory, and rescued the City from capture
and probably from sack. He received the stars of a Major-General for
his gallantry and skill, while Colonel D. A. Weisiger was promoted to the
command of the Old Mahone Brigade, as the Association composed of its
members is still proud to be called."

For the narrative of this famous fight, which must always hold a foremost position in the history of the City, we cannot do better than quote
from the excellent address delivered by Captain W. Gordon McCabe, A.
A. G., on November 1st, 1876, before the Association of Northern Virginia, entitled "The Defence of Petersburg".

"Burnside held an advanced position, carried in the assaults of the
17th and 18th of June by his own troops and Griffin's division of Warren's
corps, and succeeded in constructing a heavy line of rifle pits scarcely
more than 100 yards distant from what was then known as the Elliott
Salient. Immediately in rear of this advanced line the ground dipped
suddenly, and broadening out into a meadow of considerable extent, afforded an admirable position for massing a large body of troops, while working parties would be effectually screened from the observations of the
Confederates holding the crest beyond.

"Now, it happened that the Second Division of the Ninth Corps guard-
ed this portion of the Federal front, and as early as the 24th of June,
Lieutenant-Colonel Henry Pleasants, commanding the First Brigade of
that Division, a man of resolute energy and an accomplished mining engineer, proposed to his division commander that he be allowed to run a
gallery from this hollow, and blow up the hostile salient.

"Submitted to Burnside, the venture was approved, and at 12 o'clock
next day, Pleasants began work, selecting for the service his own regiment, the Forty-eighth Pennsylvania, most of whom were miners from the
Schuylkill region. But though Burnside approved, the Commanding General of the Army of the Potomac and the military engineers regarded the
scheme from the first with ill-concealed derision.   *   *   *   *

ery
ies
et,
*

)w-

be-
y to

As
oint
re-

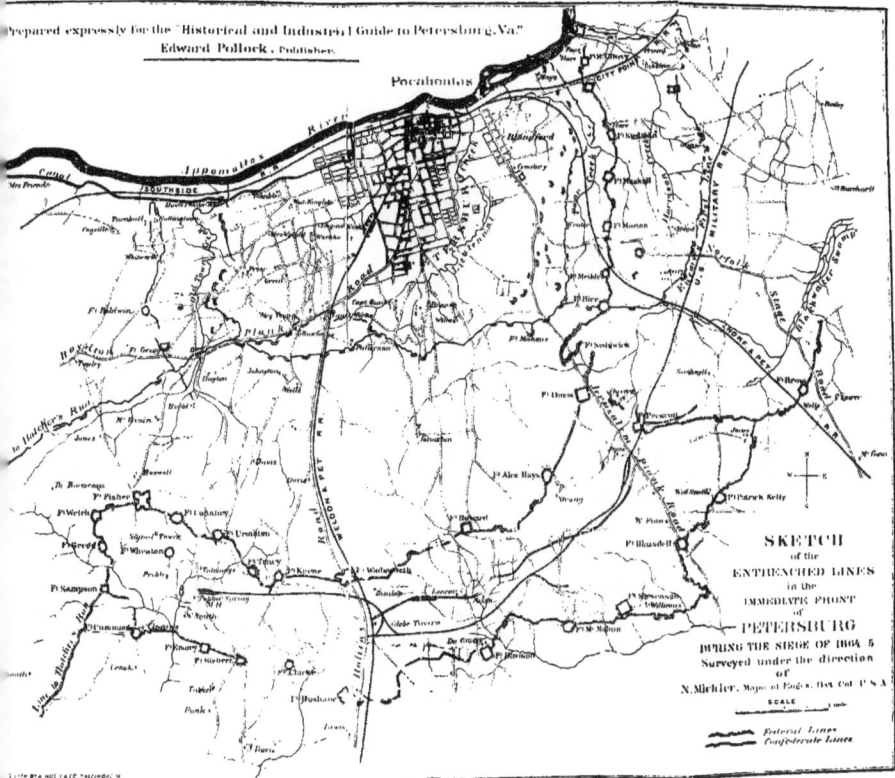

SKETCH
of the
ENTRENCHED LINES
in the
IMMEDIATE FRONT
of
PETERSBURG
DURING THE SIEGE OF 1864-5
Surveyed under the direction
of
N. Michler, Major of Engrs. Bvt. Col. U.S.A.

SCALE

Federal Lines
Confederate Lines

" By July 23d the mine was finished. It consisted of a main gallery
five hundred and ten and eight-tenths feet in length, with lateral galleries
right and left, measuring respectively thirty-eight and thirty-seven feet,
and forming the segment of a circle concave to the Confederate lines. *
* * On the 27th of July, the charge, consisting of 320 kegs of pow-

WATSON & McGILL'S TOBACCO FACTORY, WASHINGTON STREET.

der, each containing twenty-five pounds, was placed in the mine, and before sunset of the 28th, the tamping was finished and the mine ready to
be sprung.   *   *   *
" On the evening of the 29th, Meade issued his orders of battle. As
soon as it was dusk, Burnside was to mass his troops in front of the point
to be attacked, and form them in columns of assault, taking care to re-

move the abatis. so that the troops could debouch rapidly, and have his pioneers equipped for opening passages for the artillery. He was to spring the mine at 3:30 a. m., and, moving rapidly through the breach, seize the crest of Cemetery Hill, a ridge four hundred yards in rear of the Confederate lines.   *   *   *

"To cover the assault, the Chief of Artillery was to concentrate a heavy fire on the Confederate batteries commanding the salient and its approaches, and, to this end, eighty-one heavy guns and mortars, and over eighty light guns were placed in battery on that immediate front.   *   *

" Burnside, in his turn, issued his orders of assault. Ledlie was to push through the breach straight to Cemetery Hill. Wilcox was to follow, and, after passing the breach, deploy on the left of the leading division and seize the line of the Jerusalem Plank Road. Potter was to pass to the right of Ledlie and protect his flank, while Ferrero's Negro Division, should Ledlie effect a lodgment on Cemetery Hill, was to push beyond that point and immediately assault the town.

"Long before dawn of the 30th, the troops were in position, and at half-past three, punctually to the minute, the mine was fired.   *   *

"Minute followed minute of anxious waiting—a trial to even the most determined veterans—and now the east was streaked with gray, yet the tender beauty of the dim tranquility remained unvexed of any sound of war, save one might hear a low hum, amid the darkling swarm as grew the wonder at delay. *   *   * Then it was that two brave men, whose names should be mentioned with respect wherever courage is honored, Lieut. Jacob Douty and Sergeant Henry Rees, both of the Forty-eighth Pennsylvania, volunteered for the perilous service and entered the mine. Crawling on their hands and knees, groping in utter darkness, they found that the fuse had gone out about fifty feet from the mouth of the main gallery, relighted it, and retired.   *   *   *

" A slight tremor of the earth for a second, then the rocking as of an earthquake, and with a tremendous burst, which rent the sleeping hills beyond, a vast column of earth and smoke shoots upward to a great height, its dark sides flashing out sparks of fire, hangs poised for a moment in mid-air, and then hurtling downward with a roaring sound, showers of stones, broken timbers, and blackened human limbs, subsides—the gloomy pall of darkening smoke flushing to an angry crimson as it floats away to meet the morning sun.

" Pleasants has done his work with terrible completeness, for now the site of the Elliott Salient is marked by a horrid chasm, 135 feet in length, 97 feet in breadth, and 30 feet deep, and its brave garrison, all asleep, save the guards, when thus surprised by sudden death, lie buried beneath the jagged blocks of blackened clay—in all 256 officers and men of the Eighteenth and Twenty-second South Carolina—two officers and twenty men of Pegram's Petersburg Battery.   *   *   *

" Now a storm of fire bursts in red fury from the Federal front, and in
an instant all the valley between the hostile lines lies shrouded in billow-
ing smoke.   *   *   *

" It was fully eight o'clock—more than three hours after the explosion
—when Ferrero's Negro Division, the men, beyond question, inflamed
with drink, burst from the advanced lines, cheering vehemently, passed at
a double-quick over the crest under a heavy fire, and rushing with scarce
a check over the heads of the white troops in the Crater, spread to their
right, capturing more than two hundred prisoners and one stand of colors.
At the same moment, Turner, of the Tenth Corps, pushed forward a brigade over the Ninth Corps parapets, seized the Confederate line still further to the north, and quickly disposed the remaining brigades of his division to confirm his success.

PUBLIC HIGH SCHOOL, UNION STREET.

" Now was the crisis of the day, and fortunate was it for maiden and
matron of Petersburg that even at this moment there was filing into the
ravine between Cemetery Hill and the drunken battalions of Ferrero, a
stern array of silent men, clad in faded gray, resolved with grim resolve
to avert from the mother-town a fate as dreadful as that which marked the
three days' sack of Badajos.

" Lee, informed of the disaster at 6:10 a. m., had bidden his aide, Col.
Charles Venable, to ride quickly to the right of the army and bring up
two brigades of Anderson's old division, commanded by Mahone, for time
was too precious to observe military etiquette and send the orders through

Hill. Shortly after, the General-in-Chief reached the front in person, and all men took heart when they descried the grave and gracious face, and 'Traveller' stepping proudly, as if conscious that he bore upon his back the weight of a nation. Beauregard was already at the Gee House, a commanding position five hundred yards in rear of the Crater, and Hill had galloped to the right to organize an attacking column, and had ordered down Pegram, and even now the light batteries of Brander and El-

WM. E. FRENCH'S DRUG STORE, COR. SYCAMORE AND LOMBARD STREETS.

lett were rattling through the town at a sharp trot, with cannoniers mounted, the sweet, serene face of their boy-colonel lit up with that glow which to his men meant hotly-impending fight.

"Venable had sped upon his mission, and found Mahone's men already standing to their arms ; but the Federals, from their lofty 'look-outs,' were busily interchanging signals, and to uncover such a length of front without exciting observation demanded the nicest precaution. Yet was this difficulty overcome by a simple device, for the men being ordered to drop back one by one, as if going for water, obeyed with such intelligence, that Warren continued to report to Meade that not a man had left his front.

" Then forming in the ravine to the rear, the men of the Virginia and Georgia brigades came pressing down the valley with swift, swinging stride—not with the discontented bearing of soldiers whose discipline alone carries them to what they feel to be a scene of fruitless sacrifice, but with the glad alacrity and aggressive ardor of men impatient for battle, and who, from long knowledge of war, are conscious that Fortune has placed within their grasp an opportunity which, by the magic touch of veteran steel, may be transformed to swift-winged victory.

" Halting for a moment in rear of the Ragland House, Mahone bade his men strip off blankets and knapsacks and prepare for battle.

" Then riding quickly to the front, while the troops marched in single

FEDERAL HEADQUARTERS AT POPLAR GROVE, 1864-5.

file along the covered-way, he drew rein at Bushrod Johnson's headquarters, and reported in person to Beauregard. Informed that Johnson would assist in the attack with the outlying troops about the Crater, he rode still further to the front, dismounted, and pushing along the covered way from the Plank road, came out into the ravine, in which he afterwards formed his men. Mounting the embankment at the head of the covered-way, he descried within 160 yards a forest of glittering bayonets, and beyond, floating proudly from the captured works, eleven Union flags. Estimating rapidly from the hostile colors the probable force in his front, he at once dispatched his courier to bring up the Alabama brigade from the right, assuming thereby a grave responsibility, yet was the wisdom of the decision vindicated by the event.

" Scarcely had the order been given when the head of the Virginia brigade began to debouch from the covered-way. Directing Colonel Weisiger, its commanding officer, to file to the right and form line of battle, Mahone stood at the angle, speaking quietly and cheerily to the men. Silently and quickly they moved out, and formed with that precision dear to every soldier's eye—the sharp-shooters leading, followed by the Sixth, Sixteenth, Sixty-first, Forty-first and Twelfth Virginia—the men of Second Manassas and Crampton's Gap !

" But one caution was given—to reserve fire until they reached the brink of the ditch ; but one exhortation—that they were counted on to do this work, and do it quickly.

" Now the leading regiment of the Georgia brigade began to move out, when suddenly a brave Federal officer, seizing the colors, called on his men to charge. Descrying this hostile movement on the instant, Weisiger —a veteran of stern countenance, which did not belie the personal intrepidity of the man—uttered to the Virginians the single word 'forward.' Then the sharp-shooters and the men of the Sixth, on the right, running swiftly forward—for theirs was the greater distance to traverse—the whole line sprang along the crest, and there burst from more than eight hundred warlike voices that fierce yell which no man ever yet heard unmoved on field of battle. Storms of case-shot from the right mingled with the tempest of bullets which smote them from the front ; yet was there no answering volley, for these were veterans, whose fiery enthusiasm had been wrought to a finer temper by the stern code of discipline, and even in the tumult the men did not forget their orders. Still pressing forward with steady fury, while the enemy, appalled by the inexorable advance, gave ground, they reached the ditch of the inner works ; then one volley crashed from the whole line, and the Sixth and Sixteenth, with the sharp-shooters, clutching their empty guns and redoubling their fierce cries, leaped over the retrenched-cavalier, and all down the line the dreadful work of the bayonet began.

" How long it lasted none may say with certainty, for in those fierce moments no man heeded time, no man asked, no man gave quarter ; but in an incredibly brief space, as seemed to those who looked on, the whole of the advanced line north of the Crater was retaken, the enemy in headlong flight, while the tattered battle-flags planted along the parapets from left to right told Lee, at the Gee House, that from this nettle ' Danger ' Valor had plucked the flower 'Safety' for an army.

" Redoubling the sharp-shooters on his right, Mahone kept down all fire from the Crater, the vast rim of which frowned down upon the lower line occupied by his troops.

" And now the scene within the horrid pit was such as might be fitly portrayed only by the pencil of Dante after he had trod 'nine-circled Hell.' From the great mortars to the right and left, huge missiles, describing graceful curves, fell at regular intervals with dreadful accuracy and burst among the helpless masses huddled together, and every explosion was followed by piteous cries, and oftentimes the very air seemed darkened by flying human limbs. Haskell, too, had moved up his Eprouvette mortars among the men of the Sixteenth Virginia—so close, indeed, that his powder-charge was but one ounce and a half—and without intermission the storm of fire beat upon the hapless men imprisoned within.

"Mahone's men watched with great interest this easy method of reaching troops behind cover, and then, with the imitative ingenuity of soldiers, gleefully gathered up the countless muskets with bayonets fixed, which had been abandoned by the enemy, and propelled them with such nice skill that they came down upon Ledlie's men like the rain of the Norman arrows at Hastings.

At half-past ten, the Georgia brigade advanced and attempted to dislodge Wilcox's men, who still held a portion of the lines south of the Cra-

CHURCH BUILT BY FEDERAL SOLDIERS AT POPLAR GROVE. 1864-5

ter, but so closely was every inch of the ground searched by the artillery, so biting was the fire of musketry, that, obliquing to their left, they sought cover behind the cavalier-trench won by the Virginia brigade—many officers and men testifying by their blood how gallantly the venture had been essayed.

"Half an hour later the Alabamians, under Saunders, arrived, but further attack was postponed until 1 p. m., in order to arrange for co-operation with Colquitt on the right. Sharply to the minute agreed upon, the assaulting line moved forward, and with such astonishing rapidity did these glorious soldiers rush across the intervening space, that ere their first wild cries subsided, their battle-flags had crowned the works. The Confeder-

ate batteries were now ordered to cease firing, and forty volunteers were
called for to assault the Crater, but so many of the Alabamians offered
themselves for the service that the ordinary system of detail was necessary. Happily, before the assaulting party could be formed, a white hand-
kerchief, made fast to a ramrod, was projected above the edge of the Crater, and, after a brief pause, a motley mass of prisoners poured over the
sides and ran for their lives to the rear.

"In this grand assault on Lee's lines, for which Meade had massed
65,000 troops, the enemy suffered a loss of above 5,000 men, including
1,101 prisoners, among whom were two brigade commanders, while vast
quantities of small-arms and twenty-one standards fell into the hands of
the victors.

"Yet many brave men perished on the Confederate side. Elliott's brigade lost severely in killed and prisoners. The Virginia brigade, too, paid
the price which Glory ever exacts. The Sixth carried in 98 men and lost
88, one company—'the dandies,' of course—'Old Company F,' of Norfolk, losing every man killed or wounded. Scarcely less was the loss in
other regiments. The sharp-shooters carried in 80 men and lost 64—among
the slain their commander, William Broadbent, a man of prodigious strength
and activity, who, leaping first over the works, fell *pierced by eleven bayonet
wounds*—a simple captain, of whom we may say, as was said of Ridge,
'No man died that day with more glory, yet many died and there was
much glory.' "

In the four engagements of August 18th, 19th, 21st and 25th, brought
about by Grant's determination to establish himself on the Weldon Road,
the Federals, says McCabe, "acknowledge a loss of above 7,000 men, and
there is reason to believe that the occupation of the Weldon Road during
this month cost them between 8,000 and 9,000 men. The Confederate
loss was not above one-fourth of that number."

The story of this wonderful "defence " practically closes with the following passage : " On the evening of April 1st, the battle of Five Forks was
fought, and lost to the Confederates, and at dawn next morning, from the
Appomattox to Hatcher's Run, the Federal assaults began. Lee was forced
back from the whole line covering the Boydton Plank Road, and Gibbon's Division of Ord's Corps boldly essayed to break through into the
town. The way was barred by an open work of heavy profile, known as
Battery Gregg, garrisoned by a mixed force of infantry, chiefly North
Carolinians, of Lane's Brigade, and a score of artillerymen, in all 250
men. Thrice Gibbon's columns, above 5,000 strong, surged against the
devoted outpost—thrice they recoiled—but about noon the fourth assault
was ordered, and the assailants, discovered with surprise and admiration,
that of these 250 brave men, 220 had been struck down, yet were the
wounded loading and passing up their muskets to the thirty unhurt and
invincible veterans, who, with no thought of surrender, still maintained

a biting fire from the front. A splendid feat of arms, which taught prudence to the too-eager enemy for the rest of the day, for nearly 600 of Gibbon's men lay dead and stricken in front of the work, and the most daring of the assailants recognized that an army of such metal would not easily yield the inner lines. ON THAT NIGHT PETERSBURG WAS EVACUATED."

BLANDFORD OLD CHURCH, PARTIALLY RESTORED IN 1882.

During the siege, almost all parts of the City were exposed to the rain of the enemy's shell; but the people bore the danger with the same cheerful courage which they displayed under all the trying privations incident to their situation. The liberality of the citizens and the heroism of the ladies, in the relief of the sick and wounded and in the patient and calm endurance of all the perils of the siege, are far above all praise. And in leaving the subject of Petersburg's intimate and responsible connection with the fortunes of this "Mightiest Revolt in History," we heartily endorse the following beautiful tribute to Petersburg's brave sons and daughters, from the eloquent pen of Capt. McCabe :

"Her men fitted to bear arms were yonder with Lee's veterans, and now her women—suddenly environed by all the dread realities of war—discovered a constancy and heroism befitting the wives and mothers of such valiant soldiers. Some, watching in the hospitals, cheered on the

T. B. MOORE'S HAT STORE, SYCAMORE STREET.

convalescents, who, when the sounds of battle grew nearer, rose like faithful soldiers to join their comrades ; others, hurrying along the deserted streets, the silence of which was ever and anon sharply broken by screaming shell, streamed far out on the highways to meet the wounded and bear them to patriot homes. Nor shall we wonder at this devotion, for in the very beginning of those eventful days these noble women, hanging for a few brief moments on the necks of gray-haired grandsires, or pressing the mother-kiss upon the brows of eager boys, had bidden them, with eyes brimming with prayerful tears, to go and serve the State upon the outer works ; and surely, when thus duty and honor had weighed down the scale of natural love, they had learned with an agony which man can never measure, that life itself must be accounted as a worthless thing when the safety of a nation is at stake."

THE RETURN OF PEACE.

When the City had been formally surrendered by the Mayor, W. W. Townes, Major-General Hartsuff was assigned by General Grant to the command of the forces in Petersburg and its neighborhood. He made his headquarters at Centre Hill, the residence of Mr. Robt B. Bolling, and appointed Brevet Major-General Ferrero, who had been a dancing master

W. M. CAMERON & BRO.'S TOBACCO FACTORY, COR. PERRY AND BROWN STS.

in New York, to the command of the City and defences. The civil authority recognized at this time was an informal commission of citizens for the hearing and arbitration of cases arising between the two races. In due time Ferrero was succeeded by General Gibbons, who distinguished himself by suspending the *News* and imprisoning its editor, Mr. Anthony

M. Keiley, for a few days. The last Federal commandant was General Stoneman, whose administration was highly satisfactory to the citizens.

The course of municipal reconstruction was in this wise: In June, 1866, an election was held under military supervision, at which, however, none but white citizens voted, and Mr. Charles F. Collier and a council of substantial gentlemen were chosen. Mr. Collier was bayonetted out of office in two years, and Rush Burgess appointed in his stead by General Schofield. On the 1st of April, 1868, Mr. Burgess took the oath of office and the iron-clad oath of July 2d, 1862. On the 1st of April, 1869, the new iron-clad council took possession, and General W. C. Newberry, who had been a Union officer, was appointed by General Stoneman. In June, 1869, General Newberry was removed and Dr. W. G. Pearse appointed Mayor. In March, 1870, Governor G. C. Walker, under the provisions of the Enabling Act, appointed a Council consisting of representatives of all shades, the purpose being that of conciliation and practical reconstruction. Dr. Pearse resigned and the Council elected General Newberry, Mayor. On June 8th, 1870, General Newberry having resigned again, Mr. J. P. Williamson was elected Mayor by the Council. In May, 1870, Franklin Wood was elected by popular vote, the State having been admitted to the Union under the Reconstruction Acts and the negroes now exercising the right of suffrage. He took his seat for two years on the 1st of July.

In December, 1865, the Petersburg Iron Works Company was incorporated; in 1866 the Commercial Insurance and Savings Bank of Petersburg was chartered. In 1870 the City was authorized to issue bonds in the sum of $300,000, at a rate of interest not exceeding 12 per cent. for municipal purposes. In July of the same year, the Petersburg and Richmond Steamboat Company was chartered.

The people of Petersburg had accepted the results of the war with admirable spirit and fortitude. The commercial enterprise for which the City had long been noted was temporarily crippled, it is true, by the terrible ordeal of the siege and the partial laying waste of the surrounding back-country, but it was far from being stamped out. No sooner had society undergone such reorganization as the march of events had necessitated, than the repairing of shattered fortunes and the rebuilding of ruined homes were vigorously undertaken. That industry, perseverance and frugality have characterized our merchants and manufacturers in their pursuit of "Fickle Fortune," is abundantly demonstrated by the fact that Petersburg stands out to-day among her sister cities of the Commonwealth, far wealthier and much more beautiful than she ever appeared even in "those good old days before the war."

The train of events subsequent to 1870 affords but little interesting material for our narrative, as the records comprise a bare recital of ordinary local happenings and election returns.

In the early part of 1874 an Act was passed by the Legislature placing the government of the City in the hands of commissioners to be appointed by the Hustings Court. This bill, however, was vetoed by Governor Kemper, for reasons satisfactory to himself, but which failed to satisfy the friends of good government, among whom much disappointment was ex-

HARRISON & CO.'S CLOTHING STORE, COR. SYCAMORE AND LOMBARD STS.

perienced, and much severe criticism of the Governor's action indulged. In May, 1874, the Republicans, who had controlled the municipal government ever since the re-admission of the State into the Union, were defeated, and W. F. C. Gregory, the Conservative candidate, was elected Mayor.

The years between 1870 and 1880 witnessed the rapid and robust growth of the great tobacco and cotton manufacturing interests which constitute

the main sources of the City's wealth. The export tobacco trade of Petersburg has developed colossal proportions and the names of her manufacturers—as well as the choice products of their factories—are to be
found in the mouths of grateful consumers in every quarter of the
globe ; while the fabrics of our famous looms are equally appreciated by
the inhabitants of the South American Republics.

A slight shock of earthquake was experienced here in 1875, but only to
the extent of disturbing the slumbers of some few light sleepers and exciting the nervous systems of the more timid. A second shock was reported to have been felt over nearly the whole of the Atlantic slope, in
August of this year, 1884, but Petersburg was not shaken.

The story is now told. Concise and incomplete as it is admitted to be,
it is nevertheless hoped that it will be read with interest, not only by Petersburg's own people, to whom many of its facts and incidents are already familiar, but also by those at a distance, who have had no opportunity of visiting the " Cockade City," or of coming into personal contact
with its inhabitants. For all of these a hearty Virginian welcome is in
store, whenever they will claim it—no matter whence they come or whither
they would afterwards go—for the unhappy differences of the past have
been buried too deep for resurrection, while over their grave flourishes the
immortal " Fruit of Righteousness which is sown in Peace."

Many important subjects have been left untouched, or only casually referred to, in the foregoing sketch. In order that these may be more sys-
tematically treated, as well as to preserve the narrative unbroken, it has
been deemed more methodical, as well as more convenient, to devote to
these subjects a series of short chapters, which will be found to embody
many a weighty secret relating to the social virtues and commercial suc-
cesses of a happy, healthy and prosperous community, and may therefore
be considered worthy of careful perusal.

LIST OF THE MAYORS OF PETERSBURG.

1784 TO 1885.

John Banister......	1784 to 1785
Christopher McConnico.......	1785 " 1786
John Shore.....................	1786 " 1787
Robert Bolling...................	1787 " 1788
Thomas G. Peachey...........	1788 " 1789
Simon Frazer....................	1789 " 1790
Joseph Westmore...............	1790 " 1791
Richard Bate....................	1791 " 1792
Joseph Weisiger................	1792 " 1793
William Prentis.................	1793 " 1794
Thomas G. Peachey...........	1794 " 1795
Robert Bolling...................	1795 " 1796
Elias Parker.....................	1796 " 1797
William Prentis.................	1797 " 1798
J. Le Messurier.................	1798 " 1799
William Harrison...............	1799 " 1800
David Maitland.................	1800 " 1801
William Prentis.................	1801 " 1802
George Pegram..................	1802 " 1803
Robert Birchett.................	1803 " 1804
Paul Nash.......................	1804 " 1805
William Prentis.................	1805 " 1806
John McKae......................	1806 " 1807
Alexander Brown...............	1807 " 1808
James Byrne.....................	1808 " 1809
Archibald Baugh................	1809 " 1810
Joel Hammond..................	1810 " 1811
William Moore..................	1811 " 1812
Nathaniel Friend...............	1812 " 1813
William Bowden................	1813 " 1814
Edward Pegram, Jr.............	1814 " 1815
George H. Jones...............	1815 " 1816
John Hinton.....................	1816 " 1817
Samuel Turner..................	1817 " 1818
Edmund Pescud................	1818 " 1819
John H. Brown.................	1819 to 1820
Thomas Wallace...............	1820 " 1821
John Hinton....................	1821 " 1822
John Stith.......................	1822 " 1823
John H. Brown.................	1823 " 1824
Lewis Mabry....................	1824 " 1825
Jabez Smith....................	1825 " 1826
Samuel Winfree................	1826 " 1827
Lewis Mabry....................	1827 " 1828
Joseph Bragg...................	1828 " 1829
Patrick Durkin.................	1829 " 1830
Charles F. Osborne...........	1830 " 1831
Thomas Wallace...............	1831 " 1832
Samuel Winfree...............	1832 " 1833
David H. Branch...............	1833 " 1834
George W. Harrison..........	1834 " 1835
John D. Tanner................	1835 " 1836
James McFarland, Jr........	1836 " 1837
Stephen G. Wells (elected, but declined to serve)....	
George W. Harrison..........	1837 " 1838
Daniel Lyon....................	1838 " 1839
Robert B. Bolling.............	1839 " 1840
Stephen G. Wells.............	1840 " 1841
William Pannill................	1841 " 1842
Thomas Branch................	1842 " 1843
John Pollard....................	1843 " 1844
John H. Patterson............	1844 " 1845
James B. Cogbill..............	1845 " 1846
Joseph E. Cox.................	1846 " 1847
Francis E. Rives..............	1847 " 1848
J. M. B. Steward..............	1848 " 1849
Charles Corling...............	1849 " 1850
Andrew Kevan.................	1850 " 1851
John Dodson...................	1851 " 1854

In 1852 the new Constitution went into operation, and the Mayoralty became a salaried office. Mr. Dodson was the first Mayor elected by the popular vote:

W. W. Townes (continuously)	1854 to 1865
Charles F. Collier..............	1865 " 1867
Rush Burgess....................	1867 " 1868
W. B. Newberry and } W. G. Pearse.......... }	1868 " 1869
J. P. Williamson............	1869 " 1870
Franklin Wood................	1870 to 1874
W. F. C. Gregory.............	1874 " 1876
William E. Cameron.......	1876 " 1881
F. R. Archer..................	1881 " 1882
T. J. Jarratt (present incumbent)...................	1882

CITY GOVERNMENT, 1884-'85.

MAYOR : T. J. Jarratt.
TREASURER : Emmett W. Couch.
AUDITOR : Frank R. Russell.
CITY SERGEANT : J. Arthur Johnston.
COMMONWEALTH'S ATTORNEY : George S. Bernard.
COMMISSIONER OF REVENUE : George W. Hall.
CITY COLLECTOR : T. H. Bond.
HIGH CONSTABLE : W. D. Minetree.
CHIEF OF POLICE : A. S. Gittman.
CHIEF OF FIRE DEPARTMENT : P. H. Curtis.
GAUGER : W. W. Evans.
SUPERINTENDENT OF ALMSHOUSE : Michael Heelan.
KEEPER OF CEMETERY : James Muirhead.

CITY COUNCIL.

PRESIDENT : Capt. E. A. Goodwyn.   CLERK : Frank R Russell.
   First Ward : E. A. Goodwyn, J. M. Newcomb, J. H. Farley, C. W. Johns.
   Second Ward : James S. Gilliam, R. W. Collier, Augustus Wright, M. W. Pyne.
   Third Ward : W. T. Hubbard, N. T. Patteson, Bartlett Roper, W. T. Parham.
   Fourth Ward : H. R. Smith, John R. Patterson, Simon Seward, Thos. G. Gates.
   Fifth Ward : J. M. Brockwell, G. B. Eanes, H. C. Wilson, W. T. Hargrave.
   Sixth Ward : W. D. Tucker, E. L. Enniss, J. York Harris, J. M. Smith.

COURTS.

   The Corporation Court : Judge, E. M. Mann ; Clerk, J. C. Armistead. Held on the third Thursday in each month.
   The Circuit Court, of the Second Circuit : Judge, S. S. Weisiger ; Clerk, J. C. Armistead. Held in Petersburg May 30th and December 1st in each year.

The taxable property of the City of Petersburg on December 31st, 1884, was as follows :

```
Real . . . . . . . . . . . . . . . . . $5,468,112
Personal . . . . . . . . . . . . . . .   3,870,265

   Total . . . . . . . . . . . . . $9,338,377
```

The Bonded Debt of the City on the same date was $1,186,200
The Sinking Fund owns City Bonds as follows :

```
6 per cent . . . . . . . . . . . . . . $  16,600
8  "   "   . . . . . . . . . . . . . .    44,500

   Total . . . . . . . . . . . . . $  61,100
```

```
Also, cash on hand . . . . . . . . . . . $ 3,634.74
Bills receivable February, 1885 . . . . . .   2,176.53
Bills receivable February, 1886 . . . . . .   2,292.07

   Total cash on hand and bills receivable . . $ 8,103.34
```

ST. JOSEPH'S (R. C.) CHURCH.

GUIDE TO THE CHURCHES.
——:o:——

ROMAN CATHOLIC.

ST. JOSEPH'S : West Washington Street. Rev. W. B. Hanley, pastor; P. H. Curtis, Secretary and Treasurer.
Services : Sundays and Holy Days, 7 and 10 a. m. and 4 p. m. ; week days, other than Holy Days, 6:30 a. m.

PROTESTANT EPISCOPAL.

ST. PAUL'S : Union Street. Rev. C. R. Hains, D. D., rector. Services : Sunday 11 a. m. and 8 p. m ; Wednesday at 4 p. m. Sunday School 9:30 a. m. Vestry meets on the first Tuesday in each month.

GRACE CHURCH : High Street. Rev. C. J. Gibson, D. D., rector. Services : Sunday, 11 a. m. and 7:30 p. m. ; Wednesday, 7:30 p. m. Sunday School 9 a. m. Vestry meets on the first Monday in each month at 8 p. m.

ST. JOHN'S : West Washington Street. Rev. Thomas Spencer, rector. Services : Sunday, 11 a. m. and 8 p. m. ; Tuesday, 8 p. m. Sunday School 9:30 a. m. and 4 p. m. Vestry meets on the second Tuesday in each month at 8 p. m.

ST. PAUL'S MISSION : Blandford.

GRACE CHURCH MISSIONS : Old Street and New Street.

PRESBYTERIAN.

TABB STREET CHURCH : Tabb Street. Rev. J. W. Rosebro, pastor.

Services : Sunday, 11 a. m. and 7:30 p. m. ; Wednesday, 4 p. m. Sunday School 9:30 a. m. Session of Elders and Board of Deacons meet at the church on the first Monday in each month.

SECOND CHURCH : West Washington Street. Rev. S. K. Winn, pastor. Services : Sunday, 11 a. m. and 4:30 p. m. ; Wednesday, 7:30 p. m. Sunday School 9:30 a. m. Young men's prayer meeting every second Monday night. Meeting of Session the first Monday in each month at the Manse.

OLD STREET CHURCH : Old Street. Rev. W. O. Stephens, pastor. Services : Sunday, 11 a. m. and 7:30 p. m. ; Friday, 7:30 p. m. Sunday School 9:30 a. m. Monthly meeting subject to call.

METHODIST.

WASHINGTON STREET CHURCH : Washington Street. Rev. S. S. Lambeth, pastor. Services : Sunday, 11 a. m. and 7:30 p. m. ; Wednesday, 7:30 p. m. Sunday School 9 a. m. Young men's prayer meeting Sunday at 3 p. m., James B. Blanks, leader. Official meeting every Monday night.

MARKET STREET CHURCH : Market Street. Rev. J. W. Bledsoe, D. D., pastor. Services : Sunday, 11 a. m. and 7:30 p. m. ; Wednesday, 7:30 p. m. Sunday School 9:30 a. m.

HIGH STREET CHURCH : High Street. Rev. Oscar Littleton, pastor. Services : Sunday, 11 a. m. and 7:80 p. m. ; Sunday School 9 a. m.

WESLEY CHURCH, Halifax Street. Rev. W. H. Atwill, pastor. Services : Sunday, 11 a. m. and 7:30 p. m. ; Wednesday, 7:30 p. m. Sunday School 9:30 a. m.

BLANDFORD CHURCH : Blandford. Rev. J. E. R. Riddick, pastor. Services : Sunday, 11 a. m. and 7:30 p. m. ; Wednesday, 7:30 p. m.

ETTRICK CHURCH : Ettrick. Rev. Jacob Manning, pastor.

MATOACA CHURCH : Matoaca. Rev. N. J. Pruden, pastor.

BAPTIST.

FIRST CHURCH : West Washington Street. Rev. E. C. Dargan, pastor. Services : Sunday, 11 a. m. and 7:30 p. m.; Wednesday, 7:30 p. m. Sunday School, 9 a. m. Business meeting, Wednesday after first Monday in each month, after service.

BYRNE STREET CHURCH : Byrne Street. Rev. D. A. Glenn, pastor. Services : Sunday, 11 a. m. and 7:30 p. m.; Wednesday, 7:30 p. m. Sunday School, 9:30 a. m. Business meeting after morning service on the first Sunday in each month.

WEST END CHURCH : West Washington Street. Rev. C. H. Nash, pastor. Services : Sunday, 11 a. m. and 7:80 p. m.; Wednesday, 7:30 p. m. Sunday School, 9 a. m.

JEWISH SYNAGOGUE.

RODEF SHOLOM, or PURSUIT OF PEACE : Union Street. Rev. L. Freudenthal, D. D., Rabbi ; A. Rosenstock, President ; Jonas Weinberg, Secretary. Services : Every Friday at 5:30 p. m. and Saturday at 10 a. m.

SECRET ORDERS AND BENEVOLENT SO-CIETIES,

WITH THEIR PRINCIPAL OFFICERS FOR 1885.

A. F. AND A. MASONS.

MASONIC HALL—TABB STREET.

Right Worshipful John E. Townes, District Deputy Grand Master.

BLANDFORD LODGE, No. 3 : chartered September 9th, 1757. Meets on the second Tuesday in each month. John T. Parham, Master; Andrew J. Clements, Senior Warden ; Charles E. Williamson, Junior Warden ; J. Bragg Jones, Secretary.

PETERSBURG LODGE, No. 15 : chartered October 29th, 1787. Meets on the second Monday in each month. William J. Sowers, Master ; R. W. Thompson, Senior Warden ; G. E. Scott, Junior Warden ; G. W. Hall, Secretary.

POWHATAN STARKE LODGE, No. 124 : chartered December 12th, 1871. Meets on the second Thursday in each month. *Wor.* C. E. Burton, Master ; *P. M.* W. E. Drummond, Senior Warden ; J. H. Cabaniss, Junior Warden ; Louis L. Marks, Secretary,

PETERSBURG UNION ;ROYAL ARCH CHAPTER, No. 7 : Chartered December 10th, 1830. Meets on the first Monday in each month. *M. E.* John T. Parham, High Priest ; *E.* John E. Townes, King; *E.* Charles H. Kruse, Scribe ; E. B. Branch, Secretary.

APPOMATTOX COMMANDERY KNIGHTS TEMPLAR, No. 6 : Chartered May 6th, 1828. Meets on the first Tuesday in each month. *E. Sir* James B. Blanks, Commander : *Sir* John T. Parham, Generalissimo ; *Sir* William R. Nichols, Captain-General; *Sir* John E. Townes, Recorder.

I. O. OF ODD-FELLOWS.

ODD-FELLOWS HALL—SYCAMORE STREET

GLAZIER ENCAMPMENT, No. 7 : Instituted May 20th, 1840. Meets on the first Saturday and third Wednesday in each month. E. J. Bond, Chief Patriarch ; James M. Leath, Scribe.

MONROE LODGE, No. 8 : Instituted May 6th, 1837. Meets every Monday night. M. W. Nelms, Noble Grand ; Charles M. Walsh, Recording Secretary.

APPOMATTOX LODGE, No. 16 : Instituted May 1st, 1840. Meets every Friday night. E. J. Bond, Noble Grand ; E. B. Branch, Recording Secretary.

KNIGHTS OF PYTHIAS.

PYTHIAN HALL, BANK STREET.

RUTH LODGE, No. 21 : Chartered April 13th, 1871. Meets every Thursday night. R. Tucker, Chancellor Commander; H. D. Lockett, Keeper of Records and Seals.

NAOMI LODGE, No. 30: Chartered in 1874. Meets every Monday night. G. J. Hawkins, Chancellor Commander; Samuel H. Nugent, Keeper of Records and Seals. J. F. Coldwell (Ruth Lodge), Past Chancellor and Representative to the Grand Lodge of Virginia.

ENDOWMENT RANK, K. P. SECTION 222: F. A. Owen, President; Thomas H. Holt, Secretary and Treasurer. Meets on the third Wednesday in January and December in each year.

TRINITY DIVISION, No. 3, UNIFORM RANK: Meets on the second Wednesday in each month. James E. Coldwell, Commander; F. A. Owen, Recorder.

IMPROVED ORDER OF RED MEN.

WIGWAM, BANK STREET.

POWHATAN TRIBE, No. 15: Chartered July 1st, 1854. Meets every Tuesday night. E. V. Farley, Sachem; George W. Hall, Chief of Records.

APPOMATTOX TRIBE, No. 32: Chartered in 1867. Meets every Thursday night. William Newton, Sachem; Robert J. Smith, Chief of Records.

KNIGHTS OF HONOR.

PETERSBURG Lodge, No. 737: Instituted September 12th, 1877. Meets at Odd-Fellows Hall, Sycamore street, every Thursday night. G. W. Tucker, Dictator; E. B. Branch, Reporter; J. T. Morriss, Assistant Grand Dictator.

HARMONY LODGE, No. 1369: Instituted February 3d, 1879. Meets at Red Men's Hall, Bank street, on the first and third Monday in each month. M. Kleinman, Dictator; J. Peyser, Reporter. G. May, District Deputy Grand Dictator and Representative to the Grand Lodge.

FRIENDSHIP LODGE, No. 2198. Instituted May 5th, 1880. Meets at Temperance Hall, Sycamore street, on the second and fourth Tuesdays in each month. James M. Quicke, Dictator; W. D. Morriss, Reporter.

ROYAL ARCANUM.

ODD-FELLOWS HALL, SYCAMORE STREET.

SOUTHSIDE COUNCIL, No. 298: Instituted March 26th, 1879. Meets on the second and fourth Tuesday in each month. German B. Gill, Regent; P. S. Seabury, Secretary; J. T. Morriss, Past Grand Regent.

SYCAMORE COUNCIL, No. 705: Instituted August 26th, 1882. Meets on the second Wednesday and fourth Saturday in each month. W. E. Drummond, Regent; Hugh R. Smith, Secretary. J. B. Blanks, Grand Chaplain.

AMERICAN LEGION OF HONOR.

COCKADE COUNCIL, No. 65 : Organized December 29th, 1879. Meets at Odd Fellows' Hall on the first and third Saturdays in each month. J. D. Alley, Commander ; R. J. J. Spratley, Secretary. P. F. Cogbill, Past Grand Commander.

CHOSEN FRIENDS.

LEE COUNCIL, No. 1 : Instituted August 3d, 1880. Meets at Odd Fellows' Hall on the first and third Tuesdays in each month. John T. Slaughter, Chief Councillor; P. S. Seabury, Secretary.

RESCUE COUNCIL, No. 7 : Instituted March 21st, 1883. Meets at Temperance Hall, Sycamore Street, on the first and third Wednesdays in each month. W. H. Hall, Chief Councillor ; L. Lunsford, Secretary.

UNITED AMERICAN MECHANICS.

EXCELSIOR COUNCIL, No. 1 : Instituted March 6th, 1883. Meets at Pythian Castle Hall, Bank Street, every Tuesday night. E. S. Smithson, Councillor ; F. A. Owen, Recording Secretary.

JUNIOR ORDER U. A. M.

VIRGINIA COUNCIL, No. 3 : Instituted in 1878. Meets at Pythian Castle Hall, Bank Street, every Friday night. G. W. Nunnally, Councillor ; R. W. Kruse, Recording Secretary.

B'NAI B'RITH.

VIRGINIA LODGE, No. 225 : Instituted August 23d, 1874. Meets at Library Hall, Bollingbrook Street, on the first and third Sundays in each month. Joseph Mayer, President , J. Peyser, Secretary. A. S. Reinach, Sergeant-at-Arms of District Grand Lodge, No. 5. A. S. Reinach, Jacob Cohen and J. Peyser, Representatives to Grand Lodge.

FRIENDS OF TEMPERANCE.

PETERSBURG COUNCIL, No. 1 : Organized in 1866. Meets at Temperance Hall, Sycamore Street, every Monday night. J. A, Harvill, President ; L. E. Davis, Secretary. The late D'Arcy Paul, Esq., was the first president of this Council.

CHURCH TEMPERANCE SOCIETY.

NAZARITE SECTION, No. 1 : Organized January 22d, 1881. Meets at St. John's Church, West Washington Street, every Saturday night. R. H. Raney, Principal ; F. A. Owen, Recording Secretary.

ST. JOSEPH'S CATHOLIC BENEFICIAL SOCIETY.

Organized in 1877. Meets at the church school room, corner of Washington and Market Streets, on the first Sunday in each month. John P. Patterson, President ; H. C. Hailey, Secretary.

THE UPPER APPOMATTOX COMPANY,

AUGUSTUS WRIGHT, PRESIDENT.

——:o:——

The history of this ancient and important Corporation is so replete with interest, and its influence upon the material prosperity of Petersburg, as a commercial and manufacturing centre, is so strong and direct, that it has been deemed advisable to make it the subject of a separate article, in order that the true character and scope of its extraordinary powers and privileges may be clearly understood ; the more so, indeed, as the property and franchises of the Company have recently passed into the hands of a syndicate of local capitalists, who are now actively engaged in restoring and improving the river and canal along its whole navigable length, with a view to developing its usefulness, both as a water-power and a public highway, to the utmost possible extent.

The " Upper Appomattox " is that part of the river of that name lying above tide-water, into which it flows over the falls at Petersburg, and extending to Planters' Town, in Prince Edward county, a distance of about one hundred miles, passing through the important town of Farmville and traversing the counties of Dinwiddie, Nottoway, Chesterfield, Amelia, Powhatan, Cumberland and Prince Edward.

In the early history of this Commonwealth when roads were poor and far apart and settlements widely scattered, great efforts were made to utilize all the water-ways of the country, and as early as the year 1745 an Act "for the more effectual clearing of James and Appomattox rivers," was passed by the Colonial House of Burgesses (Hening's Statutes at Large, Ch. 23, p. 375), declaring these rivers to be public highways, and empowering the County Courts of Henrico, Prince George, Goochland, Amelia and Albemarle to exact penalties from all persons obstructing their navigation by felling trees into them or by building mill-dams, stone-stops or hedges, and to remove all existing obstructions, and to appoint surveyors to assist in carrying out the requirements of this Act, which was to continue in force for four years. It further defined the riparian rights and responsibilities of the owners of mill property along the river banks.

On December 17th, 1787, the General Assembly passed a second Act (Acts of 1787, Ch. 53, p. 37), "for opening and extending the navigation of Appomattox river," and appointing John Pride, John Holcombe, Joseph Michaux, John Archer, Joseph Jones, Everard Meade and Richard Crump, trustees, "for clearing, improving and extending the navigation of the said river," from Banister's mill as far up the same as they may judge it practicable, so as to have a sufficient depth of water to navigate boats, batteaux or canoes, capable of carrying six hogsheads of tobacco ; and they are authorized to take and receive subscriptions for that purpose." This Act practically gave birth to the Upper Appomattox Company, upon whom were conferred at the same time special powers to collect delinquent subscriptions, to contract for clearing and improving the river, and to remove all obstructions which might in any wise injure its navigation—duties which the counties having original authority appear to have more or less neglected. The Act also empowers the trustees, in case it should be found necessary in some parts of the river to straighten the same by cutting away the banks or by a canal, to acquire any land needed for that purpose ; the value of such land, in the event of a disagreement with the owner, to be decided by a jury. And, in consideration of the expense incurred by the company in cutting canals, erecting locks, or otherwise, it was further enacted "that the said canals and works, with all their profits, shall be and the same are hereby vested in the said trustees and their successors forever, to and for the use of the subscribers and their heirs, as tenants in common, to be apportioned among them according to the sums by them respectively subscribed and paid, and the same shall be deemed real estate, *and be forever exempt from payment of any tax, impositions or assessments whatsoever.*" Provision is also made for the levying of tolls and their legal enforcement, and for compelling the owners of mills on the said river to erect and keep in proper repair good and sufficient locks to admit the easy, safe and expeditous passage of boats.

Other enactments were made from time to time by the General Assembly conferring new powers and privileges upon the Company, and on December 21st, 1795, was passed " An Act to amend and reduce into one Act the several Acts for opening and extending the navigation of the Appomattox river," which confirms all that had gone before, and appoints the following trustees: Everard Meade, Joseph Eggleston, William Murray, Francis Anderson, John Wiley, Peter Johnson, Charles Allen, Ryland Randolph, Edmund Harrison, Alexander McRae, Drury Jones, John Johns, James Morton, Charles Scott, Richard N. Venable, John Epperson, Nelson Patterson, John Archer, John Royall, John Finney, Edward Munford, Peter F. Archer, Francis Eppes, Henry Skipwith, Buller Claiborne, Joshua Chaffin, John Nash, Jr., Samuel Carter, James Wade, John L. Crute, Roger Atkinson, Jr., James Watt, George Markham, John Purnell and Samuel Allen, who, with their successors, are thereby incorporated by the name and title of "The Trustees of the Upper Appomattox Company."

An Act to amend the last cited Act was passed November 22d. 1796 (Chap 26, p. 21), whereby it was enacted: "That the trustees therein appointed, and their successors be, and the same are hereby empowered, to clear, improve, and extend the navigation of the said river, from Banister's mills to tide-water, or as near thereto as they may deem advisable and necessary, and also as far up the said river as they may deem it practicable and conducive to the public interest. For these reasons, and to enable the said trustees and their successors thus to extend the navigation of the said river, they are hereby vested with the same powers, and shall be under the same regulations and restrictions as are given and expressed in the above recited Act."

By an Act of December 23d, 1797, (Chap. 39. p. 26), the number of trustees was reduced to thirteen, a majority of whom should compose a board for the transaction of business, and on January 20th, 1803. (Chap. 26, p. 18), was passed another Act withdrawing from the various County Courts the power hitherto possessed by them, of granting leave to build mills or dams along the banks of the river.

In 1808, and again in 1810, the General Assembly extended to the Company pecuniary assistance towards the expenses of completing the canal; and in 1813 (Chap. 34, p. 44) it was "judged expedient to authorize the trustees of the Upper Appomattox Company to extend their canal through the town of Petersburg to tide-water."

Subsequent Acts of the Legislature granted additional powers to the Company, including the right to erect mills and other useful works, and to engage in transportation and active manufacturing pursuits; and by recent legislation, April 22d, 1882, the Company is authorized to enlarge and deepen its canal and locks to a uniform depth of five feet and a width of forty feet.

It is now nearly one hundred and forty years since the Upper Appomattox, as a public highway, first engaged legislative attention, and during that extended period no less than thirty-four Acts relating to this Company have been recorded on the statute books of Virginia. By virtue of this liberal legislation the Company now enjoys an almost absolute control of a hundred miles of splendid waterway, with the privilege of navigation and right to engage in all kinds of manufactures and useful enterprises. It also has power to let, lease or sell all or any of its property or franchises, and to hold forever, absolutely exempt from taxation, whether by State, County or City, all its property now existing and that may hereafter be created.

It can easily be demonstrated, therefore, that Petersburg, in the possession of this favored corporation, with its far-reaching and inalienable chartered rights, enjoys immense manufacturing advantages over all other cities of the Commonwealth.

These advantages are briefly enumerated in a recent interesting pamphlet treating of this Company and its territory as follows:

First; The section of Virginia embraced in its area possesses most salubrious climatic advantages, freedom from the rigorous temperature of higher latitudes, and, except in most exceptional seasons, absolute free-

dom from ice obstructions ; reliable data show that delay or damage from
that cause is here unknown.

Second ; Along its river and canal banks, high above the water-line, un-
encumbered by earth or other debris, are to be found unlimited and inexhaustible supplies of the finest granite, easily worked and readily transported, which by proper enterprise could be worked to a highly profitable
degree.

Third ; Its improvement is in close proximity to unlimited supplies of
bituminous coal now worked, and it passes over the celebrated Chesterfield coal fields ; immense deposits underlie portions of its route.

Fourth ; Vast quarries of slate are adjacent to and underlie its property,
which also passes over the well known gold bearing belt, which Hotchkiss
so well describes in his work on the physical resources of Virginia ; in addition thereto it penetrates a section where the axeman has, as yet, made
little impression, and the almost virgin forest offers a tempting field to
the lumberman and the manufacturer, oak, hickory, ash, pine, etc., being
found in practically exhaustless quantities.

Fifth ; It is not subject to any practical depletion of power by droughts,
as primarily all the water in the river belongs to it, and only the surplus
water escaping over its dams can be utilized by mills below the lines of
its improvement, and it delivers its water through its own canal or race-
way into the Appomattox river at Petersburg.

It will not be questioned that the proper development of these conspicuous advantages by the judicious exercise of the extraordinary powers
possessed by this Company would result in immense benefit to the whole
community, for it would not only stimulate the commercial enterprise of
our own people and those of the tributary counties, but would also provide safe and attractive investment for an almost unlimited amount of
alien capital. Indeed, the many anxious enquiries that come from capitalists in Northern manufacturing localities, desirous to extend the field
of their operations and establish themselves nearer the base of supply, in-
dicates conclusively that this portion of Virginia must shortly become a
centre for manufacturing enterprise, especially as the causes which have
unfortunately retarded our internal industrial development are now rapidly disappearing.

A striking example of this welcome fact is found in the Upper Appomattox Company, which, as has been already stated, has been recently reorganized, and is now under the control of a syndicate composed of our
most enterprising and energetic business men, whose immediate object it
is to mature and render available, to the largest extent, the usefulness of
their vast property.

The new organization consists of thirteen trustees, the first named five
of whom are superintendents, to whom are committed the active management and control of the Company's affairs, viz. : Augustus Wright, President and Agent ; Robert W. Collier ; Russell H. Wallace, Treasurer; J.
P. Williamson, Thomas R. Moore, J. M. Quicke, G. A. Mannie, George J.
Rogers, E. B. Bain, G. W. Palmore. and R. F. Lester, Secretary.

To the good people of Petersburg it is a source of unqualified satisfaction that the working-out of this gigantic enterprise has fallen into
such excellent hands, for, under their practical management, which has
already taken shape in the vigorous pushing forward of the work of re-
cla iring, repairing and improving, some great achievement is confidently
looked for in the near future. For some time past a force has been busily

engaged clearing away obstructions, repairing dams and locks, dredging
the channel and otherwise improving the property preparatory to putting
it to its ultimate use as a magnificent water-power as well as a convenient
means of transporting such produce as tobacco, corn, hay, lumber and
cord-wood to this market, thus conferring an inestimable benefit upon the
planters and farmers of the back country as well as upon the merchants
and consumers in Petersburg.

But when all this is accomplished the great work will only have been
begun, and it is important that the numerous advantages offered to prospective participants in this enterprise should be pointed out, although
they cannot be more than briefly summed up in an article of limited compass.

Apart, then, from the exclusive rights of navigation over more than 100
miles of water-way, through a territory scarcely reached by railroad facilities, together with the practical monopoly of the whole volume of water
within the banks of the river, not only for navigation but also for milling
and manufacturing purposes, and the development of "other useful
works " along its entire length, there are other special features which already enhance the importance of this Corporation to Petersburg and her
immediate surroundings, and may be made available as a means of elevating her into one of the most prosperous commercial and manufacturing
points in the land.

1st. The physical conformation of the country through which the river
flows is most favorable to this result. Seven miles above the City and 150
feet above its mean level, the water of the river is diverted through a canal, which, by legislative enactment, may be increased to a uniform width
of forty feet, and a depth of five feet, thus giving practically unlimited
area and ample facilities for all manufacturing enterprises which depend
for success upon unfailing water-power.

2d. The property of this Corporation, of whatever kind, is absolutely
exempt from taxes and levies of every description, *forever*.

3d. The terminal point of the canal at Petersburg is within a hundred
yards of the line of the Norfolk & Western Railroad, while the Virginia
& Carolina Railroad, now in course of construction, will be equally
near. The Company and its lessees will therefore possess exceptional
facilities for distributing the products of their manufactories, while the
canal offers unusual inducements to the neighboring farmers to employ its
navigation. The Company also owns the right to connect its water-way
by canal and locks with the tidal navigation of the Lower Appomattox.

No other charter of such far-reaching scope exists under the laws of
this Commonwealth, and it needs only the hand of enterprise and capital
to make the territory adjacent to this property second to none on this
broad continent as a manufacturing and industrial centre. Nowhere else
can manufactures enjoy such exemption as is here offered, and nowhere
else can land, labor and natural force be obtained of such quality and to
such extent. The work of subdivision is easy, and small factories will be
at no disadvantage as regards position and terms, by the side of the most
colossal establishments. In this feature lies the best hope of the early ex-
pansion and solid development of large and small industrial pursuits,
which are destined to convert this section into what, by right of geographical position, it ought to be—The Great Mechanical Emporium of the
New South.

THE LOWER APPOMATTOX.

(CONTRIBUTED BY GEORGE S. BERNARD, ESQ., COMMONWEALTH'S ATTORNEY.)

Situated as Petersburg is on the Appomattox River, at the head of tide-water, only twelve miles from its confluence with the James and only eight miles above ship navigation, the City enjoys the advantage of possessing a natural highway to the ocean.

Before the introduction of railroads this highway was Petersburg's only means of communication with the outer world, and upon it was done a large business during the first half of this century. The main bulk of the articles which made up the trade of the place came or went from the town wharves. Some idea of the extent of this trade sixty odd years ago is given in a gazeteer published in 1812 (Brookes' Gazeteer or Geographical Dictionary) in the article " Petersburg," from which we make the following extract :

" This is a place of considerable trade in grain, flour and tobacco ; the exports of one year having amounted to 1,390,000 dollars."

In subsequent years the trade of the town—especially its foreign trade—considerably increased. This statement is warranted by the fact that for years several ships that plied between City Point and foreign ports were owned by citizens of Petersburg. During the decade from 1830 to 1840, James S. Brander & Co., a Petersburg mercantile house, owned the ships *Tally-Ho, Indian Chief, Caledonia, Brander, Sea* and the *Hark-Away*. Mr. L. E. Stainback, a merchant of Petersburg, owned the ships *Sarah, Scipio, Jefferson, Washington* and *Madison*. These and other sea-going vessels made regular trips, on the 15th of each month, from City Point to Liverpool, London, Rotterdam, Gottenburg and other European ports. They made also voyages to Rio. To make up the outgoing cargoes of these vessels the mills and factories of Petersburg furnished large contributions, and upon their return they brought large supplies of imported goods to fill the warehouses and stores of the merchants of the town. To transport upon the Appomattox the contributions to these ships made by Petersburg exporters and importers was the work of numerous lighters and arks, the business done by which, together with that of the lines of schooners that plied regularly between Petersburg and New York and between Petersburg and other Northern ports, during the period to which we refer, always gave the wharves of the town an appearance of life and activity in striking contrast with their appearance at the present time when the railways that radiate from the City carry so much of the freights that in former times were transported over the river.

The Appomattox, however, continues to be of the greatest practical advantage in securing to the people of Petersburg cheaper railroad rates than they would enjoy were this water-course not navigable between Petersburg and City Point. The better the navigation of the Appomattox, the more reasonable the freight rates between Petersburg and every point accessible by water, the river serving as a competing transportation route. It is not, therefore, a matter of surprise that the citizens of Petersburg have long felt the importance of improving and keeping open the navigation of this river, and at times have freely contributed money for the purpose. It is rather a matter of surprise that a ship canal to connect the town with deep water, only eight miles distant, has not been constructed. There was, indeed, in 1847, when the railroad to City Point was in a very dilapidated condition, a strong feeling among the people of Petersburg in favor of a ship canal. The Common Hall, by a unanimous vote, ordered an election to be held on the 2nd of August, 1847, to take the sense of the qualified voters of the town upon a proposition to expend $500,000 in making the proposed "ship channel," as the contemplated improvement was designated, the town to raise $300,000 of the amount, and the Legislature to be asked to subscribe the balance on behalf of the State. At the election so held, the people, by a large majority, approved the scheme, but, with strange want of forethought, the Common Hall let the matter drop, and nothing more was done about it.

As early as 1788 an Act of Assembly was passed providing for the organization of a company who were given authority to deepen the channel of the Appomattox and to collect tolls on vessels, upon condition that the company should "make the said river capable of being navigated in any season, from Broadway to Pocahontas bridge, by vessels drawing twelve feet water." In 1792 an amendatory Act was passed, allowing the collection of tolls when the river should be made navigable at any season between said points by vessels drawing *nine* feet of water. Nothing appearing to have been done under these Acts of 1788 and 1792, in 1800 an Act was passed providing for the organization of a navigation company, whose powers and privileges were substantially the same as the powers and privileges given to the company provided for under the act of 1788, but the new company was only required to make the river between Broadway and Pocahontas bridge navigable at any season by vessels drawing *seven* feet of water, as a condition to collecting tolls. In 1810 an amendatory Act gave the new company seven years from March 1st, 1810, within which "to complete the navigation of Appomattox river."

Under the Acts of 1800 and 1810 some work under the direction of Bates and others was done, but none that permanently benefitted the navigation of the river. On the contrary, the condition of the river gradually became worse, until in 1824 the depth of the water in the channel was only three and a half feet on the sand bars at mean high tide and only six inches at low tide. The engineer, Albert Stein, in a pamphlet published in 1853, referring to the condition of the river at "Stop-bar," about two miles below Petersburg, says :

"At low water, the main current passed through a very narrow winding channel across the bar, from the right to the left shore, leaving the extensive sand bank nearly dry ; and even then the channel would not admit, at very low water, in the river proper, the passage of a small canoe."

In the year 1824 the General Assembly passed an Act providing for the incorporation of the "Lower Appomattox Company," a company which still exists, the city of Petersburg being the sole owner of all the stock under an Act of Assembly passed in 1851, This Company was only required to obtain a depth sufficient for the navigation of vessels drawing *six* feet of water to entitle the Company to collect tolls. Organizing at once, the Company called to its service as engineer a foreigner, Mr. Albert Stein, to whom we have referred, and under his direction was done the first systematic work in the way of improving the navigation of the river. From 1825 to 1829 Stein was engaged in the work and in the latter year obtained the depth of water contemplated by the Act of 1824.

In 1852, when considerable interest was felt by the people of Petersburg.

in the improvement of the Appomattox, the late Dr. Benjamin H. May, then a prominent physician of the city, stated that, in 1829, when Stein had completed his work and obtained a depth of six feet at high water over the bars, he, Dr. May, learned from John Randolph, of Roanoke, that the depth obtained by Stein was about the depth of water in the river when he, John Randolph, was a boy and lived at Matoaca.

Dr. May at the same time (in 1852) mentioned another interesting fact. He said that, when Stein had obtained a depth of six feet, he (Stein) was so sanguine of his capacity to obtain a depth of twelve feet—the depth contemplated in 1788, and the depth now (1884) actually reached—as to offer to the town authorities (the Common Hall) to complete the work of getting the depth of twelve feet, *without salary*, if the town would make further advances for the purpose. The Common Hall, however, declined the proposition, having expended $60,000.

The work of Stein was done with skill, as was demonstrated by the fact that, during the period of twenty years from 1829 to 1849, although the river was entirely neglected, the depth in the channel was not only preserved but increased. This appears from a report of a committee of the Common Hall made in 1849.

In the last-mentioned year the people of Petersburg once more turned their attention to the improvement of the river, and during the succeeding eleven or twelve years they manifested the deepest interest in its navigation, and began to take steps for its improvement. In 1853 Congress made an appropriation of $22,500 for the purpose, and with this money and with appropriations from the municipal treasury, in 1861, at the opening of the late war, the river had been greatly improved. Vessels drawing nine feet of water came regularly to the wharves of the city. During this period the city grew and prospered as it had never done before. In a communication to the *Index-Appeal*, in 1881, a few days before his death, the late Henry D. Bird, whose work in planning and opening Puddledock Cut has brought him fame as an engineer, thus described the condition of things in Petersburg during the period to which we refer.

"The streets of the city were soon filled with drays loaded with freight, coming to and from the wharves, and all the signs of an increasing commerce were seen in our city. The hotels were thronged with strangers, and our merchants were beginning to feel that Petersburg was destined to become a great mart. The best proof of it is the fact that at that time the stately Iron Front Building, on Sycamore street, which would have graced Broadway in New York, was begun and finished. New warehouses and many handsome private buildings rose up in all directions, showing that the citizens were beginning to reap the benefits of their improvement of the Appomattox, and the sagacity of the Council in starting that work again."

In 1861 the work of improving the river was, of course, suspended by the war. Referring to this in his letter above mentioned, Mr. Bird, after quoting the lines—

> " Alas, with the war came in
> The soldier, hard of heart, with bloody hand,
> And conscience wide as Hell,"

says :

" We had to prepare for the horrible spectre. The work on the river was stopped, and dredging abandoned, and the same energies that had been expended in deepening the river were now devoted to the task of damming it up to prevent this awful fiend from coming up to Petersburg to ruin the City. It is hazarding little to say that if both sections of the country had devoted themselves during the four years of war to rivaling each other in the arts of peace, our river improvement would have been finished at this time.

"But it was not to be. After the war the City Council immediately recommenced. the work. The River Board was ordered to purchase a dredge, and under the direction of that indomitable veteran in managing the river improvement, Lemuel Peebles, they immediately commenced removing the dam. The Council appropriated money to resume the dredging, and all work was soon going on again."

In 1869 a new Council took up the work with increased energy and borrowed $200,000 to carry it on, with a view to obtaining a depth of twelve feet at mean high tide. In 1871 Congress appropriated $50,000 for the purpose, and has since made several other appropriations towards the improvement.

From 1871 up to the present time (1884) the improvement has been under the control of skillful engineers of the United States Army, and the fact that the depth of twelve feet at mean high water has been attained from the City harbor down to ship navigation, and that the river is now in a condition to require but little money annually to keep it in good order, attests the scientific character of the work done. During this period Lt.-Col. Wm. P. Craighill has been in charge of the work until relieved during the summer of 1884 by Captain F. A. Hinman.

Under the influence of the improvement which has been made, the river commerce of the City has greatly increased during the last three or four years, as will appear from the following statistical tables prepared from information officially furnished by Mr. E. H. Stainback, the Port Warden of Petersburg :

[Table A.]

TONNAGE OF THE PORT OF PETERSBURG FROM 1877 TO 1883 INCLUSIVE.

	No. of Vessels.	Total Tonnage.
1877	643	21,031 03
1878	666	22,802 35
1879	584	21,335 84
1880	751	30,632 53
1881	645	35,967 76
1882	917	43,391 55
1883	980	46,070 98

[Table B.]

RIVER COMMERCE OF THE PORT OF PETERSBURG.

	1880.	1881.	1882.	1883.
Inward	412,642	519,209	569,876	612,472
Outward	74,724	79,154	181,763	196,458
	$487,366	$598,363	$751,639	$808,930

THE LOCAL PRESS.

The following facts connected with the history of the Petersburg Press were mainly compiled by the Rev. E. S. Gregory, and are now reproduced in a completed form for the benefit, chiefly, of our well-beloved brethren, the "Knights of the Scissors:"

Mention has been made of the establishment of the Petersburg *Republican*, in the early part of the century. It was edited by Thomas Field, who married a sister of General Winfield Scott, and who killed in the market-place a shoemaker named John Cross, for which he was acquitted on the ground of self-defence. The next editor of the *Republican* was Colonel Edward Pescud, whose wife was a daughter of the celebrated Peter Francisco. The *Republican* was continued for many years. After its suspension, another paper of the same name was started in 1844 by J. M. H. Brunet, who sold it to William K. Drinkard, by whom it was published till 1848.

On October 1st, 1828, the first number of the *Times* (semi-weekly) appeared, with Thomas White as publisher and Francis G. Yancey as editor. It flourished for several years.

The *Constellation* was founded by Hiram Haines in 1835, and lived several years. In 1839 Mr. Haines started a short-lived paper called the *Peep O'Day*. In 1840 he began the *Virginia Star*, which also soon expired.

In 1840 the *American Statesman* was started by Burwell & Allegre, and by them sold to Charles Campbell, who discontinued it in 1843.

The *Little Cockade* had a brief existence in 1841, under H. K. Ellyson; and in 1858 the *Daily Star* had a similar experience, under the Rev. A. J. Leavenworth.

Roger A. Pryor began the *Southside Democrat* in 1849, and published it for three years, making it a specially lively and powerful organ of the Democratic party.

Mr. Hicks, of Brunswick, established, in 1855, the *Kaleidoscope*, which was issued for about two years.

In 1855 Samuel B. Paul founded the *Express*, and soon afterwards sold it to A. F. Crutchfield and Co. The paper under their management was a great financial success, and was published throughout the war. In 1865 an editorial article was published in it which the people, in that excited time, thought to lean too strongly to the Northern side, and the popularity of the paper began to decline. It was then sold to O. P. Haines and William Campbell, who in turn sold it to T. J. Clark & Co. Subsequently, under the ownership of Smith & Carp, its name was changed to the *Courier*; and when afterwards sold, first to Charles Peebles and then to E. B. Branch & Co., it reappeared as the *Progress*. In 1872 the paper was bought by Messrs. Venable, Gregory & Patteson, who re-christened it as the *Appeal*. In 1873 it was consolidated with the *Index*.

Other press ventures were the following: The *Press*, in 1857, by S. B. Paul; continued till the war. *Prices Current*, in 1858, by T. J. Clark; still published. The *Conductor*, in 1859, by J. R. Lewellen; published for several years. In 1860, the *Bulletin*, by Dr. William H. I'Anson, which was ephemeral. In 1867, the *Advertiser*, by L. Lyon and Jordan Stone; published two years. In 1873, the *Commercial*, by R. E. Cain; lasted eight months. There was an earlier *Commercial*, under Bingham & Co. In 1875, the *Star*, by Star Publishing Company, William E. Cameron, editor; lasted eight months. And the *Mail* (evening edition of the *Index-Appeal*), which was soon suspended.

In 1865, soon after the war closed, A. M. Keiley and E. B. Branch established the *News*, which, by reason of the vigor of its Southern utterances, was suppressed by order of General Gibbon. Its name was then changed to the *Index*. In was afterwards sold to Cameron, Sykes & Co., and thereafter to Chamberlayne, Sykes & Co. In 1873, as has been said, it was consolidated with the *Appeal*, making the *Index-Appeal*, which was at first published by a Company of that name, under the management of R. P. Barham, who has since become, and is now, its sole proprietor and publisher. The *Index-Appeal* is now one of the best-paying newpaper properties in the South.

In 1873 the *News* was established by a joint-stock Company, and was suspended in 1875, soon re-appearing as the *Post*, which was published by R. H. Glass & Son, during its brief span of life.

The *Rural Messenger* was founded in 1871 by Ege & Rogers, with the

WM. L. ZIMMER & CO.'S BOOK STORE, SYCAMORE ST.

late T. S Pleasants as editor. Mr. Pleasants had also been editor of the *Farmer's Journal*, published years before by Charles LeRoy. The *Southern Planter and Farmer*, now published in Richmond, was originally issued in Petersburg, and Edmund Ruffin was one of its editors.

Two Republican papers have been started in Petersburg since the war—the *Times*, edited by Dr. Leitch, and the *Virginia Citizen*, edited by Ildo Ramsdell and J. A. H. Van Auken. All of these were Northern men, and their enterprises were short-lived.

The *Weekly Letter Sheet*, formerly *Prices Current*, and the *Weekly Record*, also a commercial journal, are published every Saturday, by T. Jefferson Clark.

In January, 1883, *The Mail* was established by J. T. Pleasants and W. S. Copeland, as a morning daily newspaper, but was changed to an evening paper six months later. In January, 1884, Mr. Copeland retired from its proprietorship, and in the following June its issue was discontinued.

The *Trade Review*, a weekly journal devoted to general commercial information, was founded by David May, Jr., on October, 1st, 1883, and is well supported by our merchants.

Besides the *Index-Appeal*, daily and weekly, the *Rural Messenger*, weekly, and the *Weekly Letter Sheet*, *Weekly Record* and *Trade Review*, all of which are in thriving circumstances, Petersburg journalism is at the present time further represented by two weekly sheets known as the *Lancet* and the *Star of Zion*, devoted to the interests of the colored race and conducted by colored editors.

PETERSBURG BENEVOLENT MECHANIC ASSOCIATION.

Like many another valuable institution which has eventually proved of great practical benefit to the community in which it flourished, this Association owes it original formation to what might almost be termed an accident.

It happened in this wise : In the year 1824, the Congress of the United States had voted unanimously a resolution, requesting President Monroe to invite the Marquis de LaFayette to re-visit the United States. He accepted the invitation, but declined the offer of a ship of the line for his conveyance, and, with his son and secretary, took passage on a packet ship from Havre to New York, where he landed August 15, 1824. He was received everywhere with great demonstrations of popular enthusiasm and visited all the principal cities in the twenty-four States.

Having arrived at Richmond, a deputation from our City was sent over to escort him to Petersburg. In the mean time the mechanics of Petersburg met together at the cabinet warerooms of Macky D. I'Anson on Bank Street, and determined to do honor to the illustrious chief by erecting a triumphal arch on one of our main streets. While consulting together on the manner and means of accomplishing their purpose, information was received that the Marquis would arrive the next day at one o'clock, and as it would be impossible, in the short space of time intervening, to erect such a testimonial as would do credit to the occasion, the meeting was about to adjourn, when it was proposed to form an association of mechanics and manufacturers for a closer union, for mental improvement, for the promotion of mechanical arts and sciences and for benevolent and charitable purposes generally.

An adjourned meeting was held at the tavern of Richard F. Hannon, on Bank Street, on January 4th, 1825, at which was laid the foundation of the present prosperous Association. Luzon Whiting occupied the chair, and James Davidson acted as secretary. A week later a constitution and by-laws were adopted, together with the name and style by which the Society is known.

The following persons subscribed their names and occupations to the constitution, and then started an enterprise which has enlarged its proportions and usefulness to the present day :

Luzon Whiting, tailor ; James Davidson, burr millstone maker ; Sceva

Thayer, blacksmith ; Beverly Drinkard, carpenter ; Samuel White, cabinet maker ; William Cook, watchmaker ; George Zimmerman, tanner and currier ; Joseph C. Swan, book binder ; John T. Dejarnette, cabinet maker ; John A. Ezell, bricklayer ; Thomas Jordan, carpenter ; Edwin Badger, cabinet maker ; Herbert B. Elder, coach maker ; Daniel Lyon, bricklayer ; Wm. Shanks, cabinet maker ; John Pollard, saddler ; Robert Ritchie, weaver ; John Patterson, baker ; M. D. I'Anson, cabinet maker ; Wm. Harwood, carpenter ; Francis G. Yancy, printer ; Wm. B. Ritchie, soap and candle maker ; Thomas B. Stroud, saddler ; William Cain, tailor ; Henry Shroyer, coppersmith.

The Association was incorporated by an Act of the Legislature, passed February 2nd, 1826. The incorporators declared in the preamble to their application for a charter, that they perceived "with sentiments of deep regret " the disregard of self-culture among those practicing the mechanical arts in the town, and that they were determined to remedy the evil as far as possible, by the formation of an Association having for its object the dissemination of general and technical knowledge among that portion of the community. This was one of the first movements in the interest of

W. M. HABLISTON & CO.'S FURNITURE STORE, SYCAMORE ST.

technical education made in the United States. The Association has done a good work as a public educator, and has proved a financial success. Its property (on the corner of Sycamore and Tabb Streets) is valued at over fifty thousand dollars and its technical library is the best in Virginia. The Association also possesses an interesting museum, comprising collections of Indian implements, relics of the civil war and other curiosities, besides many creditable entomological and mineralogical specimens. The reading room is well supplied with all the leading American and English papers and magazines.

On July 14th of this year (1884) the Library Committee made the following report relative to the condition at that time of the Library and Museum :

" Since our last report the Library has been re-arranged, the books all classified, the cases numbered and labelled, and an entirely new catalogue made.

" Two hundred and twenty-five volumes have been added during the year, as follows: from the United States Government, 13 ; by donation,

13 ; by purchase, 159 ; magazines, &c., bound, 40—making the whole number of volumes now in the Library, 4,286.

"The Museum has received a number of additions in the way of ores, minerals and various other curiosities, and is steadily growing in interest."

The officers are : Wm. C. Lumsden, President ; Wm. H. Baxter, Secretary and Treasurer ; A. L. Archer, Librarian ; and the Directors are C. T. Williamson, J. M. Quicke, Wm. H. Tappey, A. A. Traylor, T. J. Greenhow, A. S. Archer and P. M. Steward.

YOUNG MEN'S CHRISTIAN ASSOCIATION.

——:o:——

As a matter of course—it might almost be said—Petersburg possesses a flourishing branch of this excellent organization, whose elevating influence is gratefully acknowledged by the whole community. It was established here in May, 1880, and has now 210 regular members. Its present officers are : Freeman W. Jones, President ; R. O. Egerton, Vice-President ; Judge Joseph S. Budd, Second Vice-President ; Augustus Wright, Third Vice-President ; Dr. J. E. Moyler, Treasurer ; J. B. Blanks, Recording Secretary, and C. A. Licklider, General Secretary. The Board of Managers consists of W. T. Plummer, W. N. Jones, W. H. Tappey, J. M. Leath, E. A. Hartley, J. A. Warwick, W. R. McKenney and J. M. Williams. The premises occupied by the Association are on the second floor of the Odd-Fellows Hall, on Sycamore street, and comprise a Reading Room, Library, Parlor, Gymnasium, etc. The rooms are open to the public from 9 a. m. to 10 p. m. daily, and are well supplied with the leading daily and weekly newspapers, magazines, and other instructive literature, while the Library books are numerous and well selected. "All are welcome," is the legend which greets the eye of the passer-by, and gives expression to the hospitable spirit which governs the Association. There is a public prayer-meeting every day at noon, and a Bible Class and Young Men's Meeting are also well sustained, in addition to an attractive course of lectures during the winter season.

THE PETERSBURG MUSICAL ASSOCIATION.

This Association, which enjoys a well-earned reputation in musical circles throughout the country, was formed on the 26th day of August, 1881, and may be regarded as the successor, as it also became the heir, of the "Petersburg Musical Club," which was dissolved about that time.

Its principal object is to create an elevated and refined taste for the most elevating and refining of all the Arts, and to provide practical instruction in the science of Music to all who will avail themselves of its benefits. That these benefits have been duly appreciated by the ladies and gentlemen of the community is evidenced by the fact that the Chorus, which in 1881 comprised twenty-one voices, now numbers eighty-five, and has attained, through constant and faithful training, an exceedingly high state of cultivation and efficiency.

The Constitution of the Association provides for two classes of membership—the regular members, whose annual subscription is $13, and the contributing members, whose subscription is $8. The latter have only the privilege of admission to the Association's entertainments, while the former enjoy the additional advantage of ownership in its property and of a voice and vote in its affairs. Music scholars, upon application by their teachers, are admitted to the entertainments of a whole season upon payment of $3.

During the seasons of 1882, 1883 and 1884, the Association gave twenty-eight entertainments, and paid out to artistes alone, during that period, about $5,500. The attendance at these concerts exceeded 16,000 persons. It has also been the means of stimulating the musical fervor of several other Associations in this State and North Carolina, members of which have attended three annual conventions, held in May of each year, in this city. On May 26th to 29th of this year (1884) there was also a grand Music Festival for both States held in our Academy of Music, which proved successful beyond the most sanguine hopes of its promoters.

The Association gives an entertainment every month during the season (October to May inclusive) besides two or three extra concerts, and a series of musical entertainments at the time of the May Convention. The highest available talent is engaged to assist the active members of the Association, and our people are thus given many opportunities of enjoyment such as rarely fall to the lot of those living at so great a distance from the Metropolis. At least once in each year nearly every great artiste in vocal and instrumental performance in the United States may be heard within the walls of our Academy of Music, and it is very much to the credit of the management and the public that the Association shows an annual increase in strength, wealth and membership.

Its present government is as follows: President, John Q. Jackson ; Vice-President, John McGill ; Treasurer, T. S. Beckwith ; Secretary, J. William Friend. Board of Directors—John Q. Jackson, John McGill, T. S. Beckwith, J. W. Friend, J. T. Young, H. Noltenius, W. H. Baxter, Dr. J. W. Bryant, Dr. S. W. Budd, A. Rosenstock, Aug. Wright, W. H. Cuthbert, George F. Jones, William R. Nichols, James M. Quicke, George J. Seay, E. B. Bain, J. E. Mason, Dr. David Steel, N. T. Patteson, Alexander Hamilton, L. H. Southall, C. D. Witherspoon, W. L. Zimmer and W. M. Habliston. Finance and Business Committee—John Q. Jackson, J, T. Young and T. S. Beckwith. Committee on Music—H. Noltenius and John Q. Jackson.

On the principle of rendering tribute where it is most justly due, and of giving expression to a sense of obligation which is shared by the members of the Association, as well as by the community at large, it should be stated that the gratifying success which has attended the career of this Society is attributable to the personal interest and efforts of the Directors in general, and, in a special degree, to the untiring energy and zeal of Mr. John Q. Jackson, the President of the Association, and Mr. H. Noltenius, the Conductor of the Chorus and Chairman of the Committee on Music—these two gentlemen being, beyond question, the leading spirits of the Petersburg Musical Association.

THE BOAT CLUBS.

—— :o: ——

Petersburg can boast of possessing two boat clubs whose names and colors are well known on the principal rivers of the State, as prominent contestants for the prizes given annually by the State Rowing Association. Last year, 1883, when the State Regatta was held at Lynchburg, our senior club, the "Appomattox," won the French Cup, which is the principal prize competed for by the several clubs forming the State Association ; and our junior club, the "Cockade City," has won at each of the last three annual Regattas, and still holds, the Fredericksburg Challenge Cup, which is given to the club taking the second place. Each club is well supplied with four-oared gigs, single sculls, pleasure-barges and other boats. The boat houses are situated on the north side of the river, immediately above Pocahontas Bridge. The initiation fee to each club is $5, and the annual dues $12.

THE APPOMATTOX B. C.

(Organized, August 1st, 1878.)

Officers : W. H. Cuthbert, President ; T. F. Heath, Vice-President ; H. L. Plummer, Treasurer ; Carter R. Bishop, Secretary.

THE COCKADE CITY B. C.

(Organized October 1st, 1880.)

Officers : R. W. Prichard, President ; E. J. Bond, Treasurer ; Eugene Jones, Secretary.

THE PETERSBURG BASE-BALL ASSOCIATION.

—— :o: ——

This Association was organized during the summer of this year, 1884, and numbers among its stockholders, of whom there are about fifty, many of our most substantial merchants and business men. The enclosed grounds of the Association adjoin the West-End Park, and are reached by the street cars, which pass the entrance gate. Considerable progress has already been made towards securing a good home nine, to compete with visiting clubs, and many excellent games were played during the opening season. The present officers are : President, W. E. Butcher ; Vice-Presidents, A. G. M. Martin, George Beadle, J. R. Belcher, R. M. Dobie ; Directors, W. E. Butcher, R. M. Dobie, A. G. M. Martin, George Beadle, C. E. Burton, J. R. Belcher, W. M. Habliston, W. E. Badger, George Davis, W. J. Jarratt ; Secretary, J. Gray McCandlish ; Treasurer, Charles C. Alley.

CENTRE HILL.

The handsome old mansion which forms the subject of this sketch, was built during or about the year 1825, and succeeded "Bollingbrook Hill" as the family residence of the Bollings. Apart from its substantial advantages, central situation and park-like surroundings, it possesses historical associations of unusual interest, as will be seen by reference to the earlier pages of this book. Its grounds cover ten acres, bounded by Jefferson, Henry, Adams and Franklin Streets. The house originally measured eighty feet square, but it was remodelled in 1850, when the east wing, fifteen feet wide, was added. It is a two-story, basement and attic building, fitted throughout with water, gas and other modern conveniences, and containing eighteen rooms, as follows : Four basement rooms, four main floor rooms—parlor, reception rooms and library—six bed chambers on the second floor and four attic rooms. It is very substantially constructed, the basement walls being three and a half to four feet in thickness. There are numerous out-houses, stables, gardeners' houses, servants' premises and other detached accommodations, all of which are in excellent order. The above engraving is taken from a photograph of the south front. The property now belongs to the several heirs of the late Robert B. Bolling, Esq., and is for sale by his Executor, T. S. Bolling, Esq., by whom liberal and reasonable terms are offered. It is already a most desirable residence, and might, with certain alterations, be made eminently suitable for a great public institution—scholastic, benevolent or charitable—such as Virginia delights to endow. The surplus land might also be sub-divided into extremely desirable building lots, fronting upon one of the best residence streets in the City. This fact alone should render the property easily saleable, and it is to be hoped that some enterprising capitalist, company or chartered institution will take advantage of the fine opportunity thus afforded.

—— :o: ——

ANDREW KEVAN, President.

It is perhaps fortunate for Petersburg that her gas supply is in the hands of a private corporation, under the management and direction of some of her most prominent citizens, instead of being controlled by the City authorities and subject to the fluctuations and vicissitudes common to all the concerns of municipal governments.

The Petersburg Gas Light Company was organized in 1851, and began to furnish gas in the latter part of that year, under a charter from the State Legislature.

The extensive gas works of the Company occupy the land at the southeast corner of Lombard and Madison Streets, and are thoroughly equipped with all the appliances necessary for the manufacture of the best gas. They use only the finest quality of coal to be had.

The capacity of the works is one hundred thousand feet of gas per day, and the supply reaches the consumers through sixteen and a half miles of gas pipes.

The capital stock of the Company is $130,000, and is all paid up. It is divided among about one hundred and twenty stockholders, more than half of whom are of the gentler sex.

The present officers of the Company are as follows : President, Andrew Kevan ; Engineer and Superintendent, William H. Baxter ; Treasurer, William F. Spotswood ; Directors,—David B. Tennant, Alexander Donnan, Dr. James Dunn, George H. Davis, and John McGill.

In addition to gas, the company deals largely in coke of an excellent quality, which is delivered to customers at reasonable prices.

It is admitted on all hands that Petersburg is as well and as cheaply lighted as any City which depends exclusively upon gas for the illumination of its thoroughfares, churches, stores and public buildings, while gas is very generally preferred to kerosene oil in the better class of residences, by reason of its good quality, cleanliness and exemption from danger of fire—for it is a well-established fact that the majority of accidental fires in private dwellings are caused by the careless handling of oil lamps. In the long run gas is the cheapest, safest and best artificial light for general use that has yet been discovered.

The offices of the Petersburg Gas Light Company are in Mechanics' Building, corner of Tabb and Sycamore Streets.

THE ANDERSON SCHOOL AND BOYKIN, BLAND & CO.'s TOBACCO FACTORY.
WASHINGTON STREET.

PETERSBURG STREET RAILWAY.

———:o:———

As is well known to the readers of history, Petersburg suffered more severely than any other Southern city from the wasting effects of the Civil
War, and when Peace returned to the fair but bankrupt land, in 1865, it
almost seemed that Petersburg's ruin had been finally accomplished, beyond hope and beyond remedy. It followed, therefore, that her recuperation was slow, when compared with other and less unfortunate trade centres, and for some years she languished and dropped behind. But the turning point was reached at last, and active vitality again became the order
of the day. New buildings and other improvements appeared on all sides;
home industries revived and alien capital came here in search of investment; but there was still something wanting, and it could not be denied
that Petersburg remained "behind the times." The street-car was not seen
on her thoroughfares, and the jingle of the car-bells was a sound as yet unknown to her people,

On November 1st, 1882, however, the following communication was received by the City Fathers, in monthly session assembled:

To the Honorable Common Council of the City of Petersburg:

Your petitioner, George Bendle, of Syracuse, in the State of New York, on behalf of
himself and such other persons as may be associated with him, respectfully represents to
your honorable body, that he and his said associates desire to lay down and operate a
street railway on the following streets in the City of Petersburg, to-wit: Second, River,
Rock, Old, Sycamore, Washington, West, Farmer, the street next adjoining the West-
End Park on the East, Oak, Halifax and Liberty Streets, and also upon such other streets
as may be selected, under the superintendence of a committee of your honorable body,
for the laying down and operating of such Railway; the cars on said Railway to be run
on every day in the week, including Sunday; to be drawn by horses, and the fare for a
single passenger not to exceed five cents; the track to be a single track, with centre-bearing
rails, with conveniently-located turn-outs, and the property to be exempt from taxation
for City purposes for a period of ten years from November 1st, 1882. And your Petitioner accordingly respectfully prays that your honorable body will grant unto him and
his said associates exclusive authority to lay down and operate upon said streets such
Railway upon the terms aforesaid, and under such reasonable regulations as your honorable body may prescribe.   [Signed]   GEORGE BEADLE.

Two days after the receipt of this petition, an adjourned meeting was held, at which the Common Council unanimously adopted an ordinance granting the prayer, with such necessary restrictions as the comfort and convenience of the public required ; and in the following month, December, 1882, the energetic proprietor began the construction of the Railway, which was completed and put into operation in September of the next year (1883.) The track, which is four miles in length, and connects the passenger and freight depots of the Norfolk and Western, Richmond and Petersburg, and Petersburg and Weldon Railroads, with West-End Park, on one line, and with the end of Halifax Street, on the other, is thoroughly well laid, having the usual bed of granite and cobble-stones and patent switches. Already there is plenty of traffic to employ the twelve cars now in use, and Mr. Beadle intends shortly to increase the number, having been granted permission to extend the Railway as far as the Central Lunatic Asylum—a distance of two miles. Besides this principal extension, it is proposed to lay tracks along South Sycamore Street to the foot of "The Heights," and also to the Cemetery, at Blandford. When this is done, all the suburbs will be embraced within this beneficent system, and every part of the City will be directly connected with the railroads, markets and principal stores ; the value of suburban property will be greatly enhanced ; building in the outskirts of the city will be encouraged ; industries will be stimulated by the easy accessibility of cheap land whereon to erect factories ; the public convenience will have been subserved to an extent almost impossible to estimate, and Mr. Geoge Beadle will have established himself still more firmly in the esteem and respect of a grateful community. During the fifteen months which have elapsed since the opening of the Street Railway, five hundred and twenty-nine thousand passengers have availed themselves of its comforts ; and the city has been no loser by its wise liberality in exempting the Railway property from taxation, for the land all along the line, and in the suburbs which it penetrates, has increased very considerably in its actual and taxable value, as a direct consequence of this improvement. The enterprise so far has been profitable to all concerned ; it is to be hoped that it may soon become lucrative to its deserving founder.

AUGUSTUS WRIGHT'S SHOE STORE,
SYCAMORE ST.

RAILROADS.

THE NATURAL BRIDGE OF VIRGINIA.

———:o:———

THE PETERSBURG RAILROAD.

About the 10th of February, 1830, an Act was passed by the General Assembly incorporating the Petersburg Railroad Company, and Commissioners were appointed to receive subscriptions to its stock, which at first was only $400,000, divided into shares of $100 each. The Road was to run "from Petersburg to some convenient point on the North Carolina line," and the survey was begun in December, 1830. A month later (January, 1831,) the contract was awarded to build the road from Petersburg to Jarratt's, in Sussex County, a distance of about 30 miles, and in the Summer of 1832 arrangements were made for extending it to Blakely, in North Carolina, about 60 miles from Petersburg, which was accomplished by the 1st of October, 1833.

The methods of railway construction in those early days were necessarily somewhat primitive. The prototype of the fine steel rail of to-day was a piece of strap iron, about three-quarters of an inch thick and two and a half to three inches wide, nailed on to the wooden rail which, in its turn, rested on the ties. The first locomotive used on this road was built in England, and the cars were modeled after the old English stage coaches and carried about eighteen passengers, inside and out. The freight cars were four-wheeled conveyances called wagons, and carried about three tons each. The first president of the Petersburg Railroad Company was Donald McKenzie. At a meeting of the stockholders held in March, 1836, Henry D. Bird, the chief engineer, reported that the Company had in use 100 wagons, 5 coaches and 7 engines. He stated that his heaviest engines weighed, including fire and water, 6 tons, 6 cwt., and were each capable of drawing from 20 to 25 wagons, carrying in the aggregate 60 to 70 tons of produce. Mr. Bird gave it as his opinion that it was injudi-cious to run a passenger train at a greater speed than 15 to 18 miles an hour. Hitherto the passenger fare had been 8 cents per mile, but this was reduced in 1836 to six cents. Ten cents per ton per mile was the charge for freight, or ten dollars for the whole distance. The Company was re-

A. ROSENSTOCK & CO.'S DRY GOODS STORE, NO. 1 IRON FRONT.

stricted by an Act of 1836 from paying dividends in excess of 15 per -cent. (!) after paying all debts and setting aside a reasonable sum for re newal, repairs and construction. Meanwhile Blakely had been abandoned as the Southern terminus of the road in favor of Weldon, N. C., and the Company had acquired the power to form connections with other roads leading South. In 1841, the Portsmouth & Roanoke Railroad had been authorized to sell one-half of that portion of their road lying South o Gary's, N. C., and half of the bridge at Weldon, to the Petersburg Rail road Company. The Board of Public Works was directed, in 1846, to sell the Portsmouth & Roanoke road, and the purchasers were incorpor ated as the Seaboard & Roanoke Company. Competition between these roads was prevented by the regulation of fares and other rates.

In 1853 the Greensville & Roanoke and the Petersburg railroads were consolidated, the charter of the latter to govern the whole. In 1861, by an ordinance of the Virginia Convention, the Petersburg Railroad and the Richmond & Petersburg Railroad were authorized to connect their rails through the City, which was done.

This road is the principal highway connecting Petersburg with the vast railroad system which traverses the whole of the Southern States and is consequently one of the principal arteries of our trade. All the cotton received here for manufacture or transmission comes over its metals. At Weldon it connects with the Raleigh & Gaston Road, leading to Raleigh, the Capital City of North Carolina. Connection is there formed with the Raleigh & Augusta Road, which intersects the Carolina Central Road at Hamlet, and so connects with Charlotte, Asheville, Columbia and Augusta—all railroad centres whence direct communication is maintained with all Southern points from the Atlantic Ocean to the Mississippi.

ALEX. WILSON'S GROCERY STORE, SYCAMORE ST.

THE CITY POINT RAILROAD.

The next Company incorporated was the City Point Railroad, whose charter is dated January 26th, 1836. Its stock was fixed at $150,000, and the charter was to expire if work was not begun within two years. Ten acres of land at City Point and two at the Petersburg terminus were permitted to be held. William E. Hinton was elected the first president. Next year the Company was authorized by the Council to extend its line into the town, and the Board of Public Works assumed six hundred shares of its stock. In 1847 the road was transferred to the City of Petersburg, by whom it was sold in 1854 to the Southside Railroad Company, and was eventually included in the Act of Incorporation of the Atlantic, Mississippi & Ohio (now the Norfolk & Western) Railroad.

The length of this road is nine miles, and connects Petersburg directly with deep water navigation. Freight is transferred at City Point to the steamships of the various lines carrying passengers and freight to and from New York, Philadelphia, Baltimore, Richmond, Norfolk, and other points North, East and South. The importance of this line to our producers, manufacturers and merchants cannot be over-estimated, for it brings the City into direct, rapid and inexpensive communication with the great markets of the Atlantic seaboard.

THE RICHMOND & PETERSBURG RAILROAD.

By an Act of March 14th, 1836, the Richmond & Petersburg Railroad Company was chartered. Books for stock subscriptions were opened at both termini, and the capital was fixed at $300,000, which was increased in 1843 to $685,000. In 1865 the Company was authorized to issue coupon bonds not exceeding $175,000 to rebuild the James River bridge and the depots, workshops, &c., destroyed at the time of the evacuation. The first president of the road was Holden Rhodes, and Moncure Robinson was its original engineer. In 1871 the controlling interest which the State had from time to time acquired in this Road was disposed of, during the "Railroad War" of that year, to Gen. J. R. Anderson, H. K. Ellyson, and other leading citizens of Richmond, for $200 per share.

At Richmond this Road connects with the Fredericksburg & Potomac and other systems, branching off in endless ramifications to all points at the North and West.

Midway between Petersburg and Richmond, at the village of Chester, a narrow-gauge line connects this road with the Clover Hill Coal Pits in Chesterfield County.

T. A. PALMER'S GROCERY STORE, HALIFAX ST.

THE NORFOLK AND WESTERN RAILROAD COMPANY.

This important system was inaugurated by the incorporation of the Southside Railroad, in 1846, and on March 13th, 1849, of the Petersburg & Lynchburg Railroad, with a capital of $1,000,000. An Act of the same date transferred to the City of Petersburg all the State's stock in the Petersburg & Roanoke Railroad, to be applied to the construction of the Southside Railroad. Ten years were allowed for the completion of the Road, and if the work was not begun in three years the subscription was to revert to the State, and the Southside Company was to extend its line so as to connect with the Richmond & Danville Road, at Burkeville. In 1850 the city was authorized, by a popular vote, to subscribe $200,000 to the stock of the Southside Railroad, and another Act authorized the increase of the stock in the sum of $800,000, to enable the Company to continue its

road to Lynchburg. The gauge of the road was required to correspond
with that of the Richmond & Danville and the Virginia & Tennessee
railroads. In 1854 the Company was authorized to buy the City Point Railroad, and to issue bonds, convertible into stock, for the purchase money.
By an Act of April 18th, 1867, the Southside Company was consolidated
with the Norfolk & Petersburg and the Virginia & Tennessee Railroad

SEWARD & MUNT'S GRIST MILL AND TRUNK FACTORY, CAMPBELL'S BRIDGE.

Companies, and became the Atlantic, Mississippi & Ohio Railroad Company, under the Presidency of General Mahone. In June, 1876, by a de-
cree of the United States District Court at Richmond, this consolidated
Road was placed in the hands of Charles T. Perkins and Henry Fink, as
receivers, by whom its affairs were administered until early in 1882, when
it was sold to satisfy the claims of the bondholders, and became the prop-

er.y of a syndicate incorporated as the NORFOLK AND WESTERN RAILROAD COMPANY.

The Norfolk & Western main line extends from Norfolk, Va., at the mouth of Chesapeake Bay, to Bristol, Tenn., the distance being four hundred and eight miles. At Bristol it connects with the East Tennessee, Virginia & Georgia Railroad. It is intersected at Burkeville by the Richmond & Danville, at Lynchburg by the Virginia Midland, and at Roanoke by the Shenandoah Valley Railroads.

The New River Division of the Norfolk and Western is seventy-five miles long, starting at Central, forty miles west of Roanoke, and having its present terminus at Pocahontas, in the great Flat Top coal region, with its inexhaustible stores of the finest coal, suitable alike for steam purposes and the production of a first-class coke for blast-furnace use. Other extensions and branch lines are also being constructed for the purpose of reaching the vast and varied mineral wealth known to exist in the sections penetrated by this Road.

The Norfolk & Western is one of the Railways forming the gigantic system known as the Virginia, Tennessee & Georgia Air Line, which, with its connections, traverses that vast section of the United States lying east of the Mississippi and its tributaries, and embracing much of Maryland, Virginia, Tennessee, Western North Carolina, Georgia, Alabama and Mississippi, which, possessing in a remarkable degree those great resources of individual and national wealth represented in the products of field, forest, mine and water-power, presents also an array of scenic attractions, unsurpassed throughout this supremely-favored land.

With coal and iron side by side in unlimited quantities and of superior quality, all through the mountainous region of Western Virginia, there is no end to the future possibilities of this great system. In writing of the advantages which the territory traversed by these lines offers to the Iron Master, Mr. Andrew S. McCreath, chemist to the State Geological Survey of Pennsylvania, writes, under date March, 1883, as follows : "The ores are abundant and generally of good quality ; they can be economically mined, for the country in many localities is broken up by numerous ravines affording natural openings for mining operations ; most of the deposits are within convenient distance of the Railroads—with easy down grades; the water supply, either for washing ore or for manufacturing purposes, is ample and permanent at all seasons ; limestone for fluxing purposes exists in unlimited quantities ; coke of the finest quality for blast furnaces can now be obtained at a reasonable cost ; and the Railroad facilities for reaching markets in every direction are unusually good—thus forming a combination of circumstances rarely equalled."

THE VIRGINIA & CAROLINA RAILROAD.

Another important line is at this time in course of construction, which, when completed, will prove a valuable feeder to our tobacco, cotton and general produce markets. Its charter name is the Virginia & Carolina Railroad, and it will run in an almost straight line from Petersburg to Ridgeway, in Warren County, North Carolina, a distance of 77 miles, traversing the Counties of Dinwiddie, Brunswick and Mecklenburg, in this State, and connecting at Ridgeway with the Raleigh & Gaston Road, which in its turn connects with the Great Southern System of Railroads.

This Company is also building a line twenty miles in length from Hamlet to Cheraw, in North Carolina, which will be continued through Camden to Columbia, Aiken and Augusta, Ga., thus completing as straight a line as could be drawn between Richmond, Va., and the last named city, and having an advantage of nearly one hundred miles over the existing routes, with lighter grades and superior construction. Road stations will be built at convenient places along the line wherever the amount of business will justify the expense.

Thus centrally situated, with railroads radiating to every point of the compass, with direct and easy access alike to the cotton fields of Alabama and Mississippi, the orange groves of Florida, the grand forests and succulent meadows of Southwest Virginia and the fertile plains of the North; the rich mineral deposits of the mountains and the varied resources of the sea; with a continuous supply of tobacco for our factories and cotton for our looms; it is not to be wondered at that the practical business men of Petersburg look forward to her future with confidence, even as they regard her past with honest pride.

OUR COMMERCIAL ORGANIZATIONS.
—:o:—

PETERSBURG CHAMBER OF COMMERCE.

This important body, which was organized on March 8th, 1881, comprising nearly all the prominent and influential merchants of the city—practical business men, whose ripe experience and high character entitle them to public confidence and specially qualify them to guide, control and protect the mercantile interests of the community.

The following is the present government of the Chamber: President, E. B. Bain; First Vice-President, David Callender; Second Vice-President, R. T. Arrington; Secretary and Treasurer, J. Gray McCandlish; Directors, R. M. Doble, J. T. D'Alton, W. T. Plummer, N. B. Prichard, W. H. Tappey, J. A. Warwick, Alex. Wilson, F. W. Jones, Aug. Wright, Jas. S. Gilliam, Jr., C. E. Burton, Samuel J. Hurt, W. H. H. Bagwell, Bartlett Roper and Mark E. Kull.

A general meeting of the Chamber is held in the parlor of the Y. M. C. A., in Odd Fellows Hall, on the second Tuesday of the months of January, April, July and October, and the Board of Directors meet at the same place on the second Tuesday of every month.

PETERSBURG TOBACCO ASSOCIATION.

The commercial and industrial life of the city may be said to be almost wholly dependent upon the Tobacco trade, in its various branches, and it is therefore of the highest consequence that this particular trade should be fostered and encouraged with the utmost solicitude, and carefully fortified against all adverse possibilities, from within or without. With these objects in view, our Tobacco Association was organized on August 15th, 1866, and has labored faithfully since that date in the fulfillment of its mission.

Its present officers are as follows; President, W. L. Venable; Vice-President, S. P. Arrington; Secretary and Treasurer, John M. Banister; Auctioneer, James T. Tosh; Board of Directors, George Cameron, Robt. A. Martin, J. M. Parham and E. B. Bain.

The Association meets daily (except Saturday) in the hall of the Tobacco Exchange, corner of Sycamore and Washington streets.

PETERSBURG RAILROAD!

THE GREAT DIRECT THROUGH ROUTE

TO THE SOUTH

AND THE SHORTEST LINE TO

ALL ATLANTIC COAST CITIES!

THREE PASSENGER TRAINS DAILY,

WITH PALACE CARS ON ALL DAY, AND PULLMAN SLEEPERS
ON ALL NIGHT TRAINS,

CONNECTING AT WELDON WITH

WILMINGTON & WELDON & RALEIGH & GASTON R. Rs.

NO CHANGE OF CARS

BETWEEN WILMINGTON AND WASHINGTON.

And Sleepers running through from BOSTON, to JACKSONVILLE,
FLORIDA. The most direct and pleasant route between the North and
South.

Through Tickets and Baggage Checks to all principal points North
and South.

FREIGHT TRAINS leave Petersburg daily, making close connections
with trains on W. & W. and R. & G. Railroads at Weldon. No transfers
between Petersburg and Wilmington or Charlotte.

R. M. SULLY,
General Superintendent.

NORFOLK AND WESTERN RAILROAD.

THE GREAT TRUNK LINE
—TO THE

SOUTH AND SOUTHWEST,
—VIA—

LYNCHBURG AND BRISTOL.

THE QUICKEST AND MOST DIRECT ROUTE TO

CHATTANOOGA,	ATLANTA,
DECATUR,	BIRMINGHAM,
JACKSON,	MOBILE,
MEMPHIS,	MONTGOMERY,
NASHVILLE,	NEW ORLEANS,
HOT SPRINGS,	GALVESTON,

—AND—

All Texas and Trans-Mississippi Points!
—VIA—

MEMPHIS AND TEXARKANA,
—OR VIA—

NEW ORLEANS AND HOUSTON.

PULLMAN PALACE SLEEPING CARS
Between Lynchburg and New Orleans, and between Lynchburg and Memphis

WITHOUT CHANGE.

☞TICKETS ON SALE AT ALL COUPON OFFICES.☜

JOS. H. SANDS, General Superintendent.
A. POPE, General Passenger Agent.
H. V. L. BIRD, Agent N. & W. R. R. Petersburg, Va.,

THE OLD RELIABLE.

Virginia, Tennessee and Georgia Air-Line.

FAST FREIGHT LINE

FROM

BOSTON, PROVIDENCE, NEW YORK,

Philadelphia and Baltimore,

AND FROM

Norfolk, Petersburg, Richmond and Lynchburg,

TO ALL POINTS

SOUTH & SOUTH-WEST.

☞ Through Rates Given and Quick Time Made. All Claims for Losses, Damages or Overcharges Promptly Adjusted.

This Line is composed of Merchants' & Miners' Transportation Co. from Boston and Providence; Old Dominion S. S. Co., from New York; Philadelphia, Wilmington & Baltimore R. R. and Clyde Line Steamers from Philadelphia; Baltimore Steam Packet Co., from Baltimore; Norfolk & Western (A. M. & O.) R. R.; East Tenn., Va. & Georgia R. R.; Memphis & Charleston R. R.; Nashville, Chat. & St. Louis R. R.; Western & Atlantic R. R.; Selma, Rome & Dalton R. R.; Alabama Central R. R.; Vicksburg & Meridian R. R.; Mobile & Ohio R. R.; Illinois Central R. R., and their connections.

Have your goods marked VIRGINIA, TENN. & GA. AIR-LINE.

Agents: C. P. Gaither, 290 Washington Street, Boston; E. H. Rockwell, India Point, Providence; Thomas Pinckney, General Eastern Agent, 303 Broadway, N. Y.; John S. Wilson, 44 S. Fifth Street, Philadelphia; W. P. Clyde & Co., 12 South Wharves, Philadelphia; W. H. Fitzgerald, 157 W. Baltimore Street, Baltimore.

W. T. PAYNE,

Agent Claims and Expenses, Norfolk, Va.

STEAMSHIP AND STEAMBOAT LINES.

————:o:————

The time was—and not much more than a quarter of a century ago—when Petersburg was regarded as a sea-port of some importance, and many ships owned by her merchants made regular trips between City Point and Europe, besides a number of smaller vessels engaged in the coasting service. In those good old days the Appomattox was a much frequented highway, and steamers of light draft were necessary in transporting outward and inward freights between the wharves of the City and the sea-going vessels at the Point. Of late years, however, this species of traffic has been almost entirely suspended, and Petersburg's direct intercourse with the outer world is now carried on principally by means of the railroads and the steamships plying between Richmond and the Atlantic ports, calling at City Point to receive and deliver Petersburg freights. Shipping facilities of this kind are plentiful for all practical purposes, the fine steamers of the Old Dominion Line carrying our passengers and freight to and from New York and Norfolk; those of the Clyde Lines, to and from Norfolk, Philadelphia and the Carolinas; and those of the Virginia Steamboat Company, to and from Richmond, Newport News, Norfolk and all the James River Landings, making close connection at Norfolk for Baltimore, and other points, the connection between Petersburg and City Point being made by the City Point branch of the Norfolk and Western Railroad.

ATTRACTIVE HOMES IN TOWN AND COUNTRY.

[CONTRIBUTED BY MESSRS. PYLE & DEHAVEN.]

Petersburg and its vicinity abound in cheap and attractive homes which offer special inducements and advantages to all classes of immigrants—native and foreign—not to to be surpassed in any other section of this country.

Five railroads centre here from different directions, and one canal. It is the terminus of navigation of the Appomattox River, and is at the head of tidewater. Schooners, ships and steamers of fifteen to eighteen feet draft come to our wharves from any of the ports of the United States or foreign countries. The export of tobacco, cotton, flour, grain, &c., from Petersburg to foreign countries is of vast importance to the agricultural and manufacturing interest.

An extraordinary vastness of natural water-power exists for a number of miles up the Appomattox River, along which are dotted, on both sides of the river, cotton mills, flouring mills, paper manufactories and other machinery, employing thousands of hands and causing marked demands for all kinds of country produce. At least twelve steam tobacco factories are located in the City, each employing from two to eight hundred hands, and purchasing at good paying prices, all the tobacco brought to the market, and thousands of dollars are weekly paid to hands employed in these factories.

The business of Petersburg extends through all of Southside Virginia, upper North Carolina and East Tennessee.

Farm lands in the vicinity range in price from $2 to $100 per acre, according to location and improvement; and the climate is not equalled in its adaptability to the cultivation of every variety of cereals, fruits and vegetables ordinarily grown in any of the States, either North or South.

Virginia will be, in a few years, one of the first farming districts in the United States. A rapid tide of immigration has turned in this direction. The large plantations are being divided up into small farms and sold to Northern, Western and European farmers, who, with their natural thrift and enterprise, are making the waste places to bloom with the various products which this climate is adapted to. No part of our country offers to settlers such a combination of advantages as Southside Virginia. Everywhere will be found, near at hand, virgin soil, original timber, unused water power and inexhaustible mineral deposits; ample facilities for transportation exist, and the best markets are near at hand. The climate is good, the winters are short and mild, and the country healthy. The land is level, free of stone, and capable of raising any kind of grain.

Tobacco, corn, cotton, wheat, oats, rye, peanuts and buckwheat are the principal crops.

Sweet and Irish potatoes, melons, and all kinds of vegetables, are also raised to a large extent. Fruits of all kinds do well here, from early strawberries and apricots to late winter apples. Early vegetables and small fruits are being cultivated for Northern markets, having several weeks' earlier maturity and thus gaining for the producer the early high prices.

Winter especially has its attractions and advantages in comparison to the North and West. Being very short and mild—with little snow or frost—farmers are enabled to work on their land through nearly the whole winter, so that the ground is ready at the earliest planting season.

Cattle and sheep require but little shelter or feeding; sheep especially are never fed unless there happens to be snow on the ground.

The above are all permanent natural advantages in favor of this section, and are rapidly developing in the minds of Northern and Western people, who are beginning to purchase while land is yet cheap—some a small farm, others a large one, and occasionally several thousand acres for a colony It is already a fact that every neighborhood consists of a large proportion of immigrant families.

[CONTRIBUTED BY CAPTAIN JOHN C. GRIFFIN.]

Few States offer so many advantages to immigrants as do all sections of Virginia. Its mild, healthy and equable climate, exempt alike from the rigorous winters of the North and the heated summers of the South; its central position, geographically considered, superior market facilities by land and water, and great diversity of soil and crops, destine her, in the near future, to take front rank among the agricultural States of the Union, as her inexhaustible mineral wealth and water power will, when developed, enable her to take prominent position with the first mining and manufacturing States. No State is better watered, being traversed by some of the finest rivers on this Continent, such as the Potomac, James, Roanoke, Appomattox, and innumerable smaller streams, which afford an easy and cheap transportation to the markets of the world of her varied products, and water power to turn millions of spindles. Her people are intelligent, kind, hospitable and law-abiding, and extend a hearty welcome to all honest and industrious immigrants settling in their midst, come from where they may, without regard to religious views or political opinions.

This portion of the State—the vicinity of Petersburg—is gently undulating, neither hilly nor level, with a soil varying from sandy loam to heavy clay—both having a fine clay sub-soil. Crops embrace everything, nearly, of grain or fruit grown in the north temperate zone. The chief staples are tobacco, wheat, rye, oats, corn, peanuts, potatoes, sweet and Irish; melons, fruits, &c., &c. Stock—horses, hogs and sheep—are also raised in considerable numbers and at paying prices.

This section is as healthy as any in America, and none is more exempt from epidemic diseases—typhoid and lung diseases are very rare—and many of the most prevalent and fatal diseases of the North and Northwest are unknown. These diseases not only do not prevail, but the climate has cured numbers who have settled here from the North since the war. These are a few of the advantages of this section, and when taken in connection with our cheap lands and public school privileges, we are constrained to think that we only need population to develop her slumbering resources—to make her future as prosperous as her past has been honorable.

In consequence of negro emancipation, an entire change has been necessitated in our labor system, and, consequently, in our mode of farming; smaller areas are cultivated than formerly, and a more thorough cultivation prevails; the result is, most of our farmers own more land than they can use advantageously, and are therefore offering their excess at very low prices, and are anxious to sell. There are others compelled to sell their entire farms; and many who, owning several farms, reserving alone their homestead, sell their remaining lands. Many of these farms are valuable old homesteads, with comfortable dwellings, necessary farm houses, fruit, timber, &c., and can be purchased, frequently, for less than the buildings cost.

C. H. PYLE.   R. W. DeHAVEN.

PYLE & DeHAVEN,

REAL ESTATE AGENTS,

—AND—

LAND BROKERS,

ALSO AGENTS OF

Virginia Immigration Society.

OFFICE IN MECHANICS BUILDING, TABB STREET,

PETERSBURG, VIRGINIA,

WE OFFER GREAT BARGAINS IN

FARMS, TIMBER LANDS

—AND—

MINERAL LANDS,

CHEAP LANDS, GOOD MARKETS AND EXCELLENT CLIMATE.
WRITE FOR CIRCULARS CONTAINING DESCRIPTIONS.

TOBACCO.

——:o:——

Sublime Tobacco! which from East to West
Cheers the tar's labor or the Turkman's rest ;
Which on the Moslem's ottoman divides
His hours, and rivals opium and his brides ;
Magnificent in Stamboul, but less grand,
Though not less loved, in Wapping or the Strand!—
—*The Island.*

Situated on the Eastern boundary of the tobacco-growing section of
Virginia, and in the direct line of railroad transportation to the sea-ports
of the Atlantic and the great cities of the North and East, Petersburg
has always enjoyed extraordinary advantages as a mart and distributing
point for the raw material, and also, of late years, as a locality eminently
suited to its manufacture. The facilities of communication which the
City has heretofore possessed with her back country are about to be increased by the development of navigation on the Upper Appomattox
and by the construction of the Virginia & Carolina Railroad, both of
which arteries pass through some of the finest tobacco land in this State
and North Carolina. Ever since her foundation, the town has been the
depot for the tobacco grown within the district naturally tributary to her
—from the days when the hogsheads were rolled along the public highway to market, down to the time when the freight cars of the old Southside and the Petersburg & Weldon Railroads offered the planters a less
expensive and far more expeditious method of transmitting their produce—and as tobacco has always been the most valuable, if not the principal, crop cultivated in the surrounding counties, it has naturally exercised a ruling influence upon the whole commercial history of Petersburg.
Until comparatively recent times, indeed, the pulses of the various markets have been very sensitive to the rise and fall in the current quotations
for leaf tobacco, and as this product has furnished an immense field for
speculation, the general commercial interests of the City have, in times
past, experienced the extremes of buoyancy and depression in response to
the fluctuations of the leaf market. This, however, was more perceptible
when Petersburg was noted rather as a depot for leaf tobacco than as the
great manufacturing centre which she has since become. The amount of
money kept in circulation no longer entirely depends, as it formerly did,
upon the weight and value of the crops, but is governed, in a great measure, by the activity or idleness of the large tobacco factories which have
grown up since the war and are to-day the main support of the City. In
the manufacture of a pound of tobacco more money is expended in wages
alone than the aggregate profits of the planter, who grows the leaf, and
the middleman, who sells it, and any one of our larger factories contributes more to the general prosperity to-day than did, in former times, the

whole host of brokers, speculators and "private buyers" whose dimin-
ished ranks are occasionally deplored. It is a noteworthy fact, moreover,
and one which very materially affects the permanent welfare of all classes
in the community, that the manufacturers for the Export Trade, of whom
there are several in the City, draw, almost exclusively, on England for
their shipments, thus introducing, on an average, about £7,000 sterling,
per week, of foreign money to be expended here in the purchase of leaf
tobacco, machinery, &c., and in wages.

The tobacco grown in this section of Virginia, and manufactured into
plug and twist in the Petersburg factories, has never lost its ancient pres-
tige in the foreign markets, in spite of vigorous and aggressive competition on the part of Western and Northern rivals ; and in Australia, New
Zealand, India and other distant lands where these products are largely
consumed, a box, to be thoroughly appreciated, must show unmistakable
proof of having been prepared of leaf grown in the land of Powhatan
and Pocahontas, where the plant attains the perfection of development,
without the rank flavor and woody stem of the Western leaf, and where it
acquires its peculiar sweetness and aroma from the exact suitability of the
soil and climate ; while in its skillful preparation for the markets of the
world, our manufacturers have no superiors, and few, if any, equals, in the
United States or elsewhere. This one article of commerce has made the
name of Petersburg familiar in every quarter of the globe, as well as in
every State and Territory of the Union, and it is always associated with
a much prized luxury, whether heard within the frozen belt of the Polar
Zone or beneath the scorching rays of the tropical sun—in the mining
camp of the Far West or on the sheep-run of the antipodes.

Our manufacturers, it must be remembered, have to compete with the
unlimited capital of the North and the indomitable "push" of the West,
and it is therefore by the intrinsic merit of their products alone that they
have been able to hold their own in the past, or can hope to do so in the
future. This applies to the Domestic as well as to the Foreign Trade,
but it is in the latter branch that Petersburg stands pre-eminent. Of the
53,539,352 pounds of manufactured tobacco exported from the United
States during the last five years, Petersburg has contributed 19,260,015
pounds, or 1,413,565 pounds more than one third ! Within the same period 26,121,000 pounds has been manufactured here for the Home Trade,
making a total of 45,381,015, or a yearly average of 9,076,203 pounds, in the
preparation of which the manufacturers expend annually in material and labor nearly $2,500,000, the greater part of which goes immediately into the
hands of our retail merchants, while the tax paid by the former during
the last fifteen years towards the support of the Federal Government ag-
gregates a sum greater than the taxable property of all kinds in the City
to-day. The value of the "plant" employed in the manufacture of tobacco in Petersburg is estimated at between $500,000 and $600,000.

An examination of the subjoined tables, compiled from official figures,
will reveal some interesting facts in relation to the Tobacco Trade of this
City.

MANUFACTURED TOBACCO

EXPORTED FROM PETERSBURG, VA., SHOWING THE MONTHLY SHIPMENTS, IN POUNDS.

1875 to 1884, inclusive.

MONTHS.	1875.	1876.	1877.	1878.	1879.	1880.	1881.	1882.	1883.	1884.	Totals.
January	244,037	157,091	270,784	302,474	132,425	205,017	280,615	415,785	281,723	238,669	2,667,560
February	275,876	202,906	312,402	423,917	303,981	251,728	132,733	223,515	253,334	272,809	2,622,391
March	191,963	280,568	516,652	262,811	270,563	270,507	315,792	125,756	296,312	966,402	3,294,726
April	445,221	447,910	366,718	412,742	249,362	244,507	271,997	309,959	336,674	297,586	3,537,576
May	211,641	372,002	508,912	373,051	507,198	382,930	280,714	458,772	303,627	297,870	3,710,138
June	218,231	345,008	163,043	508,677	206,430	128,041	359,361	431,469	353,143	377,977	3,429,107
July	290,648	529,103	404,574	475,439	208,066	101,965	365,558	360,363	130,458	271,553	3,190,977
August	271,897	395,692	466,292	313,271	275,878	343,188	214,989	397,657	215,139	273,756	3,187,550
September	301,117	471,689	543,394	574,947	299,231	230,713	290,670	409,322	353,860	344,216	3,968,608
October	286,288	413,531	414,936	380,656	293,091	299,156	318,679	118,529	389,011	275,497	3,530,977
November	213,381	454,616	396,773	409,119	202,680	396,481	363,348	355,249	396,697	367,493	3,513,657
December	331,053	497,296	217,886	370,347	469,312	327,063	311,240	350,777	360,955	497,031	3,733,439
Totals	3,284,756	4,580,446	4,867,776	4,906,641	3,266,407	3,883,156	3,462,538	4,672,555	3,609,984	3,772,069	40,087,567
Total Exports from the U. S.	11,386,046	10,581,744	11,634,951	9,808,406		10,086,132	10,826,215				111,180,645

	1883.	1884.
Inspections for the year ending September 30th.	10,760 hhds.	10,767 hhds.
Stock on hand inspected	2,207 "	1,526 "
Stock on hand for inspection	184 "	12 "
Shipments of leaf tobacco all coastwise)	4,032 hhds.	3,684 hhds.
" " " " "	412 tierces.	307 tierces.
" stems " "	783 hhds.	1,339 hhds.
Sales of loose tobacco.	5,449,544 pounds.	4,636,748 pounds.

COMPARATIVE STATEMENT OF THE TAXES COLLECTED
FROM MANUFACTURED TOBACCO.

1877 to 1883, inclusive.

YEAR.	Tax Collected from Tobacco manufactured in the U. S.	Tax Collected from tobacco manufactured in Virginia.	Tax Collected from tobacco manufactured in Petersburg.
1877	$ 27,053,072 38	$ 7,932,220 78	$1,073,508 06
1878	25,326,153 08	6,501,730 29	1,151,147 64
1879	24,703,874 90	6,448,546 88	895,171 26
1880	21,170,154 40	5,781,409 58	746,732 90
1881	22,833,287 60	6,063,105 73	966,057 38
1882	25,033,741 97	6,226,308 30	706,595 29
1883	24,834,951 86	4,764,228 40	577,033 71
Total	$170,955,236 19	$43,717,549 98	$6,116,548 64

NOTE: On June 6th, 1872, the tax on manufactured tobacco was reduced from 32 cents to 20 cents per pound. On March 3d, 1875, it was increased to 24 cents, and on May 1st, 1879, again reduced to 16 cents. On May 1st, 1883, the tax was fixed at 8 cents per pound, and so remains at the present time.

TOBACCO WAREHOUSES.

————:0:————

" From time immemorial "—which means, in this particular instance, from the early days of Petersburg's establishment as a town, and the systematic settlement of the surrounding counties—tobacco, as has already been shown, has ever been the most important factor in the mercantile welfare of this district, and the warehouses, on the floors of which the loose leaf is bought and sold and sampled, have necessarily been the vital centres of the tobacco trade. There are four of these warehouses in Petersburg, one of them, " Moore's," being in private hands, and the other three, namely, " Centre," " West-hill " and " Oaks," remaining under the control of the State authorities. Millions of pounds of loose leaf tobacco are sold at auction at these warehouses every year, and thousands of hogsheads and tierces are sampled and inspected for manufacture or shipment. Farmers bringing their produce to town find excellent accommodation for their wagons and horses at these warehouses, without charge, and every effort is made by their respective managers to insure the comfort of their guests.

S. W. VENABLE & CO.

[ESTABLISHED IN 1853.]

While it may safely be asserted that there are few dealers in tobacco throughout the length and breadth of this fair Continent, or in the more important of the markets beyond the seas, to whom the name of this firm is unfamiliar, it is by no means probable that the magnitude of its operations is generally appreciated, even within hearing distance of its factory whistle. Nor would it be easy to point out many instances, even in this land of miraculous developments and infinite possibilities, in which intelligent enterprise and persevering energy have more strikingly met with their legitimate reward, than the record of this flourishing house affords.

More than thirty years have passed into history since Mr. S. W. Venable, the head and founder of the firm, began handling tobacco in this market, and during the whole of that period the business has been steadily increasing and ranks to-day among the half-dozen largest tobacco-manufacturing establishments in the United States, if not in the World. Some idea of the rapidity of its growth may be gathered from the fact that in 1866—the year after the termination of the Civil War—the amount of tobacco manufactured and sold by this firm was about 700,000 pounds, while it now produces over 4,000,000 pounds annually, consuming between 4,000 and 5,000 hogsheads of the raw leaf.

The factory is three and a half stories high, fronting 150 feet on Byrne street, by a depth of 250 feet, and is well supplied with every device in modern machinery for the manufacture of all varieties of plug and fine bright twist tobaccos. It employs, in the busy season, eight hundred hands, thus supporting nearly four thousand persons, or about one-sixth of the whole population of Petersburg !

In 1875, Mr. S. W. Venable admitted his son, Mr. E. C. Venable, to partnership, and the firm is now composed of these two gentlemen.

The field of their home-trade is bounded only by the limits of the United States, and they export to Great Britain, Australia, India, South America and the West Indies, making a specialty of fine bright navy tobaccos for the foreign and domestic markets.

Among the principal brands manufactured by this house are "Admiration," "Amot Lyle," "The Chief," "Nimrod," "Vinco," "St. George," "Bacchante," "Hester," "Mogul," "Perfection," "Live Oak" and "E. C."

The firm also deals extensively in leaf tobacco for shipment abroad, and is one of the large buyers on the floors of our tobacco warehouses and at the Tobacco Exchange.

WM. CAMERON & BRO.

Tobacco is the staple product of Virginia, and the development of its trade must ever be matter of deep interest to all who are concerned in the welfare of the State; and, in the same ratio, its manufacture, which constitutes Petersburg's principal industry, cannot fail to engage the earnest attention of the business and professional classes of the community, for

WM. CAMERON & BRO.'S TOBACCO FACTORY, PETERSBURG, VA.

upon its success depends the very existence of a large proportion of the city's now thriving population.

Conspicuous among the pioneers of this most important branch of trade, stands the firm of Wm. Cameron & Bro., consisting of William, Alexander and George Cameron. For many years past the management of this extensive and increasing business has received the energetic as well as the progressive personal attention of Mr. George Cameron, whose skill and success have extended the firm's operations, year by year, until the present day. They are now among the largest exporters of manufactured tobacco in the country, and their many leading brands, among the best known of which may be mentioned the "Raven," "Havelock," "Two Seas," "Orion," "Canary," "Our Chief," "Peach and Honey," "Mazeppa" and "Pluck," are famous the world over, wherever the virtues of superior aromatic "Cavendish" and "Twist" are appreciated. This would appear to be chiefly the case in Australia and New Zealand, whither the bulk of Cameron & Bro.'s products are shipped, although large quantities are also consumed in India, South Africa and Great Britain. In addition to the manufactured article, Messrs. Cameron & Bro. are extensive shippers of strip (stemmed) and leaf tobacco.

On the corner of Perry and Brown Streets, in this City, stands "Cameron's Factory," a handsome, lofty and imposing structure of modern architectural design, which a city many times Petersburg's size might well be proud to own. It occupies the site of the firm's original factory, which was burned to the ground in 1878. It is four stories high, with an ornamental cupola, and has a front on Brown Street of one hundred and eighty feet by a depth on Perry street of two hundred and forty feet. The offices, warehouse, engine-house and drying-rooms occupy separate buildings, which form a spacious quadrangle, affording ample room for the special work of each department. But of still higher importance than even substantial and capacious buildings, is the machinery with which the various styles of plug, twist and navy tobacco are prepared, and in this respect Cameron's factory is splendidly equipped. In 1856 hydraulic pressure was first applied, by apparatus invented and patented by Mr. William Cameron, and ever since that date improvements have been introduced from time to time until perfection has at last been attained. The machinery, which is manufactured from designs specially prepared for this factory, is run with three boilers with capacity of two hundred horse-power, and a sixty-horse power engine.

This establishment alone employs over six hundred hands—which means, in other words, that it feeds nearly three thousand mouths. The firm also owns and operates a large and perfectly-appointed factory in Richmond, which is managed by Mr. Alexander Cameron, under the name and style of Alexander Cameron & Co.

In addition to these, the firm has in operation three extensive factories in the Australian cities of Sydney, Melbourne and Adelaide, respectively, the former of which has recently been enlarged and improved at a cost of over £20,000. At each of these factories Messrs. Cameron & Bro. have also found it necessary to establish their own bonded warehouse to facilitate the conduct of their enormous local trade, and these warehouses are under the charge of officials detailed for that special duty by the Colonial Governments. All the Australian affairs of the concern are under the personal management of the senior partner, Mr. William Cameron.

D. B. TENNANT & CO.

Among the large manufacturers of tobacco for the export trade, to whose combined success is mainly due the fame which Petersburg has acquired in the World of Commerce, the firm now under review occupies a conspicuous and honorable position.   It was founded as long ago as the year 1843, by Messrs. Robert Dunlop, now deceased, and D. B. Tennant, the surviving partner and present head of the concern, under the style of Dunlop & Tennant.   In 1865 Mr. Tennant admitted to partnership Mr. David Dunlop, a nephew of his late partner, and the name of the firm was changed to D. B. Tennant & Co.

Besides being the heaviest exporters of manufactured tobacco to the markets of the Old World, to South America, the West Indies and the Island groups of the Pacific Ocean, the house of D. B. Tennant & Co. enjoys the further distinction of seniority over every other similar establishment now existing in Petersburg.

The factory, which employs about four hundred hands, is in all respects adapted to the requirements of the large and still increasing manufacturing operations of the firm.   It comprises a splendid three-story brick building, situated on East Washington street, covering an area of 100 by 200 feet, and fitted throughout with all the latest and best adapted inventions in the way of machinery, which is driven by powerful steam engines.   This establishment is thus enabled to manufacture and export annually an enormous quantity of plug and twist tobacco, of various grades, and comprising many popular and famous brands, amounting in the aggregate to over a million and a half pounds.   Of these brands, the following are among the best known, namely : "Thomas R. Shellard," "Belle of Virginia," "Harlequin," "Elephant," "Captain Cook," "Derby," "Emu," "Lothair," "Bellevue," "Ellerslie," "Fair Maid," "Kohinoor," "Faithful Lover" and many others of almost equal popularity, and all composed exclusively of the choicest Virginia leaf.

In the markets of India, London, Liverpool and Australia, these fine tobaccos are in the greatest demand, and three of the brands, viz., "Belle of Virginia," "Kohinoor" and "Bellevue," earned the highest award—a gold medal—at the Calcutta exhibition of 1883-'84.

The firm of D. B. Tennant & Co. is regarded in commercial circles generally, at home and abroad, as one of the most substantial manufacturing houses in the United States, and the industrial interests of Petersburg are indebted, in a peculiar degree, to its progressive and long-sustained enterprise.

These gentlemen are also largely interested in Petersburg property, other than that connected with their tobacco factory, and although the cares and responsibilities attaching to them as proprietors of this important business are necessarily many and onerous, one or other of them is sure to be found on the Board of Directors of nearly every sound corporation doing business in the city, and it is to such men and such houses as D. B. Tennant & Co. that all thriving centres of trade and industry owe their credit and prosperity.

WATSON & McGILL.

The development of the Tobacco interest is so intimately allied to the past, present and prospective commercial prosperity of Petersburg, that any considerable enterprise which is calculated to foster and supplement this development must necessarily be regarded with favor by all who have the real welfare of the city at heart. Capital is the nursing mother of suc-

WATSON & McGILL'S TOBACCO FACTORY, PETERSBURG, VA.

cess, and its free but judicious application to the requirements of enlarging industry is not only a sure guarantee of a healthy and vigorous maturity, but also a decided indication that the controlling and dispensing hand is directed by those correct mathematical principles which the experience of ages has taught us to regard as well-nigh infallible. Among many legiti-mate causes for self-gratulation, Petersburg can boast of several examples

in support of this theory, and, with no desire to be lavish of compliment in
any special direction, it may be fairly said that the foregoing remarks apply with convincing force to the firm whose name is placed at the head of
this article.

For many years past, Messrs. Watson & McGill have been extensively
engaged in the manufacture of plug and twist tobacco for the foreign
trade, towards the supply of which Petersburg contributes more largely
than any other city in the United States. Gradually but surely the business of the firm has grown in importance, and has latterly assumed such
extended proportions that, in 1883, the old three-story factory on West
Washington street, although of considerable capacity and measuring two
hundred by sixty feet, was found to be quite inadequate to the increased and increasing requirements, and a handsome new wing, of equal
height and covering eighty by forty feet of ground, was added and fitted
up with the most approved appliances—the whole forming one of the most
commodious and complete tobacco manufactories in the country.

The force employed in this busy establishment numbers about four hundred experienced hands, and the article they turn out finds much favor in
the eyes—and mouths—of the dwellers in distant lands. The markets
of Europe and Australia are the principal channels through which the products of this factory find their way to the consumers, and among the numerous brands which have been most directly instrumental in spreading
the name and fame of Messrs. Watson & McGill, at home and abroad, as
among the most capable, reliable and enterprising manufacturers of Virginia's great staple product may be mentioned : "Black Swan," "Over the
Water," "New Zealand Joys," "Triumph," "International," "Peach
Basket," "La Honradez," "Le Grand" and "McRae," besides many
others, the popularity of which is necessarily limited to the markets for
which they are specially manufactured.

WILLIAMSON & ROUTH.

The most conspicuous building in the western suburbs of the city is the
three-story brick tobacco factory of this firm, situated on South Street,
near the basin of the Upper Appomattox Canal. The business was founded
in 1860, by the senior member of the firm, Mr. J. P. Williamson, who carried it on successfully for twenty years alone. In 1880 Mr. James E. Routh
was admitted to partnership and the present firm established. The factory, which is well supplied with all necessary machinery for the manufacture of all kinds of plug and twist, and for the preparation of foreign leaf
and strips, employs from one hundred and twenty-five to one hundred and
fifty hands, and is capable of putting out 5,000 pounds of manufactured
tobacco a day. Its products are shipped to Europe, Australia, India and
the West Indies, where they have become very popular and enjoy a steady
demand. The principal brands manufactured by this firm are "Vuelta
Abajo," most of which goes to Havana, and "Two Flags," which finds its
market in London. Messrs. Williamson & Routh are now giving more attention than heretofore to the process of stripping and preparing for shipment those grades of raw leaf tobacco which are most adapted to the foreign trade, and their large factory is kept busy in all its various departments.

BOYKIN, BLAND & CO.,

[SUCCESSORS TO C. A. JACKSON & CO.]

Late on the night of October 13th, 1884, during the prevalence of a high wind, and at a time when the town and country were still suffering from the effects of an almost unprecedented drought, and everything above ground was literally "as dry as tinder," the clanging bells rang out the fire-alarm with such persistence that hundreds of people who had retired to their beds turned out to ascertain its cause. The unnatural glow in the western sky and the volumes of ruddy smoke rolling southward from the Fourth Ward, plainly indicated the direction of the disaster, and it was soon known throughout the city that the magnificent tobacco factory of C. A. Jackson & Co., on High street, one of the oldest and largest in the United States, was in flames. For hours the fire raged furiously, and when it was at last extinguished there was nothing left of what had been but yesterday the busy scene of happy and profitable labor, save a shapeless heap of smouldering ruins. So great a loss had not been experienced in Petersburg for many years from a similar cause, but it was announced at once that the business of the firm would be resumed as soon as suitable premises could be secured.

"Ill blows the wind that profits nobody," sang the infallible Bard of Avon, and experience has demonstrated that some advantage may be reaped from even so destructive an event as a conflagration. However that may be, it is certain that the immense business of C. A. Jackson & Co., which was established in the year 1868, and has contributed largely since that date towards building up the industrial interests of Petersburg, had not received its death-blow, nor even a permanent injury, by the loss of the factory. This very circumstance, on the contrary, has been made the occasion of introducing new blood and reorganizing the concern, which is now composed of Messrs. Robert H. Boykin, John B. Bland and Charles A. Jackson, all practical men, of long experience in the tobacco trade, who succeed the late firm of C. A. Jackson & Co., whose famous brands of bright and dark plug tobacco they are now manufacturing. These latter are too well known to the trade and the public to require more than casual mention here, for there are few lovers of the fragrant weed in Virginia, North Carolina, Texas and the Southwest generally, who have not rejoiced in the use of "Old Hickory." "Spring" or Jackson's Best,"—the last-named having also a large demand in many of the Northern States.

The temporary premises of Boykin Bland & Co. are the buildings formerly occupied as a tobacco factory by McEnery & McCulloch, adjoining the Anderson School Building, on West Washington Street, an engraving of which is shown on page 93. It is a three-story brick building fitted with steam and hydraulic presses and all other machinery employed in preparing brands of the finest quality. It has a manufacturing capacity of 1,500,000 pounds of plug and twist tobacco a year, and employs three hundred hands. This arrangement will enable the firm to fill the most pressing orders until the burned factory has been replaced.

JOHN H. MACLIN.

This gentleman, who has been engaged in the manufacture of plug and twist tobacco in Petersburg since the year 1868, is the successor of the firm of Maclin & Wallace, of which he was also the head. He occupies and operates the fine three-story brick factory situated on the corner of Washington and Jefferson Streets. The dimensions of the main building are 120x40 feet, and the capacity of the factory is four thousand pounds a day. Mr. Maclin turns out all styles of plug and twist tobacco and ships them to the uttermost parts of the earth. In the lumber camps of Canada and in the populous cities of Europe, in the Australian "bush" and in the luxurious "bungalow" of Hindostan, on the pampas of South America and on the diamond fields of Cape Colony, on the sugar plantations of the West Indies and in the cinnamon gardens of Ceylon, wherever, in fact, the "plant divine, of rarest virtue" is known and loved—and where is it not? —such brands as "The Correct Thing at Last," "Black Hawk," "Mistletoe," "Star of Virginia," and a great many others manufactured and exported by Mr. John H. Maclin, of Petersburg, are sure to be found, claiming their fair share of public notice and receiving their fair share of public patronage.

Mr. Maclin employs about a hundred hands, and has recently reinforced his machinery with a fine forty-horse power steam engine, steam presses, lump machinery, etc., to which he contemplates making further additions very shortly. All his shipments to the foreign markets are made through Messrs. Joseph D. Evans & Co., of New York, who are sole agents for all his brands.

In addition to his plug and twist factory, Mr. Maclin is largely engaged in the purchase and re-prizing of leaf tobacco, and this department of his business is conducted in a large framed structure, 80x44 feet, on Jefferson Street, adjoining the main building. This is devoted exclusively to the finest grades of leaf tobacco for the Austrian market, and is nearly all sold to the Agent for that Government.

Mr. Maclin is one of those who are bound to progress with this progressive age. He is rapidly replacing what still remains in his factory of the "old methods" by new machinery of the most approved type, and will shortly be able to turn out a million pounds of manufactured plug and twist, annually.

W. D. BARKLEY & CO.

This enterprising firm of tobacco manufacturers, whose factory and offices are at Nos. 52 and 54 Bank Street, opposite Short Market Street, was established in 1879, and consists of Messrs. W. D. Barkley (formerly of the firm of Maclin & Barkley) and R. L. Judkins, both of whom are practical and experienced manipulators of the "sublime weed." They put up several styles of bright and dark plug and twist tobacco for the domestic and foreign trade. Their factory is run by steam and water power, and has a capacity of over two thousand pounds a day.

Their principal brand manufactured for export is "O. K." Twist, and this is mostly shipped to the South American markets and those of the West and East Indies.

For the domestic trade they prepare several special brands, among which those in the greatest demand are, "Rip Rap," "Hobson's Choice," "Barkley's Best," and "U & I." These meet with a ready sale in Virginia, Pennsylvania and North Carolina, and the factory is taxed to its utmost capacity to keep pace with the orders.

This factory also produces some very popular varieties of granulated smoking tobacco, among which should be particularly mentioned "Canary Bird," "Captain Jinks" and "I. X. I." These, and many others, have maintained their original standard of excellence for so long a period that they have become firmly established in public favor, and the demand for them is steady.

The establishment of W. D. Barkley & Co., while not pretending to rival some of the colossal manufacturing houses which are the pride of Petersburg and the mainstay of her industrial prosperity, is, nevertheless, a useful and reliable contributor to the enormous aggregate of production which has made this city one of the principal tobacco markets of the world. Petersburg has the best of reasons for glorying in her commercial importance, which has been earned for her, to a preponderating extent, by those of her citizens who are engaged in the manipulation of tobacco, either as manufacturers or dealers, and among these W. D. Barkley & Co. occupy a creditable position.

ROBERT C. OSBORNE.

Conspicuous among the many handsome and substantial edifices which have arisen within the last few years as unimpeachable witnesses to Petersburg's commercial enterprise and industrial vitality, stands the new three-story brick tobacco factory of Mr. Robert C. Osborne, 90x40 feet, which occupies the northwest corner of Henry and Fourth streets, in this city.

The business was founded in 1839 by Mr. E. H. Osborne, father of the present proprietor, and was conducted by the former until his death, in 1876. The original factory, which was situated on Jefferson Street, was destroyed by fire in 1872, when Mr. Osborne rented a temporary factory on Lombard Street, whence he has recently removed to his new building, which is fitted throughout with appropriate modern machinery.

Many well-established and popular brands of plug, twist and bright tobaccos are manufactured at this establishment, namely : "Minnie," "Myrtle," "Autumn," "Laurel Leaf," "The Surprise," "Phoites' Compliments," "Eagle," "Cabaniss," "Dolphin's Bride," "Van-Dyck," "Virginia's Offering," "Black Crow," "Otham" and "Zephyr," all of which are prepared specially for direct export to the markets of London, Liverpool, Glasgow, Norway, Sweden, Germany, Holland, Belgium, France, Spain, Austria, Portugal and South America.

For nearly half a century this house has been among the leading contributors to the export tobacco trade of the city. That the reputation of its products has been fully maintained up to the present day is evidenced by the increasing demand for the above-mentioned brands, while no surer guarantee for future excellence could well be offered than that which is afforded by the honorable and prosperous career of this establishment during the past forty-five years.

A. J. CAMPBELL & CO.

In considering broadly the immense Tobacco Trade of Petersburg, it is
only natural that attention should be principally directed to those two important branches which most materially affect the public weal, namely, the
sales of leaf—loose and in hogsheads—at the several warehouses, and the
manufacture of plug and twist, for the domestic and foreign markets, at
the splendid factories reviewed in the foregoing pages ; and it is equally
natural that, in view of these prominent interests, the more modest establishments engaged in the manufacture of Tobacco, and therefore properly
belonging to the same category, should be, to some extent, overlooked.
Among these latter, whose influence in the employment of labor, the ex-
penditure of money in material, and the spreading and cementing of Petersburg's commercial relations with other sections of the country, has been
gratefully recognized in the past and continues to be exercised and appreciated in the present, are the firm of A. J. Campbell & Co., manufacturers of
Snuff and Smoking Tobacco, and its predecessors. This business was
established in 1861, by Mr. James E. Venable, who was succeeded by
Messrs. Joseph E. Venable & Sons, and successfully conducted by them
until three years ago, when it was purchased by the present firm, the members of which are Mr. A. J. Campbell and his brother, Mr. A. C. Campbell.   These gentlemen, until recently, operated two factories, one at the
Locks and the other at the Basin of the Upper Appomattox Canal. The
former, which was the larger of the two, was destroyed by fire on October
11th, 1884, just after it had received a complete outfit of new machinery
and been enlarged to four times its former capacity. At the time of this
loss the firm employed about a hundred hands, and were grinding about
one thousand pounds of Snuff per day. The work has necessarily been
greatly reduced for the time being, but the remaining factory is working
to its utmost capacity, and the firm contemplates replacing the burned
building at an early date. Among the principal brands of Snuff manufactured by this house, are "Carolina Belle (Scotch), "Rose-scented Macca-
boy," "Rappee," etc.; and of fine granulated Smoking Tobacco, they put
up, among others, the popular and delicate "Yellow Bird," "Red Fox,"
"Macaria," and "Old Virginia." They also manufacture several kinds of
Flavorings used by tobacconists, such as ground deer-tongue, orange-peel,
etc. Most of their Snuffs are consumed in Virginia, North and South Carolina, Georgia, Alabama, Tennessee, Mississippi, Florida and Texas, while
their Smoking Tobacco finds ready markets in the Western and Southern
States, generally.

MOORE'S WAREHOUSE.

AMONG THE "ANCIENT LANDMARKS" OF PETERSBURG, THERE IS PER-
HAPS NO OTHER WHICH HAS BORNE SO LARGE A SHARE IN THE MERCAN-
TILE DEVELOPMENT OF THE CITY AS THE TOBACCO WAREHOUSE ON MAR-
KET STREET KNOWN AS

"MOORE'S."

IT DATES BACK TO THE COLONIAL DAYS, HAVING BEEN BUILT ABOUT THE
YEAR 1770 BY ONE WILLIAM BARKSDALE, AND WAS ORIGINALLY CALLED
"BARKSDALE'S WAREHOUSE." IT WAS PURCHASED IN THE FIRST YEAR OF
THIS CENTURY BY AN ENGLISH SETTLER NAMED ROBERT MOORE, WHOSE
NAME IT HAS SINCE BORNE. IT IS SUBSTANTIALLY BUILT OF BRICK AND
ROOFED WITH SLATE IMPORTED FROM WALES, WHICH HAVE SUCCESS-
FULLY WITHSTOOD THE STORMS AND RAVAGES OF A CENTURY, AND ARE
TO-DAY IN A PERFECT STATE OF PRESERVATION. AFTER THE DEATH OF
ROBERT MOORE AND HIS SON, THE WAREHOUSE BECAME THE PROPERTY
OF THE CHILDREN OF WILLIAM DAVIDSON, OF LONDON, FROM WHOSE
HEIRS IT WAS PURCHASED IN 1870 BY ITS PRESENT PROPRIETORS, MESSRS.

WATSON & McGILL,

TOBACCO MANUFACTURERS, OF PETERSBURG. IT FRONTS ABOUT TWO
HUNDRED FEET ON MARKET STREET, BY A DEPTH OF THREE HUNDRED
FEET, AND IS CENTRALLY AND CONVENIENTLY SITUATED. IT IS THE OLD-
EST TOBACCO WAREHOUSE IN PETERSBURG, AND REPRESENTS AN ENOR-
MOUS BUSINESS, PAST AND PRESENT. UNTIL RECENTLY IT HAS, IN COM-
MON WITH OTHER WAREHOUSES OF THE CITY, BEEN SUBJECT TO THE
CONTROL OF THE STATE GOVERNMENT, BUT IN FUTURE IT WILL BE CON-
DUCTED AS A "PRIVATE WAREHOUSE," UNDER THE SUPERINTENDENCE
OF MANAGERS APPOINTED BY ITS OWNERS. THE PRESENT MANAGERS
ARE MESSRS. JAMES M. PARHAM AND PERRY STOKES, BOTH BEING GEN-
TLEMEN OF LONG EXPERIENCE AS SAMPLERS AND INSPECTORS UNDER
THE OLD REGIME, WHEN THE STATE CLAIMED AN INTEREST IN THE BUSI-
NESS OF THE WAREHOUSES, AND VIRTUALLY CONTROLLED THEIR AF-
FAIRS. WITHIN THE LAST DECADE THE PREMISES HAVE BEEN THOR-
OUGHLY REPAIRED AND ENLARGED BY THE ADDITION OF AN EXTENSIVE
WING, WHICH FRONTS ON FRIEND STREET. IT AFFORDS EXCELLENT AC-
COMMODATION FOR THE WAGONS AND HORSES OF PLANTERS BRINGING
THEIR TOBACO AND OTHER PRODUCE TO THE CITY BY ROAD, WHILE ITS
CAPACITY FOR STORING HOGSHEADS IS ALMOST UNLIMITED. MOORE'S
WAREHOUSE IS WELL KNOWN TO EVERY TOBACCO PLANTER WITHIN THE
WHOLE OF PETERSBURG'S TRIBUTARY RADIUS, AND THOUSANDS OF HOGS-
HEADS FROM MORE DISTANT POINTS ARE RECEIVED AND SOLD THERE
DURING THE YEAR.

J. J. PERCIVALL, Petersburg, | W. M. FIELD, Dinwiddie.

West Hill Warehouse,

PETERSBURG, VA.

PERCIVALL & FIELD · · Samplers.

PERSONAL ATTENTION TO SALES AND PROMPT RETURNS.

OUR NEW SHEDS AND ROOMS

will soon be completed, giving us ample accommodation.

Insurance on Tobacco Free.

THE LARGEST AND MOST CENTRALLY LOCATED WARE-
HOUSE IN THE CITY.

THE VIRGINIA SLATE-ROOFING COMPANY.

———:o:———

O. O. THOMAS & CO.

For many years past, Virginia and the adjoining States have been indebted to this Company for some of the finest slate roofing ever done
within their borders, and Petersburg alone furnishes many hundreds of pal-
pable testimonials to the excellence of its work. Mr. O. O. Thomas is the
senior member of the firm and the managing director of the company. He
has had a long and practical experience in every department of his trade,
and has earned the highest encomiums from all who have employed his
services. Among the prominent buildings and residences in this city, the
Company can point to the following, as offering examples of its superior
slate roofing, namely : The Central Lunatic Asylum, the Normal School,
the Library Hall, the residence of John McGill, Esq., on Market Street
(a view of which is shown on page 45), the residence of James E. Routh,
Esq., on Washington Street, and others which might be numbered by
scores. In fact, nearly all the slating done in Petersburg during the last
seven years, is the work of this firm.

But their fame is by no means confined to this City, or even to this
State. The roof of the Eastern Lunatic Asylum, at Williamsburg, is their
work. So is the roof of Hampden-Sydney College, at Farmville, and that
of the Union Depot at Bristol, and of the Norfolk & Western Railroad
Company's Depot at Lynchburg. The roofing of the beautiful Public
Square, at Nashville, Tenn., was also furnished by them, and they have left
grand samples of their handiwork at Atlanta, Ga., Chattanooga, Tenn.,
and many other cities. The Norfolk & Western Railroad Company has
employed the services of O. O. Thomas & Co. upon many of their new
buildings during a period of several years, and has given them the highest recommendations.

There is no part of a building, whether it be a public hall or a private
residence, upon which its comfort and value so much depend as its roof,
and it is of the utmost importance that this portion of the structure should
be intrusted only to skilled and experienced hands, and there are none to
be found, North or South, better skilled or more experienced than those of
O. O. Thomas & Co., otherwise known as the Virginia Slate Roofing Company. They own and operate slate quarries, and can therefore supply the
material as well as the labor, without the expensive aid of middle-men. In
Tennessee alone, six hundred and seventy-five buildings, public and private, have been roofed by this firm, and a much larger number in Virginia
and North Carolina. In addition to Slate Roofing of all kinds, they also
furnish and lay slate flagging for pavements, as well as furnishing tin and
iron Gutters, Valleys, Ridges, etc. The offices of the Company are at No.
142 Sycamore Street, Petersburg, Va.

PEANUTS.

—:o:—

Within the last ten years the Eastern section of Virginia has developed a wonderful trade in this product, and has outstripped all other States in its cultivation. In the season of 1873-4 Virginia produced only 225,000 bushels, while in 1883-4 her yield amounted to 1,250,000 bushels. The light, sandy soil of the Tidewater Counties seems to suit the crop exactly, and the peanuts grown in Virginia command a higher price than those raised in any other State.

There are in Petersburg six peanut "factories," or cleaning establishments, which give employment to hundreds of hands, and ship their various brands to all parts of the North and West, daily. The nuts, or rather their hulls, are cleaned, polished, and assorted according to size by machinery, which does the work better and more expeditiously than was possible under the old system of washing and distributing by hand.

The peanut is of African origin, and was introduced to this country by some trading vessel—probably a "slaver." The African nut, however, is of inferior quality as an article of food, although it is extremely valuable as a commercial commodity, for it produces a large proportion of the so-called olive oil of French manufacture.

Nearly the entire crop of this State is grown in the counties lying immediately to the east of Petersburg, and a large share of the whole yield is purchased by our dealers and distributed by them to the various points of consumption.

After Virginia, the States of Tennessee and North Carolina produce the largest crops, and the following comparative statement of each year's yield since 1873, copied from Mr. Cary W. Jones' book, *Norfolk as a Business Centre*, will be found of interest to those engaged in the trade :

SEASON.	VIRGINIA.	TENNESSEE.	NORTH CAROLINA.	TOTAL.
	Bushels.	Bushels.	Bushels.	Bushels.
1873–4	225,000	175,000	60,000	460,000
1874–5	350,000	200,000	120,000	670,000
1875–6	450,000	235,000	100,000	785,000
1876–7	780,000	500,000	125,000	1,405,000
1877–8	405,000	325,000	100,000	830,000
1878–9	875,000	425,000	90,000	1,390,000
1879–80	1,350,000	750,000	120,000	2,220,000
1880–1	1,500,000	750,000	120,000	2,370,000
1881–2	825,000	250,000	75,000	1,150,000
1882–3	1,250,000	460,000	140,000	1,850,000
1883–4	1,250,000	600,000	150,000	2,000,000

D. B. DUNLOP. J. F. PEEBLES. C. J. SYME.

DUNLOP, PEEBLES & CO.,

✦✦✦✦ LEADERS ✦ AND ✦ HAND-PICKERS ✦ OF ✦ PEANUTS ✦✦✦✦

MAKERS OF CHAMPION, PHENIX AND CHALLENGE BRANDS.

Factory: No. 40 Sycamore Street, Petersburg, Va.

OUR GOODS ARE MADE FROM CHOICEST STOCK & HIGHEST STANDARD MAINTAINED.

REFERENCE:—PETERSBURG SAVINGS AND INSURANCE COMPANY.

JOS. B. WORTH,

CLEANER AND HAND-PICKER OF

PEANUTS.

Factory and Office : No. 13 Old Street, Petersburg, Va.

PROPRIETOR OF

"EAGLE AND FLAG" BRAND Fancy Hand-Picked and Polished Virginia Peanuts.

"SHIELD" BRAND Fancy Hand-Picked and Polished Spanish Peanuts.

CHOICE SPANISH SHELLED PEANUTS A SPECIALTY.

ALL QUOTATIONS AT FACTORY and subject to Fluctuations of the Market.

CORRESPONDENCE SOLICITED.

R. C. MARKS.
R. A. HARRISON.

R.C.MARKS & CO.,

Manufacturers and Cleaners of All Grades of

HAND-PICKED PEANUTS

Virginia and Spanish Shelled and Unshelled.

Petersburg, Virginia.

FACTORY: COR. LOMBARD AND THIRD STREETS.

ESTABLISHED IN 1868.   ESTABLISHED IN 1868.

GEO. DAVIS & CO.,

MANUFACTURERS AND CLEANERS OF ALL GRADES OF VIRGINIA AND SPANISH, SHELLED AND UNSHELLED

Hand-Picked Peanuts

29 BOLLINGBROOK STREET, PETERSBURG, VA.

BUTTER DISH FACTORY.

——:o:——

GEORGE A. MANNIE & CO.

It was with much gratification that the people of Petersburg received the announcement, about four years ago, that an entirely new enterprise was to be established here by some gentlemen from the North, for the purpose of manufacturing butter dishes, veneers, and other kindred articles of commerce, although it must be admitted that some doubts were entertained as to the stability and success of the undertaking. Time has confirmed the feeling of gratification and dissipated the doubts which accompanied it, and the firm of George A. Mannie & Co.—or rather "The Butter Dish Factory, by which name the concern is more generally known—has become one of the institutions of the City, and has already become an acknowledged power for good in the community, under the personal management of Mr. George A. Mannie, the resident partner and head of the firm.

The factory, which is situated on Hinton Street, in the western section of the City, covers a considerable area and employs about one hundred hands, nearly all of whom are from among the most respectable of our poorer white citizens of the weaker sex, who are physically incapacitated from engaging in the heavier labor and heated atmosphere of the tobacco factories and other important industries of the place. Hence the establishment here of such a concern as the one now under consideration could not fail to be a veritable godsend.

The capacity of the factory, with its complete outfit of steam engines and machinery, is one hundred thousand butter dishes a day, and orders for this number can be filled at a very few days' notice, except during the busiest seasons.

The output is mostly sent to New York, whence the dishes are distributed over the whole length and breadth of the United States by Messrs. D. S. Walton & Co., of West Broadway and Franklin Streets, the well-known large manufacturers of Manilla Paper, Paper Bags, etc., who are the sole agents of the butter dishes made at the Petersburg factory.

No effort has been made to establish a foreign trade for these commodities, but there is little room for doubt that such a demand could be created as would necessitate the enlargement of the factory and the employment of an increased force of hands, and both of these results are most desirable. Enterprises like this are entitled to all the support and encouragement that can be given them, and it is earnestly to be hoped that the Butter Dish Factory of Petersburg may prove a grand and permanent success.

SOUTHSIDE MANUFACTURING CO.,

PETERSBURG, VA.

JAMES E. ROUTH,

PRESIDENT AND TREASURER.

GEORGE H. BROWN,

MANAGER.

COMMISSION MERCHANTS, GROCERS AND MERCHANDISE BROKERS.

——:o:——

These three important branches of Petersburg's trade are here grouped together, for the reason that they are too closely allied to each other to admit of separate treatment. United, they cover a vast and varied field and embrace many interests. Indeed, there is no department of commercial enterprise represented in the City which employs so much capital, engages so many of our leading business men, or exercises so wide-spread an influence over the whole territory which recognizes Petersburg as its principal or central market. It is customary among our wholesale grocers to act also as commission merchants, and *rice versa*. Vast quantities of cotton, tobacco, peanuts grain, bacon, poultry and other kinds of produce, are received here for sale on commission, and the consignments are often accompanied by orders for provisions or cash. An open account is frequently kept by the planter with his commission merchant, who advances what goods, fertilizers and money may be required by his country customer, from harvest to harvest, and it occasionally happens that the latter is unable, through misfortune or some other cause, to make a settlement even at harvest time, in which event his commission merchant must "carry" him till the following year, taking a mortgage lien upon land or future crops, as security. It will be seen that considerable capital is required to carry on a business of this kind, and it is estimated that nearly a million dollars is invested in it by our merchants, about a quarter of this amount being employed by those who do an exclusively commission business and carry no stock. When it is remembered that from 25,000 to 50,000 bales of cotton, 500,000 to 600,000 bushels of peanuts, 5,000,000 pounds of loose leaf and 10,000 hogsheads of tobacco, besides other articles of produce in proportionate quantities, are received here annually, and that the greater portion passes through the hands of our commission merchants, the immense importance of their operations will appear; and it may be here stated, without fear of contradiction, that in no town in the United States can be found a more sound, solvent and successful body of business men than they, in proportion to the population and the amount of capital involved.

The Grocery Trade of Petersburg may also be quoted as holding a most satisfactory position. It is almost entirely in the hands of prudent, experienced men, of sufficient financial strength to enable them to keep on hand extensive and varied stocks of goods, and to supply the retail traders of the adjoining counties of this State and North Carolina with almost every commodity usually found in country stores. Our excellent transportation facilities by railroad, river and canal, are even now being improved and increased in every direction, and the prospects for our expanding trade are brighter to-day than they have ever been since the close of the war, in 1865. The Merchandise Brokers, of whom there are three firms in Petersburg. are auxiliary to the wholesale grocery trade, and their influence on the market is most beneficial.

R. T. ARRINGTON. S. P. ARRINGTON.

John Arrington & Sons

GROCERS AND

COMMISSION MERCHANTS,

GENERAL AGENTS FOR

Pacific Guano,
McComb Arrow Tie Company,
and Bridgewater Flour,

NOS. 31 AND 33 SYCAMORE STREET,

Petersburg, Virginia.

HANDLE ALL KINDS OF PRODUCE, COTTON, TOBACCO, PEANUTS, &C.

Bright Tobacco a Specialty.

R. T. ARRINGTON,
R. T. ARRINGTON, Jr.,

S. P. ARRINGTON.
F. W. SCOTT.

ARRINGTONS & SCOTT,

General Com'n Merchants,

Shockoe Slip,

RICHMOND, VIRGINIA.

E. B. BAIN,

COMMISSION MERCHANT,

44 SYCAMORE STREET,

PETERSBURG, VIRGINIA.

PROMPT PERSONAL ATTENTION GIVEN TO EHE SALE ON ALL PRODUCE CONSIGNED TO ME.

Leaf Tobacco, Cotton, Grain and Peanuts, Specialties.

DEALER IN

NO. 1 PERUVIAN GUANO,

AND AGENT FOR SEVERAL POPULAR

BRANDS OF FERTILIZERS.

J. GARLAND BLACKWELL & CO.,

GENERAL

COMMISSION MERCHANTS,

No. 55 North Sycamore St.,

PETERSBURG, VA.

CONSIGNMENTS OF COTTON, TOBACCO,

PEANUTS, CORN, POULTRY,

AND COUNTRY PRODUCE

WILL RECEIVE PERSONAL ATTENTION.

PROMPT RETURNS MADE AND LIBERAL ADVANCES ON PRODUCE IN HAND.

Correspondence Solicited.

ESTABLISHED 1830.

ROBT. A. MARTIN.   ROBT. R. HILL.   A. G. M. MARTIN.

MARTIN, HILL & CO.,

Grocers & Commission Merchants

NO. 11 SYCAMORE STREET,

Petersburg, Va.

FAITHFUL PERSONAL ATTENTION GIVEN TO THE SALE OF

Cotton, Tobacco, Wheat, Corn, Peanuts, &c.,

AND LIBERAL

CASH ADVANCES

MADE ON SAME.

ORDERS FOR GOODS SOLICITED FROM

PUNCTUAL, RESPONSIBLE PARTIES.

ALL ORDERS WILL BE FILLED AT FAIR PRICES.

MARTIN, HILL & CO., Petersburg, Va.

1853   1884

ALEXANDER WILSON,

DEALER IN

IMPORTED AND DOMESTIC FAMILY GROCERIES.

TEAS,

Wines, Liquors and Provisions,

No. 5 North Sycamore Street,

PETERSBURG, VA.

Sole Agent for Moerlein's Cincinnati Beer and "Appomattox" New Family Flour,

PATENT ROLLER PROCESS; (THE BEST IN THE MARKET.)

I have always on hand and am continually receiving per steamers from Baltimore, Philadelphia, Boston and New York, fresh supplies of all goods in my line.

All goods are warranted, and will be sold at the lowest market prices. The patronage of my friends in the city and surrounding country is respectfully solicited by

ALEX. WILSON.

✦ Grocer ✦ and ✦ Confectioner ✦

—:o:—

DEALER IN ALL KINDS OF

FIRST-CLASS FAMILY GROCERIES AND PROVISIONS.

ALL GOODS WARRANTED

TO BE AS GOOD AND AS CHEAP AS ANY IN THE MARKET.

A LARGE STOCK OF CANNED GOODS AND DRIED FRUITS.

NO. 202 HIGH STREET,

PETERSBURG, VA.

J. H. CABANISS.   CHAS. LUNSFORD.

CABANISS & LUNSFORD,

COMMISSION MERCHANTS,

21 OLD STREET, NEAR SYCAMORE,

PETERSBURG, VA.

Seed and Produce,   Butter and Cheese,
Flour and Feed,   Grain and Hay.

GIVE FAITHFUL ATTENTION TO

CONSIGNMENTS AND MAKE PROMPT RETURNS.

CORRESPONDENCE SOLICITED.

☞ Refer to the Bank of Petersburg.

J. HAMPDEN SLATER,

GENERAL MERCHANDISE BROKER,

GRAIN, FLOUR AND PROVISIONS, SPECIALTIES.

No. 3 Tabb Street, Petersburg, Virginia.

REFERENCES: Hinton & Dunn, Petersburg Savings and Insurance Company, and general jobbing trade.

CHARLES E. SMITH.   T. M. PERKINS.

SMITH & PERKINS,
MERCHANDISE BROKERS,

Corner Sycamore and Tabb Streets, Petersburg, Va.

In direct telegraphic communication with the New York and Chicago Markets. Offer the best service in the execution of orders in Options. ☞Flour, Grain, Provisions and General Merchandise.

JAMES DUNLOP, JR.   W. W. TOWNES.

DUNLOP & TOWNES,
GENERAL MERCHANDISE BROKERS,
43 Sycamore Street, Petersburg, Virginia.

☞BEST REFERENCES GIVEN.☜

BANKS.

———:o:———

Petersburg is under no necessity for any exceptional banking accommodations, for the reason that she is not, like Norfolk, for instance, a great seaport requiring enormous advances of cash for the purchase of whole crops of cotton, and for other kindred purposes. On the contrary, our large shippers, who are also manufacturers, draw direct on their consignees in London and other foreign points, and are the channels through which large sums of money are constantly introduced, instead of acting as drains through which the bank vaults are periodically depleted. ·Our commission merchants also rely, to a great extent, upon their own capital, for carrying on their business, and the banks, therefore, are not liable to be called upon for any extraordinary discounts, but serve rather as depositories and collecting agencies, than as mere money lenders. It thus happens that the three sound banking institutions which flourish here, although they are all kept very busy the year round, are quite able to transact all the business that seeks them, and to meet all possible demands upon their ample resources. Two of these banks are joint-stock companies and are owned and directed by our most substantial merchants, manufacturers and capitalists.

THE PETERSBURG
SAVINGS & INSURANCE COM'Y,
PETERSBURG, VIRGINIA.

Incorporated in 1860.

Capital, $200,000.
Surplus and Reserve, $94,630.

OFFICERS:

FRED. R. SCOTT, President,   D. B. DUGGER, Cashier.
ALEX. DONNAN, Vice-Prest.,   E. W. BUTCHER, Secretary.
WM. H. SCOTT, Assistant Secretary.

DIRECTORS:

STATEMENT, DECEMBER 31ST, 1883:

Cash on Hand	$ 79,702 55	Capital	$ 200,000 00
Due by Banks and Bankers	46,292 11	Certificates of Deposit	187,144 54
Loans and Discounts	693,179 84	Individual Deposits	190,870 17
Stocks and Bonds	146,040 00	Due Banks and Bankers	15,886 61
Real Estate	25,787 49	Dividend January, 1884	8,005 00
Premiums Due	10,054 50	Due Agents	43 67
Due for Rent	457 50	Insurance Losses Unpaid	5,555 08
		Reinsurance Reserve	31,026 85
		Interest Reserve	18,207 67
		Net Surplus	42,345 40
	$1,001,414 08		$1,001,414 08

THE BANK OF PETERSBURG,

PETERSBURG, VA.

R. H. JONES, JR., President.   JOSEPH CARR, Vice-President.
SAMUEL STEVENS, Cashier.

——:0:——

CHARTERED UNDER STATE LAW IN 1872.

——:0:——

CAPITAL, $64,800.

——:0:——

Transacts a General Banking Business and Solicits Correspondence.

——:0:——

Particular attention paid to Collections and Remittances made promptly.
No extra charge made for Collections when drawn with Exchange.
No charge for collections on Richmond, Lynchburg, Norfolk or Suffolk.
Exchange issued on All Principal Cities in Europe.

——:0:——

DIRECTORS :

R. H. JONES, JR.	JOSEPH CARR,	AUGUSTUS WRIGHT,
T. S. BECKWITH, JR.	ALEXANDER WILSON,	T. F. RIVES,
	WM. M. FIELD.	

FERTILIZERS.

——:0:——

During the last few years the demand for fertilizers has been far in excess of the supply of natural guano and manure, and has led to its manufacture on a very large scale. In the newly and sparsely settled Territories of the West, where the land has been under cultivation for a comparatively short period, the need of an artificial stimulus to the soil has as yet been little felt, but in the East it has become indispensable. The ground has been tilled by succeeding generations until its nourishing power is exhausted and requires periodical and systematic renewing to render it once more fertile and productive. Especially is this the case in the Eastern portion of Virginia, the Carolinas and other States where the trucking business is extensively carried on and where tobacco, cotton, peanuts and grain are raised as staples. The richest soil can only supply a certain limited amount of nutrition to the vegetation it sustains, and when that nutrition has been exhausted by over-cropping it must be restored, either by the slow process of natural recuperation or else by such artificial means as science may suggest and experience approve. The latter alternative obviously commends itself to the practical planter and farmer, and the result is that artificial fertilizers are now in almost universal use among agriculturalists, and fertilizer factories are to be found in Petersburg as well as in all other Eastern and Southeastern industrial centres. Several of our commission merchants are local agents for the brands manufactured in Richmond, Norfolk, Baltimore and elsewhere, which are best adapted to the requirements of our staple crops and the character of our soil, and the sale of this one article in Petersburg amounts annually to about $150,000.

Davie & Whittle,

MANUFACTURERS,

PETERSBURG,   VIRGINIA.

The manufacture of Cotton in and around the City of Petersburg is second in importance only to that of tobacco, and has attracted much attention, for many years past, at home and abroad. There are now in operation in and near the City, six mills and factories, having in the aggregate about thirty thousand spindles and one thousand looms, and employing nearly one thousand hands. Their products, consisting of Sheetings, Shirtings, Drills, Duck, Osnaburgs, and other varieties of Domestics, are known in all the leading markets of this country, and are sought for to some extent, by exporters in South America and the West Indies, where they are regarded with much favor and command the highest prices paid for similar cotton goods. Among the stockholders and directors, of these mills and factories, are several of the wealthiest capitalists and merchants of the City, and there is good reason for feeling encouraged with regard to the future of this important industry, for the re-opening of the Upper Appomattox Canal and the extensive improvements recently completed upon their river property will render available a large supply of magnificent water-power, hitherto wasted, which will, in all probability, attract capital and enterprise to the City and its neighborhood, for the purpose of engaging in manufacturing pursuits. Petersburg lies within the boundaries of the great cotton-producing region of the South, and enjoys direct access to its very centre, as also to the inexhaustible coal-fields of Western Virginia, which insures to her all the steam-power she could require upon very favorable terms, in addition to the excellent water-power referred to above. There is no valid reason, therefore, why this City, possessing, as has been shown, unsurpassed advantages, and having at hand the raw material as well as the wherewithal to convert it easily and economically into merchantable fabrics, should not enter upon a spirited and successful competition with her less favored but more enterprising rivals at the North, and become as great a Cotton-manufacturing centre as any in New England.

Swift Creek Cotton Manufacturing Company,

R. T. ARRINGTON, PRESIDENT.

PLUMMER & MORGAN, AGENTS.

MANUFACTURE BROWN DOMESTICS IN A VARIETY OF STYLES.

MILL AT SWIFT CREEK, CHESTERFIELD COUNTY.

Office: 44 Sycamore St., Petersburg, Va.

Petersburg Cotton Mills,

CANAL STREET, Near Head of Old Street.   J. M. KITCHEN, Superintendent, and
BOLLINGBROOK STREET, Blandford.   G. R. WILLIAMS, Superintendent,

F. E. DAVIS, President.   BARTLETT ROPER, Secretary and Treasurer.

170 LOOMS.   **6,000 SPINDLES**

CAPACITY 7,000 YARDS OF CLOTH A DAY.

Manufacture Several Varieties of BROWN DOMESTICS.

Ettrick Manufacturing Company.

—:0:—

D. D. Tennant, President.   R. R. Hill, Vice-President.

—:0:—

DIRECTORS :

D. B. Tennant,   R. R. Hill,
Alexander Donnan,   Dr. D. Steel,

George H. Byrd.

—:0:—

David Callender, Agent.   W. H. Wheary, Superintendent.
C. L. Barksdale, Secretary.

—:0:—

7,500 Spindles.   **250 Looms.**

Manufacturers of Sheeting, Drills, Duck and Osnaburgs.

Matoaca Manufacturing Company.

—:0:—

Alex. Donnan, President.   John McGill, Vice-President.

—:0:—

DIRECTORS :

Alexander Donnan,   John McGill,
James E. Routh,   D. B. Tennant,

George H. Byrd.

—:0:—

David Callender, Agent.   W. H. Wheary, Superintendent.
C. L. Barksdale, Secretary.

—:0:—

9,000 Spindles.   **250 Looms.**

Manufacturers of Sheetings, Shirtings and Drills.

Battersea Manufacturing Company.

—:0:—

Dr. D. Steel, President.   J. Wesley Friend, Vice-President.

—:0:—

DIRECTORS :

Dr. D. Steel,   J. Wesley Friend,
D. B. Tennant,   Alexander Donnan,

George H. Byrd.

—:0:—

David Callender, Agent.   W. G. Radcliffe, Superintendent.
C. L. Barksdale, Secretary.

—:0:—

3,600 Spindles.   **100 Looms.**

Manufacturers of Drills, Shirtings, Duck and Osnaburgs.

Old Dominion Cotton Mills, Manchester, Virginia,

S. P. ARRINGTON, President.
EDWARD GRAHAM, Agent and Treasurer.

9,000 SPINDLES.   **250 LOOMS.**

Manufacture all kinds of BROWN DOMESTICS. Capacity Ten Bales Cotton per day.

SUMAC.

——:0:——

This section of country abounds in Sumac of a very fine quality, which is destined to become an important factor in the industrial and commercial life of Petersburg. The most valuable leaf comes from Sicily, and with this the Virginia product compares very favorably in the matter of strength. The principal fault found with our domestic Sumac is that it is gathered carelessly. There is too much stem picked with the leaves, which are also frequently brought to market with a liberal mixture of sand. If dealers in the country would take more care in this respect, the price would soon advance and the domestic article would compete on something like even terms with its Sicilian rival.

The directions for gathering Sumac properly are simple enough, and might easily be complied with. Pick only the leaf and leaf stem. Be careful that no sand becomes mixed with it. Cure in the shade, and turn frequently until dry. When dry it is ready for the market.

The millers of Petersburg are always ready to furnish sacks, free of cost, and to pay the highest price for prime leaf Sumac.

W. N. JONES.   **B. B. VAUGHAN.**   **A. M. HILL.**

W. N. Jones & Co.

MANUFACTURERS OF

OAK BARKS AND SUMAC.

APPOMATTOX MILL, Petersburg, Virginia.

HIGHEST CASH PRICES PAID FOR LEAF SUMAC AND STICK-BARK. Correspondence solicited

Rialto Mills, Petersburg, Virginia.

JAMES M. WILLIAMS, MERCHANT MILLER,

KEEPS AT ALL TIMES A SUPPLY OF THE BEST CORN MEAL. PROPRIETOR OF THE

GALIEO SUMAC MILLS.

ORDERS RESPECTFULLY SOLICITED.

THE VIRGINIA HOG CHOLERA CURE,

INDISPENSABLE TO FARMERS AND ALL WHO RAISE HOGS..
THE MOST VIOLENT AND VIRULENT CASES OF "HOG
CHOLERA" OR "SWINE PLAGUE" YIELD
READILY TO ITS CURATIVE
POWER.

The remedy which we now offer, and which is known as "THE VIRGINIA HOG CHOLERA CURE," has proved itself an absolute safeguard against not only Cholera, but also against all other forms of "Swine Plague," and is a General Condition Powder of the most valuable and positive character. Wherever used it has completely eradicated the disease and caused the rapid growth and fattening of hogs. For poultry it has no superior, curing Chicken Cholera, keeping out Vermin, and securing a generally Healthful Condition.

We are confident that its use will result in unlimited benefit to the farmer, insuring him against loss and rendering it as easy to raise hogs as if the Cholera were a thing unknown. After the disease has appeared it can be easily and quickly checked, it matters not at what stage it may be taken, unless, indeed, the hog or hogs are actually in the throes of death. The ingredients contained in "THE VIRGINIA HOG CHOLERA CURE" are expensive, some being procured from widely separated countries, but in their combination they are but the gathered forces provided by Nature for the cure of these evils. For two years we refused to offer it for sale, and in all instances where applicants proffered the money we declined, preferring that our preparation should be thoroughly and practically tested by hog raisers before putting it upon the market.

It is now made up, nicely labeled with directions for using it, in one-pound and one-half-pound packages, and these packages are put up in substantial wooden cases, made to contain from twelve to twenty-four pounds, convenient for shipping.

Where the party ordering is not known to us, the money must invariably accompany the order. If our farmers will club together and always keep a few packages of VIRGINIA HOG CHOLERA CURE convenient for use, or use it every few days as a preventive, they will keep out all kinds of disease, and their hogs will fatten more rapidly and keep in fine condition. To wait until the disease has obtained a foothold, before ordering, is to invite the Plague and consequent loss. The value of ONE hog invested in the VIRGINIA HOG CHOLERA CURE will prevent the loss of several hundred hogs and positively prevent the Plague. Our patrons frequently request that packages be sent them by mail. The preparation is a fine powder, and the postal laws prohibit the transmission in the mails of all merchandise that will be likely to damage the contents of the pouches in the event of accident, hence we make all shipments by freight or express, and our customers will please note the fact that the charges upon one pound are about the same as upon a case containing twelve pounds. If your Druggists or General Stores do not keep it, address letters to us, and they will receive prompt attention.

We want reliable agents in every County in the Southern and Western States, and we will furnish terms upon request.

BUTLER, WINSTON & Co., Manufacturers,

P. O. Box 648,   Norfolk, Va..

E. B. BAIN, Agent for Petersburg Va.

HOTELS AND RESTAURANTS.

———:o:———

Owing, perhaps, to the proximity of "big Richmond," as well as to the frequency of trains running to and from Petersburg in every direction, there does not appear to be the same necessity for many large hotels here as there would be if the City were less centrally situated or less favored in the matter of Railroad schedules. As it is, we have three excellent hotels and numerous restaurants, and visitors from far and near will find ample accommodation, combined with every comfort, and a hospitable welcome. Our markets overflow with fish, game, poultry, fruits, vegetables and other luxuries for the table, and the bills of fare at our hotels and restaurants would not disgrace those of much larger cities. The hotels are conveniently situated as regards the Railroad depots, banks, principal stores and public buildings, and are all within a stone's throw of the street railway. Moreover, they are all in the hands of experienced and careful proprietors, and are therefore well managed, and exempt from many of the discomforts which usually render hotel life anything but attractive.

HOTEL GARY,

Tabb Street, Next Door to Postoffice,

PETERSBURG, VA.

———:o:———

Centrally Located.   Appointments First-Class.

TO MEET THE WANTS OF

Tourists and Commercial Travellers.

BOLLINGBROOK HOTEL,

M. A. PETTIT, - - - Proprietor.

PETERSBURG, VA.

BOARD, - - - $2.00 AND $2.50.

Fine Bar and Billiard Hall,

HOT AND COLD BATHS.

New Furniture.   Newly Papered.

☞It is the purpose of the Proprietor to have EVERYTHING FIRST-CLASS.

The Exchange and Ballard Hotels,

Corner Fourteenth and Franklin Streets,

These Well-Known Leading Hotels

Have Been Thoroughly Renovated,

AND CAN NOW OFFER UNSURPASSED ACCOMMODATIONS
FOR SIX HUNDRED GUESTS.

The Halls and Dining Rooms are HEATED BY STEAM, which renders the House particularly attractive for Invalids and the Travelling Public generally.

The Two Houses are connected by a COVERED SUSPENSION BRIDGE, which makes them practically ONE HOTEL.

Particular attention given Letters or Telegrams requesting that rooms be reserved. PRIVATE PARLORS WITH SPECIAL SUITES OF ROOMS, with or without Baths, for Travelling Parties.

Our COMFORTABLE COACHES will be found at all arriving Trains.

J. L. CARRINGTON, Proprietor.

THE NEW PURCELL HOUSE,

NORFOLK, VIRGINIA.

PHIL. F. BROWN & BRO.,

(OF BLUE RIDGE SPRINGS, VIRGINIA,)

PROPRIETORS.

RECENTLY RENOVATED AND GREATLY IMPROVED.

DINING-ROOM, PARLORS, HALLS, &C., HEATED BY STEAM.

Electric Bells in All the Rooms.

HYDRAULIC PASSENGER ELEVATOR RUNS AT ALL HOURS.

THE PURCELL

Is Conveniently Located in the Very Centre of Business.

Street Cars pass immediately by the Hotel. connecting with Steam Cars to Ocean View and Virginia Beach, or Steamboat for the famous Hygeia Hotel at Old Point Comfort.

IT WILL BE THE EARNEST EFFORT OF THE PROPRIETORS

TO PLEASE ALL.

WHO GIVE THEM A CALL.

TERMS: $3 AND $2.50 PER DAY.

✦QUINCEY'S ✦ EUROPEAN ✦ HOUSE,✦

CHRIS. QUINCEY, Proprietor.

DEALER IN

Wines, Liquors, Cigars and Tobaccos.
Fine Imported Goods in Stock.

FIRST-CLASS RESTAURANT.

Ladies' and Gentlemen's Dining and Luncheon Rooms.
Bar, Lunch Counter and Pool Room.

128 Sycamore Street, Petersburg, Va.

JULIUS LIEBERT,

**Wine and Spirit Merchant, Dealer in Cigars, Tobacco,
Cigarettes, Etc.**

Manufacturer of SODA, GINGER ALE and SARSAPARILLA, and Bottler
of BERGNER & ENGLE'S LAGER BEER.

Is About to Remove from His Present

SALOON, BILLIARD HALL AND RESTAURANT,

No. 10 Lombard Street, to his Handsome and Extensive New Premises,

NO. 18 BOLLINGBROOK STREET,

Petersburg, Va.

EICHBERG'S SALOON AND RESTAURANT,

No. 4 Bank Street, Petersburg, Virginia,

THE CHOICEST BRANDS OF WINES, LIQUORS, TOCACCO AND
CIGARS always on hand.

The Table is furnished with all the Delicacies in Season—FISH, GAME,
OYSTERS, &c.

Special Terms made with Regular Boarders by the Day, Week or Month

Walthall's European House.

Rooms Furnished with New Furniture.

Table Supplied Wrth the Best the Market Affords.

FINEST

Wines, Ales, Liquors, &c.,

208 & 210 SYCAMORE STREET,

PETERSBURG, VIRGINIA.

"I Board There."   "I Don't."

IRON WORKS, AGRICULTURAL IMPLEMENTS AND HARDWARE.

:o:——

Among the most obvious essentials to an important manufacturing town, which is also the centre of an extensive and fertile agricultural district, such establishments as foundries and manufactories of farming implements and machinery stand at the head of the list, for it would be impossible to operate tobacco works, grist or saw mills, engines or any other kind of mechanical contrivance, unless the means of supplying, renewing and repairing were always at hand. In this respect Petersburg is very well off, having several first-class establishments of this kind, where Tobacco and and Cotton Presses, Locomotive and Stationary Engines, Boilers, Saw, Grist and Sumac Mills, Elevators, Steamboat Work, Dredges, Castings, Forgings and all other varieties of Steam and Hydraulic Machinery are manufactured and repaired at short notice, and with most skillful workmanship. The numerous Saw Mills and other industries carried on through the surrounding rural districts, help to keep our foundries busy all the year round, while the manufacture and repair of agricultural machinery and implements also furnish them with a large amount of work. In addition to our local foundries, others at distant points are represented here by agencies, and the farmer who makes Petersburg his market can find at one or other of our iron works or stores any variety of plow, wagon, reaper, mower, or other implement that he may fancy or require. Petersburg's hardware stores ar unequalled in the South as regards the size and variety of the stocks they carry, which include every conceivable article in their line, from a stove to a carpet tack, besides gunsmiths' wares, fishing tackle, musical instruments, clocks, ammunition, etc.

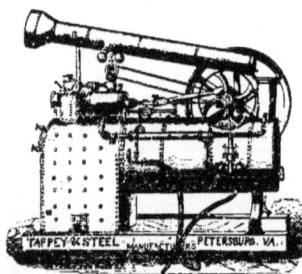

THE

✦Appomattox ✦ Iron ✦ Works ✦

33 AND 35 OLD STREET,

PETERSBURG, VIRGINIA,

MANUFACTURERS OF

Agricultural Implements.

Mill Gearing, Shafting, Pullies,

And Machinery of All Descriptions.

Tobacco Fixtures,

HYDRAULIC PRESSES, &C.

◁MACHINE WORK TO ORDER.▷

Farming Implements in Stock.

THE LIGHT RUNNING
DOMESTIC
❖⁘SEWING⁘MACHINE,⁘❖

SCHOOLS AND COLLEGES.

——:o:——

Any attempt to advance original ideas upon the momentous question of Education which is universally admitted to be one of paramount importance in every civilized and progressive community, would but weary the reader, and at the same time prove a lamentable failure; for the subject has been worn almost threadbare by the preachers and lecturers, commentators and statesmen, of all generations; and is still, as it is probably destined to remain, an unsolved problem. But it is gratifying to know that our own people enjoy exceptional advantages in their efforts to secure this "pearl without price," and that the system in force here is as perfect and efficacious as any that has yet been discovered. Besides the public Primary and High Schools, Petersburg numbers among its scholastic institutions several private Seminaries of the very highest order, for boys and girls; and many of Virginia's most distinguished scholars and statesmen received their education at a Petersburg school.   This State has always been famous for the number and high rank of her Schools and Colleges, and Petersburg has always done more than her just share towards establishing this enviable reputation. There is hardly a State or Territory in the Union which is not represented by a bright young son or daughter among the students at one or other of our Seminaries.   This City is eminently adapted to institutions of this kind, for, in addition to the excellence of the education they afford, the climate is extremely healthy the water pure and plentiful, and society as refined and genial as any in the land.   Numbers of our young men go up every year to some of the great Universities, and there graduate with high honors, thus giving the best possible proof of the thoroughness with which they have been trained while attending Petersburg Schools. By far the most popular University among the people of this State and section is that far-famed seat of learning, the University of Virginia; while the medical profession is indebted for many of its ablest recruits to the Medical College of Virginia, at Richmond.

FOUNDED 1865.

THE

UNIVERSITY SCHOOL,

PETERSBURG, VA.

W. Gordon McCabe, (U. of Va.,) Head Master,

Instructor in Ancient Languages, French, German and Early English.

ASSISTANT MASTERS:

JAMES ROY MICOU, (U. of Va.,) *Instructor in Mathematics.*
JOHN DUNN, M. A., (U. of Va.,) *Instructor in Mathematics and German.*
W. G. MANLY, (U. of Va.,) *Asst. Instructor in Ancient Lang. and English.*
J. CALVIN LESTER, *Asst. Instructor in Mathematics and English.*

Continuous Session from October 1st to June 30th.

THE UNIVERSITY SCHOOL is mainly preparatory to the UNIVER-SITY OF VIRGINIA, the Professors of which institution endorse it most heartily. (See Catalogue.) During the past nineteen years it has also prepared and sent up to Princeton, West Point, Annapolis, Boston Institute of Technology, Stevens' Scientific Institute, (Hoboken,) Columbia School of Mines, and other institutions of high grade, a great number of pupils whose uniform success is the best guarantee of the thoroughness of the instruction in the school.

For Board, Tuition. Washing, Fuel and Lights, Per Session of Nine Months,
(Payable Half-Yearly,).. $34.00

The Head Master takes into his own Family a limited number of boarders. As these places are usually taken promptly, early application is advisable.

☞ *No boarding pupils are received for less time than the whole session.*

The health of Petersburg is excellent.
For Catalogues and detailed information address

W. GORDON McCABE, Head Master.

ST. PAUL'S FEMALE SCHOOL,
PETERSBURG, VA.

CORPS OF TEACHERS:

J. G. GRISWOLD,
FERDINAND SCHWENCK,
MISS LAURA M. RUSSELL,
MISS JESSIE DONNAN,
MISS V. L. MAJOR,
MISS LOSSIE HILL,
MISS MITTIE PATTERSON,

The Session Begins the Middle of September.

FOR PARTICULARS ADDRESS

J. G. Griswold, A. M., Principal.

UNIVERSITY OF VIRGINIA.

—:o:—

The Session begins on the FIRST OF OCTOBER, in each year, and continues until the Wednesday before the 4th day of July ensuing.

The institution is organized in Separate Schools, on the Eclectic System, embracing FULL COURSES OF INSTRUCTION in Literature and Science and in the Professions of Law, Medicine, Engineering and Agriculture.

THE EXPENSES

of the student, (except such as enter the practical laboratories,) exclusive of the cost of text books, clothing and pocket money, are from $356 to $391, according to schools selected ; or, for those who economize by messing, these expenses are from $266 to $300. No charge for tuition to candidates for the ministry unable to meet the expense.

Apply for Catalogues to WM. A. WINSTON, Secretary. P. O. University of Virginia, Albemarle County, Va.

JAMES F. HARRISON, M. D., Chairman of the Faculty.

PLANTERS' HYPOTHECATION WAREHOUSE,

PETERSBURG, VA.

GENERAL STORAGE

FOR TOBACCO, COTTON, PEANUTS AND MERCHANDISE GEN-
ERALLY.

DRAYS, LUMBER WAGONS AND CARTS ALWAYS ON HAND.

WOOD, HAY, PROVENDER AND MILL FEED FOR SALE

L. W. DUGGER, Lessee.

DRUGS, PAINTS AND OILS.

——:o:——

The business done in these important commodities, in Petersburg, is
much more considerable than would be supposed by the uninitiated, and is
conducted by four wholesale and about a dozen retail houses, employing together a cash capital of about $100,000. The stocks kept by these establish-
ments are large and varied, and several of our druggists have earned a
wide and honorable reputation through the excellence of the goods they
supply, as well as through the agency of certain "specialties" which they
put up. Besides Drugs, Paints and Oils, all our wholesale and some of our
retail houses carry full lines of Window Glass, Perfumery, Spices, Seeds,
Patent Medicines, Fancy and Toilet articles, and numerous other goods
not strictly akin to pharmacy, to-wit: Tobacco, Cigars, etc. Our principal
wholesale drug trade is carried on with central Virginia, the two Carolinas
and Georgia, while all the Southern States have been made more or less
familiar with Petersburg's enterprise in this line.

JOSEPH CARR,

WHOLESALE AND RETAIL DEALER IN

DRUGS & PATENT MEDICINES

Paints, Oils, Glass, Dyes, Varnishes, Brushes, Perfumery, &c., &c

CORNER SYCAMORE AND WASHINGTON STS.,

PETERSBURG, VA.

BECKWITH'S
ANTI-DYSPEPTIC PILLS.

The best and most reliable Anti-Dyspeptic Medicine ever offered to the Public.

When such distinguished men as the late President MARTIN VAN BUREN, GEORGE E. BADGER, late Secretary of the Navy; Gov. EDWARD STANLY, of California; Gov. IREDELL, of North Carolina; Senators TALMAGE, of New York; PRESTON, of South Carolina; HENDERSON, of Mississippi; Judge H. POTTER, of U. S. Court; Judge Thomas GHOLSON, of Virginia; Hon. BEVERLY TUCKER, of Virginia; Gen. McCOMB, of Georgia; W. H. APPLETON, of New York; Rev. Dr. F. L. HAWKS, of New York; Doctors MINGE and CORBIN BRAXTON of Virginia; Drs. T. L. JOHNSON, of Mississippi; YOUNG, of Tennessee; BOND, MANNING and JONES, of North Carolina; and a host of other such men give strong certificates of the value of a medicine, *IT MUST HAVE INTRINSIC WORTH.* All this is true of BECKWITH'S ANTI-DYSPEPTIC PILLS, and to-day they are as good as when these certificates were written.

READ THE FOLLOWING CERTIFICATES.

HON. MARTIN VAN BUREN,
Late President U. S.

"Beckwith's Anti-Dyspeptic Pills for eight years have saved me from the necessity of employing a physician in a single case. I cannot trust myself without them."

HON. GEORGE E. BADGER,
Late Secretary of Navy.

"I believe them myself to be the best Anti-Dyspeptic medicine ever offered to the public."

HON. BEVERLY TUCKER,
Late Professor William and Mary College.

"I suffered for fourteen years from diseased liver, disordered digestion and a constitution in ruins. From the use of Beckwith's Anti-Dyspeptic Pills, I can now eat what I please, do what I please, sleep soundly and enjoy life as much as any man."

JUDGE THOMAS S. GHOLSON,
of Virginia.

"I take no other medicine. I confidenty recommend them to the public."

MADISON, IND., March 10th, 1842.

"My attention was drawn to these pills many years ago by the Hon. Geo. E. Badger, of North Carolina, while suffering under some unpleasant derangement of the stomach. I experienced then, and have since, great relief from their use. I have no hesitancy in recommending them as an agreeable remedy for the diseases enumerated in your circular."
J. H. WOOLFORD.

CEDAR FALLS, Iowa, March 22, 1841.
"I am using your Pills with great benefit. I think they are the best anti-dyspeptic pills I ever used. I travel a good deal, and carry them with me."
W. S. GARRISON.

A host of other certificates of equal strength are in the hands of the proprietor. For more than seventy years this medicine has maintained its high reputation. Now what is Dyspepsia? It is one or more of the following: Heartburn, Sick Stomach, Headache, Tasting your food after eating, Spitting up your Food, Constipation, Torpid Liver, Indigestion, Colic, Nervous Irritability, Dizziness, Disturbed Sleep, with distressing dreams and untold sufferings. BECKWITH'S ANTI-DYSPEPTIC PILLS have cured thousands of such sufferers, and will do it again. No medicine was ever sustained by such undoubted testimony. Try them. E. R. Beckwith, pharmacist, now manufactures these invaluable Pills from the Original Recipe of his grandfather, Dr. John Beckwith.

FORTY PILLS IN A BOX--PRICE TWENTY-FIVE CENTS.

E. R. BECKWITH, Pharmacist,

COR. MARKET AND HALIFAX STS., PETERSBURG, VA.

SOLD BY DRUGGISTS GENERALLY.

WM. F. SPOTSWOOD,
APOTHECARY,
CORNER BOLLINGBROOK & SYCAMORE STS.,
PETERSBURG, VA.

WM. H. CAMP,
Wholesale Druggist,
225 Sycamore Street,
PETERSBURG, VA.

GEO. C. STARKE, M. D.
Druggist,
37 NORTH SYCAMORE ST.,
PETERSBURG, VA.

R. W. THOMPSON,
DEALER IN PURE AND RELIABLE DRUGS AND MEDICINES,
Fancy and Toilet Articles, Paints, Oils, Glass and Putty, Cigars and To-
bacco and everything usually kept in a First-Class Drug Store.
Use CARBOLATED DENTALINE for the Teeth.

Cor. Scyamore and Tabb streets, Petersburg, Va.

VALENTINE'S MEAT JUICE WORKS,

RICHMOND, VA.

There is, perhaps, no name which has been more directly instrumental in spreading the fame of our State's Capital, as a great manufacturing city, than that of Mann S. Valentine, whose Meat Juice is not only an important article of commerce, but has also been long accounted one of the richest blessings known to invalids of all the nations upon earth. This invaluable extract has earned and secured the hearty endorsement of the Medical Faculty in all lands, and has been awarded medals and diplomas at the "Centennial Exposition (Philadelphia) in 1876, the "Exposition Universal" (Paris) in 1878, the "Domestic and Scientific Exhibition" (Brighton, England), in 1881, and the "Medical and Scientific Exhibition (London) in 1881.

But more significant than even these high testimonials of genuine worth, is the substantial commercial success with which Mr. Valentine's enterprise and perseverance have been attended. As the virtues of this wonderful essence became gradually known and appreciated, orders began to pour in from all sides with ever-increasing volume, and before long it was found impossible to supply the demand without additional accommodation. From time to time extensions were made, until every available inch of the old premises was utilized ; but the relief was only temporary, and at last it became necessary to erect new works, suitable for the requirements of this large and growing trade. A convenient site was accordingly purchased and the handsome four-story-and-basement structure on the corner of Cary and Sixth Streets, completed and occupied during the summer of 1884, testifies alike to the enterprise, good taste and practical judgment of Mr. Valentine and his associates.

The building is of course constructed with direct reference to the various stages through which this famous extract must pass before it assumes its commercial form as "Valentine's Meat Juice," and no expense has been spared in making the works complete in every department. The machinery and all the intricate combinations of pipes, pumps, syphons, stop-cocks etc., which the proper treatment of the essence requires, were mainly designed by Mr. Valentine himself, who has offered a standing prize for any improvement in the appliances of the works, by any of his operatives, which will save labor or make perfection more perfect. The building fronts seventy-eight feet on Cary Street by a depth of one hundred feet on Sixth Street, and is built of brick, with iron front and granite basement. It is very handsomely fitted up inside, and finished in oiled and highly-polished heart-pine and walnut.

It is impossible, within the limits of this article, to describe the various departments and their uses, for their name is Legion. Suffice it to say that from the time the beef is received in the "treatment room" until the

Meat Juice is bottled for shipment, it must pass the most delicate and severe tests in each stage of its manufacture, and must finally conform to that standard of purity, density and clearness which has been established by Mr. Valentine, as the result of careful study and practical experience extending over many years.

Valentine's Meat Juice is extracted from the flesh of only the healthiest and finest beef cattle, from fifteen to twenty thousand pounds of which is slaughtered daily for the purposes of this one specialty.

At the Centennial Exposition, in 1876, Valentine's Meat Juice received the highest award for "Excellence of its method of preparation, whereby it more nearly represents fresh meat than any other extract of meat, its freedom from disagreeable taste, its fitness for immediate absorption and the perfection in which it retains its good qualities in warm climates." Since then it has attained world-wide popularity, simply and solely by virtue of its own intrinsic merit. It is easily portable, and is therefore of special benefit to the traveller by land or sea. It is absolutely unaffected by change of temperature or climate, having proved itself of equal value in the tropics, where its consumption is rapidly increasing, and in the Polar Seas, whither it was taken by the medical officers connected with the Greely Relief Expedition.

Mr. Valentine has associated with him in the several departments of his business, Mr. Ira W. Blunt, and his four sons, Messrs. G. G., M. S. Jr., B. B. and F. S. Valentine.

Having Thoroughly Equipped Our Mill with the Most Perfect Machinery for Manufacturing

BY THE ROLLER PROCESS,

We are enabled to offer the Trade the very best Flour that can be had.

OUR STANDARD BRANDS:

DUNLOP PATENT FAMILY,   PIONEER FAMILY,   McCANCE XXX,   OLIVE BRANCH,
MANCHESTER GEM,   JAMES RIVER FALLS FAMILY,   AURORA XX,   SHOCKOE,

ARE MADE OF SELECTED WHEAT, AND FOR PERFECT UNIFORMITY IN THEIR BAKING AND BREAD MAKING QUALITIES

CAN BE HIGHLY RECOMMENDED.

The DUNLOP PATENT FAMILY, of which we are making a SPECIALTY, cannot be surpassed, for FAMILY USE, by any brand upon the market, whether of Spring or Winter Wheat, and in all respects will please the most fastidious taste. The saving of time and trouble in handling an article certain to give entire satisfaction makes

THE BEST FLOUR THE CHEAPEST.

BRAN, BROWN STUFF AND SHIP STUFF ALSO FOR SALE.

DUNLOP & McCANCE,

RICHMOND, VIRGINIA.

☞ SAMPLES AND PRICES FURNISHED TO DEALERS ON APPLICATION.

INSURANCE.
—:o:—

To the nervous person in moderate circumstances, regardless of age, sex or occupation, there are few things capable of yielding such solid comfort as the possession of a sufficient Policy of Insurance—fire or life—with a first-class Company. Indeed, no prudent man will leave his property unprotected against the risk of fire, or his family unprovided for in the event of his death, when a trifling outlay in the form of premiums will absolutely insure him against pecuniary loss—possibly ruin—and his family, after he is gone, from poverty. When a man's property, whether it be his factory, warehouse, store or dwelling-house, is covered to its full value by reliable insurance against the accidental spark or the malice of the incendiary, the peal of the fire-alarm is robbed to his ear,'of half its customary terrors, for it awakens in him no dread of personal disaster; and when he knows that immediately upon his death those nearest and dearest ones who now depend upon him for support, will receive a sum of money sufficient to guard them at least against want, if not enough to supply them with their accustomed comforts, his last days are unclouded by those tortures of apprehension which would otherwise necessarily assail him. Nay, more; it is an established medical fact that a comparatively mild form of disease is not unfrequently aggravated until it becomes fatal, by just such anxiety as an insurance policy would allay or avert; and it follows, therefore, that the Life Insurance Companies are often actually instrumental in prolonging life, as well as in fulfilling the avowed beneficent objects of their incorporation.

As in business transactions generally, so in the matter of fire or life insurance, the wise man will have no dealings with other than sound and respectable companies, and there are so many of this class represented in Petersburg, each offering some special advantage or attraction, that the intending insurer is puzzled to make a selection, while he would be perfectly —perhaps equally—safe with all. Besides the Petersburg Savings and Insurance Company, whose stockholders and directors are among the most prominent and responsible of our manufacturers, merchants and professional men, nearly every first-class Insurance Company doing business in the United States is represented in Petersburg by its duly authorized and appointed agent, and their aggregate assets amount to scores of millions of dollars. There are also several Benevolent Societies established in the City, having a life-insurance element which has proved very attractive and led to the enrollment of numerous members.

Risks and possible evils of all kinds should be continually provided against, as a matter of business and as a matter of principle, and every uninsured person who estimates his property as worth protecting and his family as worth providing for, and who also duly appreciates the blessing of a mind unburdened of unnecessary care, will remedy the omission as speedily as possible by taking out policies, according to his means, on his life and worldly possessions.

The Petersburg Savings and Insurance Co.

INCORPORATED 1860.

FRED. R. SCOTT, President.   D. B. DUGGER, Cashier.
ALEX. DONNAN, Vice-President.   E. W. BUTCHER, Secretary.
WM. H. SCOTT, Assistant Secretary.
CAPITAL, - - - - - $200,000.

CARTER R. BISHOP,

Insurance Agent.

OFFICE: 62½ SYCAMORE STREET, PETERSBURG, VIRGINIA.

Cuthbert & Sons,

FIRE AND LIFE INSURANCE AGENTS.

37 Bank Street, Petersburg, Va.

BENJAMIN HARRISON,

INSURANCE AGENT,

110 Sycamore Street (Over Petersburg Savings and Insurance Company),
PETERSBURG, VIRGINIA,

Representing some of the Largest Companies in the United States.
☞ FIRE INSURANCE respectfully solicited.

JONES & STEVENS,

GENERAL INSURANCE AGENTS.

LIFE, FIRE, MARINE AND ACCIDENT.

106 Sycamore (Opposite Tabb) Street, - - - Petersburg, Va.

DR. J. E. MOYLER.   R. O. EGERTON.

J. EDWARD MOYLER & CO.,

General Insurance and Real Estate Agents,

FOR RENTING PROPERTY.

Office: Masonic Building, - - - - - Petersburg, Va.

B. B. PEGRAM,

INSURANCE AGENT,

ROOM 1 MECHANICS' BUILDING,

Corner Tabb and Sycamore Streets, Petersburg, Va.

DRY GOODS, NOTIONS, CARPETS, ETC.
———:o:———

What pen, especially it it be of the masculine persuasion, shall attempt to depict the wonders of that "Woman's Paradise," a first-class Dry-Goods Store, a mere catalogue of whose ordinary stock would fill many a close-writ page! Let not the reader be troubled, for the attempt will not be made here. Suffice it to say that Petersburg can show as handsome and as well-stocked establishments devoted to this particular class of merchandise as any city in Virginia, or elsewhere in the South. Our principal Dry Goods and Notions Stores are in the Iron-Front Building, an engraving of which is shown on page forty-nine. It comprises five lofty stories and basement. All the stores referred to carry heavy stocks of Dry Goods, Notions, and other kindred articles. The wholesale departments do a very satisfactory business, which is mostly confined to Virginia, the Carolinas and Georgia; but the area covered by this trade is gradually being extended. Most of our Dry Goods houses are also supplied with full lines of Carpets, of all descriptions and the products of all lands, as well as mats, rugs, druggets, and other similar wares. All their goods are guaranteed not to exceed Northern prices, and their assortments are as complete as are to be met with in any other city. The capital involved in the Dry Goods Trade, and those affiliated with it, is necessarily very large, and the sales for the year 1884 are estimated to have exceeded $400,000.

G. L. CROWDER & BRO.

Have greatly Improved and Enlarged their Premises, and now carry a Much Larger and Better Assorted Stock of

DRY GOODS, FANCY GOODS, NOTIONS,
CARPETS, MATTINGS, OIL CLOTHS,
WINDOW SHADES, LACE CURTAINS,
BOOTS, SHOES, HATS, CAPS, CLOTHING,
LADIES' AND CHILDREN'S CLOAKS,
UNDERWEAR, UMBRELLAS, PARASOLS, JEWELRY,
RIBBONS, COTTONS, EMBROIDERY SILKS, YARNS,

SCHOOL BOOKS, SLATES, STATIONERY,

GLASS WARE, LAMPS, CLOCKS, PICTURE FRAMES, &C.

☞We pay special attention to having the BEST BARGAINS that can be offered in BLACK CASHMERES and other BLACK GOODS and CRAPES.

Trunks at Factory Prices.   Suits Made to Order.

Come and see us and we will please you.

G. L. Crowder & Bro.,

238 Old Street Near the Head, - - - Petersburg, Virginia.

ESTABLISHED 1859.

A. ROSENSTOCK & CO.

FOREIGN AND DOMESTIC

DRY GOODS,   NOTIONS,

CARPETS.   TRUNKS.

FANCY GOODS,

Men's Furnishing Goods,

WHOLESALE AND RETAIL.

No. 1 Iron Front Building, - - - - - Sycamore Street,
PETERSBURG, VA.

WEARING APPAREL.

—:—:——

The above words are intended only to apply, in this instance, to Boots and Shoes, Hats and Caps, Clothiers' and Tailors' Goods, and Men's Furnishing Goods generally, and not to those unfathomable mysteries of feminine attire which are distracting even to think upon, and cannot possibly be either enumerated or described. These combined interests require considerable capital, and it is estimated that in Petersburg not less than $150,000 are invested in them. The Boot and Shoe business, in its wholesale department, is very far-reaching, and goods supplied by Petersburg houses are to be found in every portion of Central and Western Virginia, in the two Carolinas, Georgia, Alabama, Tennessee and other Southern States. One of our Boot and Shoe houses, that of Augustus Wright, has a flourishing branch establishment at Roanoke. Hats and Caps also form another link in the chain which binds us commercially to the people of adjoining States, and sales in this line are heavy, especially in Virginia and North Carolina, where the bulk of the business is done. The same may be truly said of Clothiers' and Tailors' Goods and Men's Furnishing Goods, the trade in which is extending gradually, and will doubtless some day overspread a much more extended territory. All these different branches of Petersburg's business are in the hands of sterling business men, who are intimately acquainted with the wants of their respective trades, and thoroughly understand them in their most minute details. Having sufficient working capital, they are enabled to take advantage of every depression in the market, and to buy up at low figures whatever may be suitable to their business. By these means they can often sell to the retail trade and individual consumers at better prices than the manufacturer would be willing to accept during his busy season.

———————

THOS. R. MOORE,

WHOLESALE AND RETAIL DEALER IN

AND STRAW GOODS.

HATS, CAPS, FURS,

Ladies' and Misses' Cloaks,

17 NORTH SYCAMORE ST.,

PETERSBURG, VA.

HARRISON & CO.

ON THE CORNER,

CLOTHIERS,

148 SYCAMORE (Cor. Lombard) ST.,

PETERSBURG, VIRGINIA,

OLD DOMINION SHIRT FACTORY

A. SIMON,

(Successor to Salamonsky & Co.,)

MERCHANT TAILOR,

16 N. Ninth Street, Richmond, Virginia.

Being compelled to reside in Richmond in order to personally superintend his large business in that city, will in future attend to the wants of his Petersburg friends by visiting them twice a month with a full line of samples.

W. E. BUTCHER.   J. M. QUICKE.

W. E. BUTCHER & CO.,

MERCHANT TAILORS,

No. 8 NORTH SYCAMORE STREET, Petersburg, Va.

NOAH WALKER & CO.,

Clothiers & Merchant Tailors,

ALEX. F. SHORT, J. GEO. WILKINSON, AGENTS.

143 SYCAMORE STREET, Petersburg, Virginia.

FURNITURE.

This trade has assumed much importance in Petersburg of late years, and now employs a cash capital of about $100,000. Ordinary household necessaries could always be obtained here as well as elsewhere, but the handsomer and more expensive articles and sets were generally sought in Richmond, or even still further away, until those now engaged in the business took advantage of the opportunity thus opened to enterprise. Our furniture warerooms now contain large and varied assortments of stock, and every taste and every pocket can be suited, at factory prices, whether the articles be required for parlor, drawing-room, dining-room, chamber, office or school. There are several firms engaged here in this business, and they can afford to sell their goods at reasonable figures, for the reason that they make their purchases at the manufactories and obtain the most favorable terms. Central Virginia and North Carolina find this a most advantageous market at which to make their purchases, and each year brings increased business to our dealers. Here, as in other places, there are those to be met with who refuse to acknowledge genuine excellence unless they import it direct from some distant market, but experience has taught the great majority of consumers that it is more economical, as well as infinitely more satisfactory, to deal with merchants whom they know personally and meet every day, reliable and responsible business men, who are always accessible when, through some accident or unsuspected flaw, a guarantee may have to be made good.

ESTABLISHED 1858.

JAMES T. MORRISS,

UNDERTAKER,

NO. 2 SOUTH SYCAMORE STREET,

PETERSBURG, VA.

———:o:———

A COMPLETE ASSORTMENT OF

Metallic and Wooden Coffins and Caskets,

PLAIN, CLOTH-COVERED AND ORNAMENTAL.

Also Burial Robes in Several Varieties.

☞All orders by letter or telegraph will receive PROMPT ATTENTION.
I have had twenty-seven years' experience in the Undertaking business,
and guarantee satisfaction in all respects.

JAMES T. MORRISS.

BOOKS, STATIONERY, PIANOS, ETC.

————:o:————

The quality and quantity of reading matter in circulation among the people of any community will be found to be a very accurate test of their intellectual capacity and refinement.   Where there are well patronized circulating libraries and book stores, carrying large and well-selected assortments of standard literature, there will also most certainly be found a large proportion of cultivated and well-informed readers. And this may justly be claimed for Petersburg, where the book business is conducted by men whose own high education and mental culture eminently qualify them to cater to the intellectual requirements of their neighbors.   The Circulating Library of Messrs. T. S. Beckwith & Co. is worthy of special mention, as a most important contributor to the education and enjoyment of our intelligent people of all ages. It contains about three thousand well-selected volumes, which are constantly being added to, and comprises every class of entertaining and instructive literature. We have several handsome and well-stocked book and stationery stores, where all commodities usually kept by first-class establishments of the kind are to be found in great abundance and endless variety, including choice paintings, engravings photographs, and a host of other articles which may be grouped under the generic term "fancy." Combined with the book and stationery business is that of Pianos, Organs and Music, and our dealers represent the most famous factories in the country, and always keep on hand a large selection of first-class instruments.

DEALERS IN

PIANOS,   ORGANS,

BOOK AND SHEET MUSIC,

PUBLIC AND PRIVATE SCHOOL BOOKS.

⊹FANCY+GOODS,+STATIONERY,+&C.⊹

PIANOS.   ORGANS.

WEBER, KNABE,   ESTEY,
DECKER, HARDMAN,   CHASE,
NEW ENGLAND, PEASE,   PELOUBET.

THE VERY BEST INSTRUMENTS MANUFACTURED.

BOOKS AND FANCY ARTICLES of all kinds.
ALBUMS, BIBLES, PRAYER-BOOKS and other Publications suitable
for presents.

A Large and Select Circulating Library.

☞ Strangers and Visitors are invited to make themselves at 'home' in
the spacious READING ROOM, where Books, Papers, Magazines and Writing
Materials are always at their service.

108 Sycamore Street, Petersburg, Va.

CARRIAGES, HARNESS, ETC.

———:o:———

One of the first things noticed by an observant visitor to a strange town is the number and style of the carriages moving upon its thoroughfares, and it may be stated, without boasting, that in this respect Petersburg will compare most favorably with any other Southern City. The reason for this is easily explained. Among our most enterprising citizens are several experienced and practical dealers in Carriages and Buggies, and manufacturers of Harness and Saddlery, who thoroughly understand their business and force trade by offering the very best articles at prices which absolutely defy competition. Every variety of private equipage, from the family coach to the racing "sulky," can be procured here, at one or other of our carriage repositories, together with every style and make of harness, saddlery, whips, lap-rugs, and other items of stable outfit. The planters and farmers who bring their produce here also find it very much to their advantage to deal with our harness manufacturers, whose goods they find cheap and serviceable. The most famous carriage factories in the country are represented by our dealers, while the harness and saddlery of their own manufacture is guaranteed to be of the best material and workmanship.

P. F. JOHNSON & CO.,

MANUFACTURERS OF AND DEALERS IN

Harness, Saddles, Bridles, Collars,

AND ALL KINDS OF

HORSE FURNISHING GOODS.

7 LOMBARD STREET,

PETERSBURG, VIRGINIA.

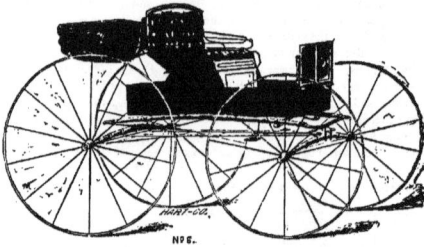

WM. H. HARRISON,
MANUFACTURER OF
Harness of All Kinds.

ALSO DEALER IN
Carriages, Buggies & Wagons,
NO. 9 BANK STREET, PETERSBURG, VA.

BAGS AND BAGGING.

The enormous increase in Petersburg's trade in Cotton, Fertilizers and Peanuts—especially the latter—created an opening two years ago for the manufacture of bags, and already this industry has become extremely beneficial to those who use its products, and profitable to its enterprising founders. There is only one Bag Factory in the City, and it is kept busy at all seasons filling orders not only from Petersburg houses, but also from those of Richmond, Norfolk and other manufacturing centres, where its work has given unqualified satisfaction. The burlap, of which the bags are made, is manufactured in Scotland and comes here direct through the agents in New York. Our supply of bags was formerly drawn from the Northern factories, with which our Petersburg factory now competes at the same or even lower prices for exactly the same material, thus saving the consumers the item of freight, at least—a small item, it is true, when estimated upon a single bag, but an important saving upon a year's consumption.

VIRGINIA BAG FACTORY,

PETERSBURG, VIRGINIA.

CARTER R. BISHOP & CO.,

MANUFACTURERS OF

BURLAP AND COTTON SACKS

---FOR---

Peanuts, Fertilizers, Grain, Flour, Meal, Sumac, &c.,

PLAIN OR PRINTED.

Headquarters for Sacks, Bags and Bag Twine.

OUR FACTORY IS RUN BY STEAM, AND HAVING RECENTLY
DOUBLED OUR CAPACITY, WE ARE NOW PREPARED
TO EXECUTE ALL ORDERS WITH NEATNESS
AND DISPATCH.

OUR LARGE AND RAPIDLY GROWING TRADE DEMONSTRATES

THAT OUR GOODS

ARE AS WE REPRESENT THEM AND OUR PRICES MODERATE.

MISCELLANEOUS.

——:o:——

In the preceding pages special attention has been directed, under distinctive headings, to each of the principal branches of trade and industry which engage the manufacturing and mercantile classes of Petersburg, and it must be admitted that not only does the present condition of her affairs make a most creditable showing, but also that her existing advantages are in a fair way to be considerably augmented, and that her future is rich in promises of continually increasing prosperity—promises which will certainly be redeemed, provided the people remain faithful to themselves and to their traditions. In addition to the more prominent subjects already reviewed, there are others, too numerous for separate classification, and yet too productive of good, in their combined influence upon the community, to justify their being passed by without mention. Among Petersburg's manufactories there is one which has flourished here for more than forty years, devoted to the production of that most indispensable article, Soap. Another, although comparatively young, has killed competition through a large section of the Southern Country in the matter of Trunks, Valises and the like. The Butter Dish and Fruit Basket Factories, already noticed, are doing an excellent and ever-growing trade with all sections of the country, and giving employment to hundreds of white women of the poorer classes, who could find no other form of manual labor suitable to their sex which would enable them to earn their living respectably. Cotton, hair and shuck Mattresses are made in considerable numbers at a Petersburg factory and distributed through the adjoining counties. The City Cemeteries and rural graveyards for many miles around, are supplied with beautiful marble shafts and tomb-stones which bear the "imprint" of the Cockade Marble Works, as do also many of the ornaments that adorn our handsome residences. Our Florists and Nurserymen are without superiors in the various details of their interesting trade and the choice est flowers can be had in profusion, at an hour's notice, during any month in the year. The windows and show cases of our Jewelry Stores sparkle with rich gems and present a most attractive assortment of watches, clocks, gold and silver ware, and such other articles as pertain to this department of trade. Such goods as China and Glass Ware are to be found here in as great variety and at as low prices as in the large Northern Cities. Our plumbers, paper-hangers, tinners, boot and shoe makers, builders, blacksmiths and mechanics of all kinds, furnish excellent work, each in his own line; while our photographic artists turn out first-class work in all styles, and faithfully reproduce, in most becoming manner, the very superior efforts of those other artists, the Milliners and Tailors. The City is also well supplied with Livery and Sale Stables; buggies, hacks and saddle-horses are numerous and can be hired at moderate rates. In short, for a city of its size and population, there cannot be found one anywhere in which the necessaries, comforts and luxuries of life, in all conceivable forms, are more abundant or more easily obtainable than they are in Petersburg, and if those who have been accustomed to send to distant points for their supplies will only give us a fair trial, they will certainly have no cause to regret the experiment, which will no doubt result in securing their permanent patronage for our " home trade."

SEWARD & MUNT,

COPPER AND LEAD

TIN, BRASS, ZINC, NICKEL AND WOOD STRAPS, &c.

Millers and Trunk Manufacturers.

MILL AND FACTORY AT CAMPBELL'S BRIDGE.

OFFICE: 5 BOLLINGBROOK STREET, - - - - PETERSBURG, VIRGINIA.

Established 1865.

CHARLES MILLER WALSH,
COCKADE MARBLE WORKS.

MANUFACTURER OF

MONUMENTS, HEADSTONES, TABLETS,

Crosses, Tomb-Stones, Grave-Stones,&c.,

OF EVERY DESCRIPTION.

Designs Sent to Any Address Free.

☞ WRITE FOR DESIGNS AND PRICES.

SYCAMORE STREET - - - (*Opposite Halifax*),

PETERSBURG, VIRGINIA,

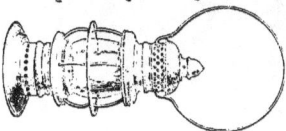

W. D. POYTHRESS,
FLORIST,

Greenhouse and Bedding Plants.

Hybrid, Perpetual and Everbloom- ing Roses.

FLORAL DESIGNS, MONOGRAMS OF THE FINEST FLOWERS. MADE TO ORDER ON THE SHORTEST NOTICE.

BYRNE ST. 239 BYRNE ST.

CUT FLOWERS A SPECIALTY.

ORDERS BY MAIL OR TELEGRAPH PROMPTLY FILLED AND SATISFACTION GUARANTEED.

239 BYRNE STREET, Petersburg, Va.

J. M. WHITEHURST,
MANUFACTURER OF

Hair, Shuck and Cotton-Top Mattresses,

ALSO WHOLESALE AND RETAIL DEALER IN

Wall Papers, Window Shades, Oil Cloths, Mattings, Rugs and Door Mats,

Lace Curtains & Curtain Material

Upholsterers' Supplies, Bedding Material, Chromos, Cornices, Picture Frame Mouldings, &c., &c.

No. 117 SYCAMORE STREET, Petersburg, Va.

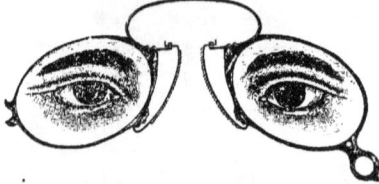

C. F. LAUTERBACK,

(FORMERLY WITH THE LATE E. RICHTER,)

✦ Watchmaker and Dealer in Fine Jewelry, ✦

Silver-ware, Watches, Clocks. &c.

☞ REPAIRS EXECUTED AT SHORT NOTICE. ☜

144 Sycamore Street, - - - - - Petersburg, Va.

D. BUCHANAN,

Practical Watchmaker, Manufacturing Goldsmith and Jeweler,

113 SYCAMORE ST., PETERSBURG, VA.,

Is about to remove to the elegant new store, No. 111 BROAD STREET, RICHMOND, where he will be glad to see his friends and patrons, and to retain at least a portion of their patronage. The business and stock in Petersburg is now for sale, and GREAT BARGAINS are offered.

JAMES SMITH.   HUGH R. SMITH.

JAS. SMITH & SON,

Soap Manufacturers,

PINE STREET, (Near Washington,) PETERSBURG, VA.

Tallow and Grease of all kinds bought and sold.

ESTABLISHED 1858.

J. B. BRADY,

GAS AND STEAM FITTER,

No. 7 Bollingbrook St., Petersburg, Va.

ESTABLISHED 1867.

ROB'T. T. STONE.   JOHN W. FRIEND.

STONE & FRIEND,

SALE, LIVERY AND HIRING STABLES,

A fine assortment of HACKS, BUGGIES AND SADDLE HORSES always on hand. Good accommodation and ample room for drovers.

NO. 40 LOMBARD ST., Petersburg, Va.

Established 1875.

GEORGE A. FRITZ,

Livery, Sale and Exchange Stables,

NO. 18 BANK STREET, Petersburg, Va.

J. D. BOWIE,

DEALER IN

FISH, OYSTERS, WILD GAME AND ALL KINDS OF COUNTRY
PRODUCE.   All orders filled with promptness and dispatch.

NO. 12 BOLLINGBROOK ST., Petersburg, Va.

A. J. MANN,

UPHOLSTERER, PLAIN AND DECORATIVE

PAPER-HANGER.

ROOMS NEATLY PAPERED AT SHORT NOTICE.

144 SYCAMORE STREET, Petersburg, Va.

LUMBER, WOOD AND COAL.

—:o:—

The central position occupied by Petersburg, renders her an important depot and distributing point for the commodities embraced by the above heading. She is within easy reach, by rail and water, of the great pine, oak, gum and poplar forests of Virginia and North Carolina, and her commerce with the Northern markets in lumber, boards, planks railroad ties and fire-wood, is considerable. There are several saw-mills in and near the city, as well as door and window-sash, wooden-dish and basket factories. The surrounding country also abounds in saw-mills, and the axe and adze of the woodman are heard incessantly in the forests. Direct railroad communication with the famous coal-fields of Virginia and the adjoining States, insures to us an abundant and cheap supply of soft or bituminous coal ; while the mines of Pennsylvania and Maryland furnish us with the excellent hard coal for which they are celebrated. Some of our coal and lumber dealers also handle lime, plaster, cement and other builders' materials, besides straw, hay, oats, etc. These trades, separate and combined, are in the hands of experienced, enterprising and reliable firms, with plenty of capital to conduct and expand their business according to the opportunities legitimately offered.

COOPER & SPOTSWOOD,

LUMBER DEALERS.

Tobacco Box Lumber a Specialty.

WASHINGTON STREET, - - PETERSBURG, VA.

LOUIS L. MARKS.   ALFRED FRIEND.

MARKS & FRIEND,

General Commission and Shipping Merchants,

DEALERS IN

✤HAY, GRAIN, COAL, LIME AND LUMBER.✤

MANUFACTURERS OF

AGRICULTURAL LIME.

➤✻✦LUMBER✦BILLS✦CUT✦TO✦ORDER✦✻◆

NO. 113 RIVER STREET,

PETERSBURG, VIRGINIA.

J. W. PHILLIPS,

DEALER IN

COAL, WOOD, LUMBER, BRICKS,

RAILROAD TIES, HOOP POLES, &C.

Office and Yards at Head of High Street, on the Basin,

PETERSBURG, VA.

☞ ORDER THROUGH TELEPHONE.

WM. J. CHAPPELL,

✦Builder✦and✦Contractor,✦

38 TABB STREET,

PETERSBURG, VA.

JOHN L. HOBSON,

DEALER IN ALL GRADES OF HARD AND SOFT COAL.

CUMBERLAND COAL A SPECIALTY.

Office : No. 3 Ta b Street and Pocahontas Bridge, Petersburg, Virginia.

WM. R. NICHOLS, Coal and Wood Dealer.

Offices : Cor. East Tabb and Sycamore Sts. and Pocahontas, Petersburg, Va.

ANTHRACITE, SPLINT, BRIGHT HOPE

AND STEAM COALS AND WOOD.

Very Lowest Market Prices Always Guaranteed.

GEO. V. SCOTT.   RICHARD C. SCOTT.

GEORGE V. SCOTT & SON,

Lumber, Coal & General Commission & Shipping Merchants.

Office on the Wharf, Petersburg, Va.

W. T. HARRISON.   E. M. BARKSDALE.

HARRISON & BARKSDALE,

DEALERS IN LUMBER, LATHS, POSTS, WOOD, &C., &C.

Second Street, below the Bollingbrook Hotel, Petersburg, Va.

☞ Estimates furnished and Bills of Lumber filled at LOWEST FIGURES.

ESTABLISHED 1874.

GEORGE J. ROGERS,

DEALER IN WOOD AND RAILROAD TIES.

COR. BOLLINGBROOK AND FIFTH STREETS, PETERSBURG, VA.

CONFECTIONERY.

——:0:——

The wholesale and manufacturing Confectioners of Petersburg have always done their full share in building up and maintaining the City's trade with the outer world ; and it is gratifying to know that their efforts have been duly appreciated, and rewarded by the increasing number of orders for their delicious products, which include candies, cakes, crackers, pies, and other articles calculated to tempt and delight the appetite. Our confectioners are also large dealers in native fruits of all kinds, fresh, dried and crystalized, as well as in imported fruits and confectionery. Affiliated with this branch of trade, although not exactly belonging to it, is the wholesale and retail dealing in toys of all descriptions ; cigars, tobacco and cigarettes ; fireworks and other articles which might be classified as "fancy goods." At certain seasons,—the Christmas holidays, for example—the business done by these establishments is enormous, and the employees are kept working night and day, filling orders for city customers and dispatching cases of goods to the villages and hamlets for miles and scores of miles around. The sales effected by our wholesale and retail confectioners during the year 188; aggregated nearly a quarter of a million dollars.

◁PROFESSIONAL CARDS▷
(ALPHABETICALLY ARRANGED.)

ATTORNEYS-AT-LAW.

GEORGE S. BERNARD.   D. M. BERNARD, JR.
G. S. & D. M. BERNARD,
ATTORNEYS-AT-LAW.
Nos. 4 and 6 Mechanics' Building,   -   -   -   Petersburg, Va.

GEORGE T. CLARKE.   R. D. GILLIAM.
CLARKE & GILLIAM.
ATTORNEYS-AT-LAW.
SURRY COURT HOUSE, SURRY COUNTY, VA.
COURTS :—Surry, Prince George and Isle of Wight Counties, United
States Courts at Richmond and Norfolk, and Supreme Court of Appeals
at Richmond, Va.

J. J. COCKE.   RO. GILLIAM, JR.
COCKE & GILLIAM,
ATTORNEYS-AT-LAW,
OFFICES: No. 114 Sycamore street (Corner of Court House Avenue),
PETERSBURG, VA.
Practice in Courts of Petersburg and surrounding Counties, and in the
United States Courts and Court of Appeals at Richmond.

CHAS. F. COLLIER.   JOSEPH S. BUDD.
COLLIER & BUDD,
ATTORNEYS-AT-LAW.
LAW OFFICES: 62½ Sycamore street, Petersburg, Va.
Will practice in the Supreme Court of Appeals at Richmond, Va., in
the Courts of the City of Petersburg and in those of the adjacent counties.

E. M. COX,
ATTORNEY-AT-LAW AND NOTARY PUBLIC.
No. 212 Exchange Building, Bank street, Petersburg, Virginia.
Will practice in all the Courts of the City and surrounding Counties.

ROPER DAVIS,
ATTORNEY-AT-LAW,
PETERSBURG,   -   -   -   -   -   VIRGINIA.

ALEXANDER DONNAN.   ALEXANDER HAMILTON.

DONNAN & HAMILTON,
(ESTABLISHED JULY 8TH, 1874.)
ATTORNEYS-AT-LAW,

No. 24 BANK STREET,   -   -   PETERSBURG, VIRGINIA.
Attend regularly all the Courts held for the City of Petersburg and the
Counties of Dinwiddie, Chesterfield, Prince George, Sussex, and occasionally those of Greensville, Amelia and Surry. The collection of debts
and winding up of estates particularly attended to. They also practice in
the District and Circuit Courts of the United States at Richmond, Va.

J. WESLEY FRIEND.   RICHARD B. DAVIS.

FRIEND & DAVIS,
ATTORNEYS-AT-LAW.

OFFICE: Over Petersburg Savings and Insurance Company's Offices,
PETERSBURG, VA.

Practice in Courts of Petersburg and surrounding Counties, and in the
United States Courts and Court of Appeals at Richmond.

ROBERT H. JONES, JR.,
(LATE OF JONES & MCKENNEY,)
ATTORNEY-AT-LAW.

EXCHANGE BUILDING, BANK STREET, PETERSBURG, VA.

Subscriber to Hubbell's Legal Directory, Sloan's Legal and Financial
Register, and member of the Continental Collection Union.
Courts of the City of Petersburg and surrounding Counties, United
States Courts and Court of Appeals at Richmond.

David A. Lyon, Attorney - at - Law,
NO. 110 1-2 SYCAMORE STREET,
PETERSBURG, VIRGINIA.

Practices in all the courts of the State of Virginia, and in the United
States Courts.

W. B. McILWAINE.   GEORGE MASON.

McILWAINE & MASON, Attorneys-at-Law,
No. 3. Mechanics Building, Petersburg, Va.

COURTS: City of Petersburg and counties of Chesterfield, Dinwiddie,.
Prince George, Surry, Sussex and Greensville.

W. R. McKENNEY, (Late of Jones & McKenney,)
COUNSELLOR-AT-LAW, Exchange Building, Bank Street,
PETERSBURG, VIRGINIA.
Commissioner in Chancery and Notary Public.

Courts of the City of Petersburg and surrounding counties, United
States Courts, and Court of Appeals at Richmond.

W. L. & THOS. G. WATKINS,

ATTORNEYS AND COUNSELLORS AT LAW,

No. 114 Sycamore Street (Cor. of Court House Avenue), Petersburg, Va.
Practice in the Courts of Petersburg and surrounding Counties, United
States Courts and Court of Appeals at Richmond.

R. T. WILSON, Attorney-at-Law,

No. 114 Sycamore Street (Cor. of Court House Avenue), Petersburg, Va.

OFFICE HOURS : From 9 A. M. to 3 P. M.

COURTS : Petersburg and surrounding Counties, Court of Appeals and
United States Courts at Richmond. Specialty of business in Surry, Sussex and Dinwiddie.

DENTISTS.

Thos. Jay Burgess, D. D. S.,

DENTAL OFFICE.

NO. 5 SYCAMORE STREET, (Over Alex. Wilson's.

PETERSBURG, VA.

DR. B. F. COSBY, Surgeon Dentist,

Graduate of the Baltimore College of Dental Surgery. Resident Prac-
titioner for Thirty Years.

Office: 23 1-2 North Sycamore St., Petersburg, Va.

DR. L. T. FUQUA, DENTIST.

OFFICE AT RESIDENCE,

First Door from Augustus Wright's Shoe Store.

NO. 8 FRANKLIN STREET, Petersburg, Va.

DR. JOHN H. HARTMAN, Dentist,

NO. 44 BANK STREET,

(OPPOSITE THE ACADEMY OF MUSIC.)

PETERSBURG, VIRGINIA,

PRINCIPAL MANUFACTURING AND MERCANTILE HOUSES OF PETERSBURG.

———:o:———

While none of our citizens are possessed of such colossal wealth as to make them the financial equals of the Vanderbilts, the Goulds and the other score or two of millionaires of whom the Metropolis of the United States can boast, we have among us many substantial business men, whose talent, energy and enterprise have secured comfortable fortunes for themselves and at the same time contributed largely towards building up the commercial importance of the city.

By such men as these the objects of this publication have been appreciated and endorsed, as is evidenced by the material support they have given it by identifying themselves, through its advertising pages, with the undertaking, and also by the liberal aid they have given in securing its wide circulation.

It is impossible to give every business house in Petersburg a separate notice without expanding the volume indefinitely. The following, which are given *gratuitously*, are therefore limited to those who have sustained the publisher's efforts to promote the public welfare, in the manner above mentioned.

Petersburg has a noble history, full of interest to all who love personal courage, public patriotism, commercial integrity and social virtue. May her future historians find many another bright page to add to her story!

————

The Upper Appomattox Company.—(See page 75.)
The Petersburg Gas Light Company.—(See page 92.)
Petersburg Street Railway, George Beadle, Proprietor.—(See page 93.)
The Petersburg Railway.—(See pages 95 and 102.)
The Norfolk & Western R. R. and **The Va., Tenn. & Ga. Air-Line.**—(See pages 98, 103 and 104.)

STEAMSHIP AND STEAMBOAT LINES.

Clyde's Coastwise and West India Steam Lines.—The fine Steamships of this Company (W. P. Clyde & Co., of Philadelphia and New York) run regularly between all the ports on the Atlantic Seaboard of the United States and the seaports of South America and the West Indies, carrying enormous quantities of freight and conducting a profitable trade. Several of Clyde's propellers run regularly between Philadelphia and Richmond, calling at Norfolk, and, in the cotton season, at West Point, Va., reciving and delivering Petersburg freights at City Point. This line has exercised a powerful influence upon the development of commercial interests in this section. Captain James W. McCarrick is the General Southern Agent, with his office at Norfolk, and Mr. Charles H. Shelton, is the agent in this city. (See page 105.)

Old Dominion Steamship Company.—This wealthy and powerful Company was organized in 1867, and succeeded the New York and Virginia Steamship Company. Its head offices are at 197 Greenwich Street, New York, and its principal officers are: Commodore N. L. McCready, President; W. H. Stanford, Secretary; and H. A. Bourne, Superintendent. Captain John M. West is the agent for Petersburg and City Point. The Company is one of the wealthiest and most influential in the country, and owns a large fleet of magnificent iron propellers, which ply between New York, Norfolk City Point and Richmond. The passenger accommodation on board these steamships is most luxurious, and during the eighteen years of its career not a single life intrusted to the Company's care has been lost. (See page 106.)

Virginia Steamboat Company.—Nothing more enjoyable can be imagined than a trip down the beautiful James on board one of the comfortable steamers of this line. They call at all the principal landings on the river between Richmond and Norfolk, and are supplied with every comfort. The scenery is superb and replete with historical interest, and the fare is only one dollar! Passengers going to Baltimore and the North can go down the river by this line to Norfolk, where close connection is made with.

the Steamships of the Old Dominion and Baltimore Steam Packet Companies. Mr. L. B. Tatum, of Richmond, is Superintendent of the Line, and Mr. Charles H. Shelton is the Petersburg Agent. (See page 106.)

REAL ESTATE BROKERS.

John C. Griffin.—This gentleman has had many years' experience as a land broker and dealer in Farms, Timber, and Mineral Lands and City Property, and has supplied many a settler with a comfortable home. Those who contemplate purchasing land in Virginia would do well to communicate with Captain Griffin before committing themselves finally, lest they should discover too late that, under his advice, they might have made a better bargain. (See page 100.)

Pyle & De Haven.—A pushing, enterprising and reliable firm, whose members are practically familiar with all the details of their business. They always keep a good list of desirable Farm and Mineral Lands and City Property for sale or exchange. They are also agents for the Virginia Immigration Society, and give special attention to the requirements of settlers from the North or from the Trans-Atlantic States. Their circulars, containing most valuable information, will be sent to all applicants. (See page 110.)

TOBACCO MANUFACTURERS.

S. W. Venable & Co.—(See page 115.)

Wm. Cameron & Bro.—(See page 116.)

D. B. Tennant & Co.—(See page 118.)

Watson & McGill.—(See page 119.)

Williamson & Routh.—(See page 120.)

Boykin, Bland & Co.—(See page 121.)

John H. Maclin.—(See page 122.)

W. D. Barkley & Co.—(See page 123.)

L. D. Inge.—For several years connected with the Tobacco Trade of Petersburg. Has recently removed to 21 Lombard Street, where he manufactures several brands of Export and Tax-paid Tobacco. (See page 123.)

Robert C. Osborne.—(See page 124.)

W. H. Hall.—Manufactures Cigars and Smoking Tobacco of several kinds and of all grades at his factory, No. 49 Bank Street. Has a large local trade and is well-supported in the surrounding counties. He contemplates enlarging his premises shortly, in obedience to the demands of his increasing business. (See page 124.)

James E. Winston.—Has established a good and growing trade in the City, as well as in Western Virginia and in the adjoining State of Tennessee, where his Cigars are in great demand. He also deals largely in several popular brands of Chewing and Smoking Tobacco, and is regarded as a most reliable manufacturer and dealer. (See page 124.)

A. J. Campbell & Co.—(See page 125.)

TOBACCO WAREHOUSES.

Moore's.—(See page 126.)

Centre.—A commodious and centrally situated warehouse under the management of Mr. F. W. Jones, of Brunswick, and Mr. W. T. Harvey of Nottoway, who give their best personal attention to the sampling of Hogsheads and the sales of Loose Tobacco. The warehouse is situated on Washington Street, opposite the depot of the Petersburg Railroad, and is most convenient for farmers entering the town from the counties lying to the westward. Good accommodation is given, without charge, to wagons and horses —and their drivers, if desired. (See page 127.)

West Hill.—The largest and most centrally located warehouse in the City, under the control of two experienced and popular Samplers, Mr. J. J. Percivall, of Petersburg, and Colonel W. M. Field, of Dinwiddie County. New sheds and rooms for the accommodation of horses and drivers are in course of construction and will very shortly be completed. All the Tobacco brought to this warehouse is insured, without expense to the owner. (See page 128.)

The Virginia Slate Roofing Co.—O. O. Thomas & Co.—(See page 129.)

PEANUT CLEANERS.

M. Levy & Co.—This firm has been actively engaged in the general Commission business for the past fifteen years, and is also one of the largest and oldest handlers of Peanuts in the City. They own several well-established brands of cleaned and hand-picked Peanuts, Virginia and Spanish, such as "Eureka," "Crown," "Prince George," etc. Their factory on Bollingbrook street, corner of Second, is fitted with all the necessary machinery. The house also deals largely in Hides, Furs, Beeswax and general Produce. (See page 131.)

Walter S. Phillips & Co.—Are engaged exclusively in the Peanut Trade, and have earned an excellent reputation as cleaners, hand-pickers and dealers. Their best known brands are "Lights," "Flags," "Champion," "Crescent" and "Extra Virginias." They solicit correspondence and furnish quotations on application. They own and operate a large and well-equipped factory, at No. 20 Bollingbrook Street, which is also the office of the firm. Their branch office in New York is at No. 233 Fulton street. (See page 132.)

Dunlop, Peebles & Co.—A recently-established firm, but composed of practical and experienced handlers of Peanuts. Their factory and office are at No. 40 Sycamore street, where they make and put up the "Champion," "Phœnix" and "Challenge" brands, from the best stock to be obtained in the market. Their work is first-class in every respect and thoroughly reliable. They refer to the Petersburg Savings & Insurance Company, and solicit correspondence with the trade all over the country. (See page 133.)

Joseph B. Worth.—Has devoted the last six years to the Peanut business, and his brands have met with great success at the North, South and West. His factory, at No. 13 Old street, has a capacity of one hundred and fifty bags of cleaned and hand-picked nuts a day, and his goods are guaranteed to be first-class in every respect, and fully up to grade. He pays the highest market price for his Peanuts and invites a trial of his brands, which include the "Eagle and Flag," fancy hand-picked and polished Virginias, and the "Shield," Spanish. Mr. Worth makes a specialty of choice Spanish shelled Peanuts. (See page 134.)

R. C. Marks & Co.—Manufacture and clean all grades of Hand-picked Peanuts, at their factory, corner of Lombard and Third streets. The firm is comparatively young, but the gentlemen comprising it, Messrs. R. C. Marks and R. A. Harrison, are old and reliable Petersburg merchants, who have secured a large and growing business connection among their friends in the adjoining counties and the Peanut dealers all over the country. (See page 134.)

George Davis & Co.—This is the oldest house now engaged in the Peanut Trade in Petersburg, having been established in 1868. In the summer of 1884 their factory was destroyed by fire, but they are at work again and are manufacturing and cleaning all grades of shelled and unshelled hand-picked Peanuts, Virginia and Spanish. (See page 134.)

WOODEN DISH AND BASKET FACTORIES.

George A. Mannie & Co.—(See page 135.)

The Southside Manufacturing Co.—Several entirely new industrial enterprises have been started quite recently in Petersburg, which have already proved of considerable value to the City, and bear promise of greatly increased importance, as they become better known. Conspicuous among these is the Company now under review. The business was founded scarcely a year ago, and was lately reorganized, with Mr. James E. Routh as President and Treasurer, and Mr. George H. Brown as manager. The factory, is situated on Commerce Street, and its object is the manufacture of Brown's Patent Fruit and Berry Baskets, Berry Crates, Veneers, Egg Crates and other like articles for facilitating the safe transportation of the products of Virginia's orchards, and those of other States in the Sunny South, to the distant markets of distribution and consumption. It goes without saying that such perishable articles as peaches, grapes, strawberries, etc., must be packed with great care, if they are to escape injury and command a fair price when exposed for sale in the Northern and Western markets, and growers fully realize the importance of using only the best—which are also the cheapest—crates and baskets for this purpose. That the wares manufactured by the Southside Company meet this demand in every respect is demonstrated by the high estimation in which they are held wherever they have been used. The factory employs from a hundred to a hundred and fifty hands, according to the season, and has a capacity of thirty thousand baskets per day. Two storehouses on Sycamore Street receive the overflow from the factory. So great a demand has already been created for these baskets that the Company is compelled to accumulate at least two millions of them by the time the fruit season opens, in order to fill the first rush of orders. Mr. George H. Brown, the experienced manager of the factory, is the inventor and patentee of the baskets and crates turned out by this Company. They are peculiarly adapted to the requirements of the delicate and luscious fruits in which this favored climate is so prolific, and there are strong indications that it will soon be necessary to enlarge the factory, so as to keep pace with the increasing trade. All the hands employed by this Company are white, and a large proportion are females. The company has recently been chartered under the State laws, with an authorized capital of $50,000. (See page 136.)

COMMISSION MERCHANTS, GROCERS, ETC.

Allen & Prichard.—A well-known, old-established and reliable firm, doing a large wholesale and jobbing business, in all kinds of groceries and country produce. Also agents for Oriental Gum Powder and the Baltimore United Oil Company's Kerosene Oil. As Commission merchants they enjoy a large and profitable country connection, and offer special inducements to promptly-paying and cash customers. (See page 138.)

John Arrington & Sons.—Established in 1866, and are among the largest handlers in Petersburg of Cotton, Tobacco, Peanuts, and farm produce of every variety. They make a specialty of bright tobacco for wrappers. They are also wholesale grocers and hold several important agencies, including those for Pacific Guano, the McComb Arrrow Tie Company and Bridgewater Flour. (See page 139.)

Arringtons & Scott.—Richmond. Va., composed of the members of the firm last noticed (Messrs. R. T. and S. P. Arrington) and Messrs. R. T. Arrington Jr. and F. W. Scott. Their business, that of General Commission Merchants, is conducted by the two gentlemen last named. They are building up a fine trade in connection with the Petersburg establishment of John Arrington & Sons. Their warehouse is at Shockoe Slip, very convenient to railroad and water transportation. (See page 139.)

E. B. Bain.—This gentleman is the surviving partner and successor of the late firm of Bain & Parrack. He is one of the oldest and best trusted of Petersburg's merchants, and is President of the Petersburg Chamber of Commerce, and a Director of the Petersburg Tobacco Association. The business was established in 1874, since which time it has grown and prospered and commanded universal confidence. Mr. Bain is a very large buyer of Tobacco, Cotton, Grain and Peanuts. He is also a large dealer in No. 1 Peruvian Guano and Agent for several popular brands of Fertilizers. He is widely known, throughout this whole section of country, as a perfectly trustworthy, conscientious gentleman, as well as a prudent and reliable merchant. (See page 140.)

J. Garland Blackwell & Co.—Established in 1881, and now doing a large Commission business with the planters and farmers of several neighboring counties—Lunenburg, Mecklenburg, Prince George, Dinwiddie, Greenville, Brunswick, Prince Edward and Halifax. They give strict personal attention to all their consignments of produce, and obtain for them the full market value. (See page 141.)

Davis, Roper & Co.—One of the largest firms of Wholesale Grocers in the City. They always keep on hand a large and varied stock of goods, and are satisfied with moderate profits. They do an enormous business with the retail trade of Petersburg and the surrounding districts, and solicit consignments of produce and merchandise, for which they invariably get the best prices. They represent, as agents, the City Mills Milling Company's flour, meal and mill feed, and invite orders for the same. (See page 142.)

Green & Burton.—An active, energetic and thriving firm, who deal largely in Cotton, Tobacco, Corn, Wheat Peanuts and other country produce, for which they solicit consignments, always giving the same their prompt attention. They are also agents for the famous Patapsco Guano and Allison & Addison's Star Brand Fertilizers, which command a ready sale for all crops. (See page 143.)

Jones & Callender.—For three years past engaged in the purchase and sale, on commission, of General Plantation and Farm Produce. making a specialty of Cotton, Leaf Tobacco, Peanuts and Wheat. As Wholesale Grocers they enjoy exceptional facilities, and all orders are promptly filled at the lowest market prices. They are agents for "National" Tobacco and Cotton Manure, and for "Orchilla" Guano. They invite custom and consignments, and guarantee complete satisfaction. (See page 144.)

Martin Hill & Co.—In 1830 this venerable commercial house was established, the original name of the firm being Martin, Jones & Bragg, the partners in which were N. M. Martin,* A. Sydney Jones* and D. Wilson Bragg.* About a year later Mr. Jones

* Now deceased.

withdrew from the concern and the business was carried on by the two remaining partners, under the style of Martin & Bragg. This last named firm was dissolved about January 1st, 1835, and the senior partner, Mr. Martin, associated with him Mr. David Dounan, Jr.,[*] and the firm name became N. M. Martin & Dounan. On the 1st of January, 1839, this firm was in turn dissolved, and Mr. Martin formed a partnership with Mr. Robert A. Hamilton (father of our townsman, Mr. Alexander Hamilton), under the firm name of N. M. Martin & Hamilton. The last-mentioned partnership did not last long, and was succeeded by N. M. Martin & Dounans, composed of N. M. Martin, David Dounan, Jr. and John Dounan, Jr. On January 1st, 1846, this firm established a branch house in Richmond, under the style of N. M. Martin & Company, the senior partner moving with his family to that City. The firm in Richmond was afterwards changed to N. M. Martin, Bro., & Company. Robert A. Martin having been admitted to partnership. On New Year's Day, the latter withdrew from the Richmond house and returned to Petersburg where he entered the firm of McIlwaine, Brownly & Company (afterwards McIlwaine, Son & Company), with whom he remained as a partner for five years. On January 1st, 1855, the partnerships existing in Richmond and Petersburg between N. M. Martin, David Dounan, Jr. and John Dounan, Jr., were dissolved, and at the same date Robert A. Martin withdrew from the firm of McIlwaine, Son & Company to join his brother, N. M. Martin, as partner in both the Richmond and Petersburg houses, the former adopting the style of N. M. Martin, Son & Company, and the latter, N. M. Martin, Brother & Company—the same as had been the style of the Richmond firm years before. The members of these two houses, when they were established in 1855 were N. M. Martin and his son, Walter K. Martin, Robert A. Martin, Henry L. Plummer, Jr. and Robert Tennhill.[*] Mr. Plummer subsequently withdrew, and N. M. Martin, Jr.[*] was admitted to partnership in both houses, without, however, any change of name occurring until January, 1st, 1861. On that date (the founder of the firm, or firms, having died in the previous year) Walter K. Martin, R. H. Cunningham, Jr.,[*] Robert A. Martin, N. M. Martin, Jr. and Robert Tannhill, reorganized both houses and continued the business in Richmond as Walter K. Martin & Company. These two firms were dissolved in June, 1865, Walter K. Martin continuing the business on his own account in Richmond, where he is now the head of the firm of Walter K. Martin & Company, and Robert A. Martin and Robert Tannhill succeeding to the Petersburg business under the firm name of Martin & Tannahill. Shortly afterwards this last-mentioned firm consolidated with McIlwaine & Company, of Petersburg, and established a house in New York, under the style of Tannahill, McIlwaine & Company, which was managed by Mr. Tannahill, who removed to that City. On July 1st, 1868, the firms of Martin & Tannahill, of Petersburg, and Tannahill, McIlwaine & Company, of New York, were dissolved. Mr. Tannahill continued the New York business and remained at its head until his death, in 1881. It is now conducted by his heirs, under the name of Robert Tannahill & Company. In July, 1868, Mr. Robert A. Martin formed a copartnership with Mr. Robert B. Hill, and continued the Petersburg business as Robert A. Martin & Company until 1877, when Mr. A. G. M. Martin, son of the senior member of the firm and grandson of the late A. G. McIlwaine (who was, in his day, one of Petersburg's most prosperous merchants), was admitted as a partner, and the concern, for the first time, assumed its present name of Martin, Hill & Company. It will thus be seen that from the house founded in 1830 by Mr. N. M. Martin (and who was for several years at the head of the Richmond firm, also), two branch houses, both of which now probably eclipse the parent establishment, have descended. To the wisdom, business talent and unimpeachable integrity of the original founder of the concern, much of the success which, since his death, has attended the old house and its branches, may doubtless be attributed. At any rate, they can say what few firms of their age can, namely: that not one of them, from their foundation, has ever suspended or gone to protest, and that to-day, although in no way connected with each other, they are all "live concerns." It will be noticed that, since its establishment in 1830, and during its whole long life of fifty-five years, "Martin" has always been the first name of the firm in Petersburg, and it may be prophesied with absolute safety that so long as the old house and its branches conduct their business on the principles laid down and practised by the original founder, Nathaniel Macon Martin, their friends will never have cause to complain of "confidence abused." He was the very soul of honor in all his dealings, socially as well as commercially, and his precept and example have borne good fruit in those whom he has trained up as his successors in business. (See page 145.)

Robinson, Tillar & Co.—Deal extensively in Groceries of all kinds, Fertilizers, Bagging, Ties, etc., and receive consignments of Cotton, Tobacco, Corn, Peanuts and other produce, for sale on commission. They make quick sales at top prices, and

---

[*] Now deceased.

render prompt returns. They are Agents for several leading manufacturers of Chemicals and Guanos, and warrant all they sell to be genuine and reliable. Mr. J. C. Robinson, the senior partner, manages the affairs of the firm in Petersburg, and Mr. B. D. Tillar, who resides at Hicksford, attends to its outside business. (See page 146.)

Alexander Wilson.—For more than thirty years Mr. Wilson has held front rank as a dealer in Foreign and Domestic Groceries, and now stands at the head of the trade in Petersburg. His stock embraces every variety of Goods to be found in first-class establishments of the kind, besides a complete assortment of Wines, Liquors and General Provisions. He is sole Agent for Moerlein's Cincinnati Beer and "Appomattox" New Family Flour. Teas, Coffees and Spices are among the articles of which Mr. Wilson makes specialties. He is also a director of the Bank of Petersburg. (See page 147.)

George S. Prichard.—This gentleman has been in his present business for the last six years, during which period he has built up an excellent connection in the City by always keeping his stock of Family Groceries, Confectionery, Canned Goods, Tobacco and Cigars, at a very high standard of excellence and at very low prices—the two qualities which most directly commend themselves to the thrifty housekeeper. He warrants his goods to be as good and as cheap as any in the market. (See page 148.)

Cabaniss & Lunsford.—Succeeded the firm of Cabaniss & Co. a year ago, when Mr. J. H. Cabaniss admitted his associate, Mr. Charles Lunsford, to partnership. This firm conducts a very extensive general Commission business, a large proportion of which comes from the western portion of the State, beyond Lynchburg. They make specialties of Seed, Butter, Cheese, Flour, Grain, Hay and Feed. They give as their reference the Bank of Petersburg, and solicit correspondence. (See page 118.)

T. A. Palmer.—Keeps a complete assortment of Choice Family Groceries, Wines, Liquors, Cigars and Tobacco, and makes specialties of Teas, Coffees and Canned Goods. He has had a long experience in the Retail Trade and has secured a large and profitable business connection. (See page 149.)

John F. Peebles.—An active, prudent and successful Merchant, who deals largely in Peanuts, Foreign and Domestic Fruits, Dried Fruits, Potatoes and general Farm and Dairy Produce, for which he pays the highest cash price. He is also a member of the firm of Dunlop, Peebles & Company, peanut cleaners. Mr. Peebles has enjoyed an active experience, covering seventeen years, in the wholesale produce and fruit trade, and is known everywhere as a thoroughly reliable dealer. (See page 149.)

Samuel J. Hurt.—One of the oldest and most highly esteemed of Petersburg's Wholesale Grocers and Commission Merchants. He attends personally to the sale of all the Tobacco, Cotton, Wheat, Corn and other produce received by him from his numerous country customers, and is regarded as an excellent salesman and most energetic man of business. He carries a large assortment of Groceries for the Wholesale Trade. (See page 149.)

T. J. Jarratt & Son.—A well-known and prosperous house, for many years large handlers of Cotton, Tobacco, Peanuts and other Country Produce, the sale of which receives the faithful supervision of the firm, whose senior partner and founder, Mr. T. J. Jarratt, was elected to the Mayoralty of the city in 1882, and is now serving his second consecutive term in that office. His son, Mr. Walter J. Jarratt, was admitted to partnership in 1883. (See page 150.)

Patterson, Madison & Co.—Have been largely engaged in the Wholesale Grocery business for the past sixteen years, and are among the most active and pushing of our merchants. They keep a good stock of general Groceries and Provisions, which they sell at the lowest market prices, being content with a narrow margin of profit. (See page 150.)

D'Alton & Co.—A thoroughly business-like house, careful and judicious in the selection of its stock, which is the largest and best-assorted in the city. The head of the firm, Mr. James T. D'Alton, is also the junior member of the firm of D'Alton & Son, carrying on a kindred business on Old Street. As wholesale grocers, D'Alton & Company stand at or very near the top of the list. (See page 150.)

E. J. Bond & Bro.—Composed of Edward J. and William A. Bond, the former of whom has for many years held, and still holds, a position of trust with the Petersburg Savings & Insurance Co. The firm is still young, but it is gradually working into a good business and already enjoys the confidence of all who have had dealings with them. They keep a full line of fine Family Groceries, pure, wholesome and well-selected; also a choice stock of Cigars and Tobacco, and they invite their friends and the public to give their goods a trial. (See page 153.)

Joseph W. Wheary.—Established in 1874, and has occupied hlss present eligible premises for the past six years. His proximity to Campbell's bridge, combined with his business ability and the excellence of his large stock of Assorted Groceries, has resulted in securing to his establishment a large trade in town and country. Mr. Wheary is prompt and reliable in all his dealings, and his success in business testifies to the esteem in which he is held. (See page 151.)

Alfred Archer.—For nearly ten years an active and successful retail grocer, taking a decided lead in the Southwestern section of the City. He keeps a full line of Family Groceries, and makes specialties of Teas, Wines, Liquors and Cigars. He is, in all respects, justly entitled to the wide popularity and confidence which he enjoys. (See page 151.)

Bagwell and Williams.—Established in 1880, and now carrying on a large and successful business as Wholesale Grocers and general Commission Merchants. They occupy the end store in the handsome "Iron Front Building," which affords ample storage accommodation and enables them to handle enormous quantities of goods and farm produce. (See page 151.)

W. T. Hubbard & Co.—Have recently removed into their handsome new premises on Sycamore Street, between Franklin and Washington Streets, the building of which was necessitated by the expanding business of the firm in Cotton, Tobacco, Wheat and other staple crops, which engage their special attention. The house was established nearly twenty years ago, and has secured a large and flourishing trade. The firm is composed of Messrs. W. T. Hubbard and J. L. Peebles, the former of whom represents the Third Ward in the City Council. (See page 151.)

F. H. Curtis & Co.—Occupy a most eligible site on Franklin Street, adjoining West Hill Warehouse, and are large dealers in Groceries, Wines, Liquors, etc. The business has been established nearly four years, previous to which Mr. Curtis occupied a store on Halifax Street, and dealt principally in Liquors, Cigars and Tobacco. Mr. Curtis is the Chief of the City Fire Department, to which office he was appointed three years ago. (See page 151.)

J. C. Blake.—Extensively engaged in the Wholesale and Retail Commission Trade and deals in all varieties of Groceries, Ship Stores and general Produce, such as Flour, Corn, Meal, Oats, Hay and Ground Feed, for horses and cattle. He gives special attention to Poultry and Game, and is the inventor and patentee of "Blake's Arctic Refrigerator," an invaluable and simply-constructed chest for preserving such perishable articles as fish, game, butter, milk, etc., during the hot summer months. (See page 152.)

Gray & Inge.—Established in 1880 by Messrs. James H. Gray and Vincent Inge. In 1883 Mr. George M. Inge, son of the last-named gentleman, was admitted to partnership. With the close of the year 1884, Mr. Vincent Inge retired from the business, leaving the firm name unchanged since its first adoption. Messrs. Gray & Inge do a general Commission trade, making specialties of the sales of Cotton, Grain and Leaf Tobacco. Their connection is wide and includes the counties of Lunenburg, Charlotte, Brunswick, Nottoway and Prince Edward, in addition to those in close proximity to Petersburg. (See page 152.)

Spratley & Kidd.—An old and reliable firm, who deal principally in Lime, Plaster, Cement, Oats, Hay and Seed, giving special attention to the last-mentioned commodity. They are also General Commission Merchants, and receive consignments of general Farm Produce, which they dispose of for their customers, always obtaining the best market prices and making prompt returns. (See page 152.)

Daniel Rahily.—One of the best-known Wholesale Grocers, Liquor Dealers and Commission Merchants in Petersburg. His roomy and well-stocked store at the foot of Sycamore Street, known as the "Old Confederate Commissary," presents at all times a busy scene, being a popular resort of retail dealers and individual consumers from the country. Mr. Rahily makes liberal advances on consignments, fills country orders promptly, and sells his goods "cheaper than the cheapest." (See page 152.)

W. B. Deaton.—For a dozen years, or more, an active and successful Wholesale Grocer and Jobber of all kinds of Twist and Plug Tobacco, with which he supplies the trade at factory prices. He always keeps on hand a large and choice assortment of goods, and may be relied on to sell the best articles at the very lowest prices. His large store, No. 1 Old Street, occupies one of the best business sites in the City. (See page 152.)

A. W. Frice.—This gentleman has been known for years as a successful wholesale and retail dealer in Groceries, Wines, Liquors, Cigars etc., doing business on Halifax Street, opposite Centre Market, whence he has recently removed to 36 Sycamore Street, at the entrance to Westhill Warehouse, his increasing business requiring greater space and a more central situation than his original premises afforded. (See page 152.)

Plummer, Bain & Co.—One of the youngest firms in Petersburg, but possessing all the essential elements of success, for its component members, Messrs. H. L. Plummer, Jr., and George W. Bain, have enjoyed exceptional advantages in their commercial training and varied experience in the purchase and sale of Cotton, Tobacco and other produce. Already this energetic young house has created for itself a far-reaching business connection and ships its goods to New York and other markets at the North and West. (See page 152.)

MERCHANDISE BROKERS.

J. Hampden Slater.—Represents various kinds of business and has regular established correspondents in all parts of the United States. Makes specialties of Flour, Grain and Provisions, General Groceries, Syrups, Coffees, etc., and refers to Hinton & Dunn, bankers; the Petersburg Savings and Insurance Co., and the general jobbing trade. (See page 153.)

Smith & Perkins.—Removed here from Richmond early in 1884. They are industrious, enterprising and ambitious. They have placed themselves in direct telegraphic communication with the markets of New York and Chicago, and have already secured a good business. They give special attention to Flour, Grain, Provisions and General Merchandise, and to the faithful execution of orders in options. (See page 153.)

Dunlop & Townes.—Experienced, conscientious brokers, well known to the whole community and held in the highest esteem. They have regular correspondents all over the country, and are not only energetic in seeking orders but are also perfectly reliable in promptly executing them. The firm is composed of Messrs. James Dunlop, Jr., and W. W. Townes, son of the late Mr. W. W. Townes, who honorably served the City as Mayor from 1854 to 1865. (See page 153.)

BANKS.

The Petersburg Savings and Insurance Co.—A sound and healthy financial institution, which has withstood, without injury to its capital or credit, the wars and shocks and panics of a quarter of a century. That its affairs have been ably and judiciously managed is shown by the fact that its surplus and reserve fund amounts to nearly $100,000, and is regularly increasing. It is careful in selecting its loans and discounts, prompt in the payment of all proper demands, and is one of the very few Banking and Insurance Companies—if not the only one—that passed through the Civil War and, at its close, met all its obligations in full. (See page 154.)

The Bank of Petersburg.—Was incorporated in 1872, and has enjoyed a liberal public patronage from the first. It possesses special facilities for making collections, which it results promptly, making no charge for those on the cities in Virginia. It issues exchange on all the principal cities of Europe, and transacts a general Banking business. Its management is excellent and its Board of Directors comprises some of the most substantial merchants and professional men in the City. (See page 155.)

FERTILIZERS.

Davie & Whittle.—These gentlemen—Messrs. Pascal Davie and Fortescue Whittle—formed their partnership in the fall of 1883, and began the manufacture of Guano under the general trade mark of the "Owl Brand," divided into several grades, according to the requirements of the various crops for which they are designed. Their factory is at the river front, and they have received most flattering reports as to the efficacy of their products, from all sections of Virginia, the Carolinas, Georgia, Tennessee and Alabama. They have enjoyed many years' experience in the manufacture and sale of Fertilizers, and that they have turned this experience to good account is evidenced by the hundreds of testimonials to the merits of their "Owl Brand," which have reached them from all quarters. They will mail their Almanac for 1885, containing copies of these testimonials, to all who apply. (See page 156.)

Freeman, Lloyd, Mason & Dryden—E. B. Bars, Agent.—The factories of this firm are at Norfolk, Va., and at Pocomoke, Md., where the business was established in 1876. The famous "Pocomoke Super-Phosphate" and "Fish Hawk" Guano are manufactured by this house, and have given complete satisfaction to the planter, farmer and trucker, under crops of every description. For many years past the goods produced by this firm have been steadily improving in quality and stand "A 1" in the estimation of all who have used them. (See page 157.)

COTTON MILLS AND FACTORIES.

Swift Creek Cotton Manufacturing Co.—(See page 158.)
Petersburg Cotton Mills.—(See page 158.)
Ettrick Manufacturing Co.—(See page 159.)
Matoaca Manufacturing Co.—(See page 159.)
Battersea Manufacturing Co.—(See page 159.)
Old Dominion Cotton Mills.—(See page 160.)

SUMAC MILLS.

W. N. Jones & Co.—Have been engaged in manufacturing Oak Barks and Sumac for ten years, and for half of that period they have occupied their present premises, the Appomattox Mill. They export nearly all their prepared Bark and some Sumac to foreign markets. Most of the latter product is sold in the United States. They offer the highest cash price for leaf Sumac and stick Bark, and solicit correspondence. (See page 160.)

James M. Williams.—Proprietor of the Galleo Sumac Mills and the Rialto Corn Mills. Also a member of the firm of Bagwell & Williams, Commission Merchants. A practical and experienced Merchant Miller, who has secured a good business by persevering industry and the acknowledged merits of his products. (See page 160.)

The Virginia Hog Cholera Cure—E. B. Bain, Agent.—This wonderful medicine has been pronounced by hundreds of grateful farmers to be an absolutely infallible remedy for this plague, which has proved so disastrous to swine-raisers. No prudent farmer should be without it. (See page 161.)

HOTELS AND RESTAURANTS.

Hotel Gary.—A comfortable, well-kept and handsomely appointed house, situated in the very centre of the business quarter, and close to the Postoffice, banks and principal stores. Its proprietors are Messrs. George C. and Thomas R. Gary, who spare no effort to contribute to the comfort of their guests. (See page 162.)

Bollingbrook Hotel.—The largest hotel in the City, and conveniently situated, being only two squares distant from the depots of the Norfolk & Western and the Richmond & Petersburg Railroads. Its proprietor, Mr. Pettit, has been many years in the hotel business and thoroughly understands its various details. The house has been recently re-furnished and re-papered, and affords every comfort to its guests at very moderate rates. First-class accommodation is provided for a hundred guests. A fine bar and billiard hall are among the attractions, and the table is supplied with the best of everything. (See page 163.)

Exchange and Ballard Hotels, Richmond, Va.—This magnificent establishment constitutes one of the most attractive features of Virginia's Capital City. Its reputation is national, and antedates the Civil War. It consists, really, of two separate houses at opposite sides of Franklin Street at its intersection with Fourteenth—the Exchange Hotel, built in 1840, and the Ballard House, built in 1860. Since the erection of the latter, the two houses have always been under one management, and have been connected by a covered suspension bridge, spanning Franklin street, at the second story. Twenty years have passed since the present courteous and hospitable proprietor of this double hotel, Colonel J. L. Carrington, became its lessee, and under his management the "Exchange and Ballard" has ever been the leading hotel in Richmond. Six hundred guests can be entertained without unusual effort, and the hotels are rich in their appointments throughout. Colonel Carrington was a resident of Petersburg before the war, and was proprietor of the Bollingbrook Hotel. (See page 164.)

New Purcell House, Norfolk, Va.—This fine hotel has always been distinguished for its excellent accommodations and equally excellent fare. From time to time it has undergone many changes and has recently been renovated, beautified, refurnished and supplied with all modern conveniences. Under the able and hospitable management of its present experienced proprietors, Messrs. Philip F. and Benjamin R. Brown, the Purcell House has advanced still further in popular favor, and visitors to Norfolk will find it very much to their advantage and comfort to make the New Purcell House their headquarters. Mr. Philip F. Brown is also the proprietor of the far-famed Blue Ridge Springs. (See page 155.)

Quincey's European House.—As the name implies, this Hotel is conducted on the so-called "European" plan, which is well understood in this country. The reputation of its proprietor, Mr. Chris. Quincey, as a genial host and almost peerless caterer, is by no means limited to this section or State, for thousands of visitors to Petersburg, of late years, have had reason to remember his hospitality and skill with gratitude. His house has recently been much improved by the addition of a billiard hall and other attractions, while the accommodations and fare are in all respects first-class. (See page 166.)

Julius Liebert.—Shortly after the close of the war this gentleman settled in Petersburg, and has for nearly twenty years been regarded as among the most enterprising and successful of her business men. His Saloon, Billiard Hall and Restaurant, at No. 19 Lombard Street, are much frequented by town and country people, among whom the excellence of his fare is proverbial. Mr. Liebert carries on an extensive business as bottler of Berguer & Engel's famous Philadelphia Lager Beer, and also as manufacturer of Soda, Ginger Ale and Sarsaparilla. He has recently purchased the premises No. 18 Bollingbrook Street, formerly occupied by the peanut factories of George Davis & Co. and R. C. Marks & Co., destroyed by fire in the summer of 1884, and has nearly completed a handsome new building, which he will shortly occupy. The spacious lot extends back to Lombard Street, and it is Mr. Liebert's design to convert the rear portion into a genuine German Beer Garden, such as have attained great popularity at the North and West. The new building will be elegantly furnished with special regard to the comfort of its patrons, and Mr. Liebert will enjoy increased facilities for meeting the demands of his large wholesale and retail business. (See page 166.)

Eichberg's Saloon and Restaurant.—The proprietor, Mr. A. Eichberg, came to Petersburg in 1848, and has been engaged in business here since 1853. He is an experienced Saloon-keeper and Restaurateur, and his stock of Wines, Liquors, Cigars, etc., are always of the choicest brands, while his table is regularly furnished with all the delicacies in season. His establishment, No. 4 Bank Street, is centrally situated, and is a most convenient house of call for visitors from the country arriving by the Norfolk & Western or the Richmond & Petersburg Railroads. Mr. Eichberg gives special terms to regular boarders by the day, week or month. (See page 166.)

Walthall's European House.—A comfortable house in competent hands. Its proprietor, Mr. O. J. Walthall, has had a long experience in the hotel business in Petersburg and Richmond, and knows exactly how to make his guests comfortable. His rooms are all newly furnished and his table is supplied with the best that the market affords. Being a "European" house, the guests call for what they want and pay for what they get. The bar is stocked with the finest Wines, Ales, Liquors etc. (See page 166.)

Heinemann's Exchange.—This popular Saloon and Restaurant is situated in one of the most central and desirable localities in the City, and enjoys a liberal patronage from the business men of Petersburg, as well as from their country friends, by whom our thoroughfares are crowded at certain seasons of the year. The Saloon occupies the ground floor of the handsome and time-honored Exchange Building, the upper portions of which is used as offices, etc., the whole being the property of Mr. Henry Heinemann, who conducts the Saloon, and keeps nothing but the very best Wines, Liquors, Cigars and Tobacco. The chief attraction, however, to the tired and thirsty, is the delicious Export Lager Beer, from Ballantine's Brewery at Newark, N. J. This is admitted to be the purest, best and most refreshing Lager Beer brewed in this country. An excellent free lunch is served daily between the hours of 10 A. M. and 3 P. M. Mr. Heinemann has been engaged in this business in Petersburg for the past twelve years, and has occupied his present premises for nine years, so he is too well known to require further recommendation. (See page 167.)

Ocean View Hotel, Ocean View, Va.—A charming watering place on Chesapeake Bay, opposite Fortress Monroe and in full view of Capes Charles and Henry. It is opened for the accommodation of guests on May 1st of each year, and is within half an hour's run from Norfolk by rail. Its situation is most desirable, affording excellent surf-bathing and fishing, while the fresh sea breezes are most invigorating. (See page 167.)

IRON WORKS, HARDWARE, ETC.

The Petersburg Iron Works.—Established in 1851. The property of H. T. Morrison & Co., experienced manufacturers of Steam Engines, Mill and Factory Machinery, dredges, tug boats and all other classes of machinery for use on land or water, ordinarily manufactured at a first-class foundry. They make specialties of Steam Dredges, Dredging Machinery and Tug Boats. All work turned out by this firm has given coun-

tiru satisfaction. They also give special attention to Pile-drivers and Hoisting Engine
of various sizes, and to locomotives for tram-roads. (See front inside cover.)

Farmers' Friend Plow Works.—These celebrated works are situated at
Jericksburg, Va., and are the property of Mr. Charles E. Hunter, who has a large
branch establishment in Petersburg, under the able management of Major J. S. Cary,
by whom thousands of these popular plows are sold during every season. In addition
to implements manufactured at these works, the Petersburg house keeps in stock all
kinds of Agricultural Implements, Steam Engines, Grist and Saw Mills, Cotton Gins,
Separators, Reapers, Mowers and other varieties of machinery, and is one of the most
extensive depots in the State. It deals also in Stoves, Wagons, and scores of other commodities indispensable to the farmer and planter, and a visit to Major Cary would be
time well spent by any one interested in Agricultural Implements or Machinery. (See
back inside cover.)

Tappey & Steel.—An old and responsible house, having flourished for forty
years, formerly under the firm name of Tappey, Lumsden & Co. Their extensive and
well equipped foundry is situated on Washington Street, opposite the terminus of the
Petersburg & Weldon Railroad. They are large manufacturers of all kinds of Engines,
Tobacco and Cotton Presses, Saw and Grist Mills, Mill Irons, Plows, Castings, Elevators for stores and factories, etc. They keep New and Second-hand Engines for sale,
and guarantee satisfaction in all their dealings. (See page 168.)

The Appomattox Iron Works.—Manufacturers of Machinery of all descriptions, Mill Gearing, Shafting Pulleys, Agricultural Implements, etc., making a specialty of Tobacco Fixtures, Hydraulic Presses, etc. They keep all kinds of Farming Implements in stock, and execute machine work to order. Prompt, skillful and reliable
in all their transactions, they have earned an excellent reputation and a large trade. (See
page 169.)

Charles Leonard.—Established in 1845, and now the largest hardware house in
the South. Occupies very extensive premises on both sides of Bank Street, which are
stocked with an endless variety of Hardware, Carriage Materials, Belting, Saw Mill,
Ship Chandler's and Fishermen's Supplies, Musical Instruments of all sorts, Cutlery,
Clocks, Spectacles, and a thousand other articles which cannot be here enumerated. Mr. Leonard is also agent for the "Household" Sewing Machine, the "Howe"
Scales and "Dead Shot" Powder, which is warranted to be the best made. There are
very few articles within the wide range of the general Hardware Trade which are not to
be found at Mr. Leonard's mammoth establishment, and everything he sells may be relied upon as of the best quality. (See page 170.)

R. B. Shelburn.—Represents the famous Light-running "Domestic" Sewing Machine, which, for the facility with which it executes all varieties of work, stands
at the head of the long list of Sewing Machines. Mr. Shelburn invites an inspection of
his stock, guarantees every machine he sells, and offers prices and terms to suit all classes of buyers. He thoroughly understands his business, having been engaged in it for
more than ten years. (See page 171.)

Plummer & Wheeler.—Extensive and reliable dealers in all kinds of Imported
and American Hardware. They keep a full line of goods in their handsome store in the
Iron Front Building. (See page 172.)

G. W. Brooks.—Manufactures on a large scale all kinds of Tin Ware and deals
by wholesale and retail in Ranges, Stoves, China, Lamps, Earthen Ware, Glass and Tin
Ware, and keeps a large and varied stock of goods which are guaranteed to give satisfaction as to quality and price. (See page 172.)

SCHOOLS AND COLLEGES.

The University School, W. Gordon McCabe, Head Master.—This famous
School was founded in 1865, and has been in successful operation for the past
twenty years. During that time it has prepared and sent up to the University of Virginia, to Princeton, West Point, Annapolis, Boston Institute of Technology, Stevens'
Scientific Institute, Columbia School of Mines and other institutions of high grade, a
great number of students, whose uniform success testifies to the excellence of the instruction given at this School, which is, however, mainly designed as preparatory to the University of Virginia, from the Faculty of which Mr. McCabe has received the highest testimonial's. The Head Master takes into his house a limited number of boarders. His
house, and the adjoining cottages built for the pupils, have all modern improvements.
Beginning in 1865, with only seventeen pupils, the School has now upon its roll over one
hundred and twenty-five, representing eleven States, from New York to Texas. The

moral tone of the School is something unique, and the students themselves would not allow a boy to remain after he had been found guilty of falsehood or other dishonorable conduct. The *morale* is controlled, in great measure, by the elder pupils, whom Mr. McCabe has drawn closely to him, as Dr. Arnold, of Rugby, did "the Sixth," and through their influence finds it easy to maintain a high standard of truth and honor. (See page 173.)

St. Paul's Female School.—J. G. GRISWOLD, Principal.—The advantages presented in this institution under the present management, are somewhat exceptional. The School was originally established by Bishop Wingfield, the Rector of St. Paul's Church, and under his control was strictly a Church School. Some twelve years ago the institution, with all its appurtenances and privileges, passed into the hands of Prof. J. G. Griswold, who at once wrought many radical changes, not the least of which was the discarding of the religious bias of the School. Under its present management it has proved an eminent success, and has established for itself an enviable reputation. Prof. Griswold, who graduated as A. M., completed his education in Europe and subsequently filled the Chair of Modern Languages at the University of San Cristobol, Havana, Cuba, and, later, hold a like Professorship at the University of Alabama. (See page 174.)

The University of Virginia.—It is generally admitted that this Institution ranks among the very first seats of learning in the country, and sends out as finished scholars in the various branches of Literature, Science and the Professions of Law and Medicine, as any of the Northern Universities. Special attention is given to instruction in the more practical schools of Engineering and Agriculture, while no charge is made for the tuition of those candidates for the ministry who are unable to meet the expense. The session begins on October 1st and closes on the Thursday before July 4th in each year. (See page 174.)

The Medical College of Virginia.—For nearly half a century this institution has been the honored exponent of the Medical Science and the Healing Art for Virginia, and, to a great extent, for the other Southern States. Its Professors' Chairs are filled by men of great learning in their profession, who are also all actively engaged in its practice. It has also an able corps in its Adjunct Faculty, composed of active younger men, who render valuable service to the students in the thorough drilling of their daily examinations and supplementary lectures. The College affords the best opportunities for medical education, and sends out men who at once assume prominence in the able and intelligent practice of their chosen Science—men of whom Virginia and her sister States are justly proud. That the College not only holds its ancient high standing in public esteem and confidence, but is also rapidly acquiring increased popularity, is shown by the attendance of students, whose numbers have been tripled within the last three years. The Catalogue can be had on application to Dr. M. L. James, Dean of the Faculty. (See page 175.)

Planters' Hypothecation Warehouse.—A substantial brick structure 75x 200 feet in size, situated on Second Street, in the rear of the Bollingbrook Hotel and in close proximity to the passenger and freight Depots of the Norfolk & Western and Richmond & Petersburg Railroads, with enormous storage capacity. It is used for storing Tobacco, Peanuts, Grain or any other kind of Produce or Merchandise, at most reasonable charges and with an absolute guarantee of safety and freedom from damage. Drays, Lumber Wagons and Carts are kept for hire, and Wood, Hay, Provender and Mill Feed for sale. For years past Mr. L. W. Dagger has been the efficient manager of this important business. He is now the sole lessee. (See page 176.)

DRUGS, PAINTS AND OILS.

Joseph Carr.—A well-known wholesale and retail dealer in Drugs, Patent Medicines, Paints, Oils, Varnishes, Glass and other commodities of a like nature. Mr. Carr is Vice-President of the Bank of Petersburg. (See page 176.)

Wm. E. French.—One of the most experienced, enterprising and reliable business men in Petersburg. A very large dealer in Drugs, Chemicals, Spices, Tobacco and Cigars, by wholesale and retail. Manufacturer of "French's Superior Cologne" and "French's Virginia Tonic Bitters," which have gained for him a most enviable reputation throughout the South. (See page 177.)

E. R. Beckwith.—For twenty years a careful student of Pharmacy and a large dealer in Medicines, Chemicals, Spices, Soaps, Toilet Articles, etc. He has established himself firmly in the confidence of the public, and is known through the whole Continent as the proprietor of Beckwith's Anti-Dyspeptic Pills, made from the original recipe of his grandfather, Dr. John Beckwith. These Pills have been working miracles on behalf of suffering humanity for over seventy-five years, and Dyspeptics everywhere should them a fair trial. (See page 178.)

Wm. F. Spotswood.—One of Petersburg's most highly esteemed citizens. He is an apothecary of rare ability, and has built up a large and steady trade. (See page 179.)

Wm. H. Camp.—The wholesale trade established by this gentleman extends all over Central Virginia and North Carolina, and is still spreading in every direction, while his retail business in the City is also very large. His store is well stocked with every variety of goods usually kept in first-class Drug Stores. (See page 179.)

C. L. Wright.—In spite of the lamentable fact that this gentleman declines to advertise in this volume—see his announcement to that effect on page 179—it is only fair and proper to state that he is an energetic and conscientious practical druggist, who has secured an excellent trade through his own ability and the excellent quality of his goods. He makes a specialty of Garden and Truck-farm Seeds, and is sole manufacturer of Dr. Hartman's Aromatic Odonto and Pearl Tooth Powder.

Geo. C Starke, M. D.—One of the oldest and most generally trusted Druggists in the City. His handsome new store, 37 Sycamore Street, contains a complete assortment of Drugs, Medicines, Chemicals, Perfumery, Toilet Articles, etc., and the greatest care and skill are employed in the preparation of prescriptions. (See page 179.)

R. W. Thompson.—Dealer in pure and reliable Drugs, Medicines, Paints, Oils, Glass and Putty, Fancy and Toilet Articles, Tobacco, Cigars etc., and proprietor of the famous Carbolized Dentaline, one of the most delicious and refreshing preparations for the mouth and teeth ever discovered. (see page 179.)

Valentine's Meat Juice Works.—Richmond, Va. (See page 180.)

Dr. D'Armstadt's Anti-Dyspeptic Drops.—(See page 181.)

Dunlop & McCance, Richmond, Va.—The large flour mills owned and operated by this firm have recently been thoroughly equipped with the most perfect machinery for manufacturing by the Roller Process—a vast improvement upon the old burr-stone method—and they now offer the trade the very best flour that can be had. Their many famous brands, of which the "Dunlop Patent Family" is their specialty, are all made of carefully-selected wheat, and can be highly recommended. They are very popular with the domestic trade and are exported largely to Brazil and other South American markets. The business was established in 1853. (See page 182.)

INSURANCE.

Petersburg Savings and Insurance Co.—(See pages 154, 185 and 232.)

Carter R. Bishop.—Represents the Hartford Fire Insurance Company, of Hartford, Conn. (See page 185.)

Cuthbert & Sons.—Represent The Royal Insurance Co., of Liverpool, Eng.; The London & Lancashire, of Liverpool, Eng.; The Northern, of London; The Fire Insurance Association, of London; The Hamburg & Bremen, of Hamburg, Ger.; The Phœnix, of Brooklyn; The Connecticut, of Hartford, Conn., and the Westchester, of New York. (See page 185.)

Benjamin Harrison.—Represents the following Fire Insurance Companies, namely: The North British and Mercantile, of London; The Home and New York, of New York; The Norwich Union, of Norwich, Eng., and The Lion, of London.

Jones & Stevens.—Represent the following Companies: Fire:—The Niagara, of New York; The Williamsburg City, of New York; The Queen, of Liverpool; The London Insurance Corporation, of London; The Scottish Union and National, of Edinburgh; The Portsmouth, of Portsmouth, Va. Marine:—The Phœnix, of Brooklyn. Life:—The Equitable Life Insurance Society, of New York; The Accident Insurance Company of North America, of New York. (See page 185.)

J. Edward Moyler & Co.—Represent the Liverpool & London & Globe, of Liverpool, Eng.; The Virginia Fire & Marine, of Richmond, Va.; The British-American Assurance Company, Toronto, Canada; The Virginia State Ins. Co., of Richmond, Va.; The Western Assurance Co., of Toronto, Canada; The Travelers' (Accident) Ins. Co., of Hartford, Conn., and the Life Insurance Co. of Virginia, of Richmond, Va. (See page 185.)

B. B. Pegram.—Represents The Washington Fire and Marine Ins. Co., of Boston, Mass.; The New York Underwriters' Agency, of New York; The Germania, of New York; The Imperial of London; The Northern, of London; The Virginia Home, of Richmond, Va. (See page 185.)

DRY GOODS, NOTIONS, ETC.

G. L. Crowder & Bro.—An enterprising and trustworthy firm of long standing, whose experience enables them to select their stock judiciously and to sell at lowest figures. Their increased business has enforced the enlargement of their premises, and they carry a large and well-assorted variety of all goods in their line. (See page 186.)

A. Rosenstock & Co.—For over a quarter of a century leading wholesale and retail dealers in Foreign and Domestic Dry Goods, Notions, Carpets, Trunks, Fancy Goods, Men's Furnishing Goods etc. They occupy one of the largest and handsomest stores in the State, and carry an enormous and carefully-selected stock of all the various lines of goods they handle. This is the oldest and largest Dry Goods establishment in Petersburg, and has earned, during its long life of usefulness and integrity, the confidence and respect of the trade and the public. (See page 187.)

J. E. Rockwell.—Has occupied his present handsome and eligible premises for the past fourteen years, and has been eminently successful in his business from the start. He deals mostly in the finer grades of Dress Goods, Millinery, Silks, Velvets, Black Crapes and Mourning Goods and makes a specialty of Bridal Trousseaux. He guarantees satisfaction, and his past honorable dealings, during his life-long residence in Petersburg, are the best evidence of what may be expected in the future. (See page 188.)

Geo. H. Davis & Co.—A most honorable and reliable house. Large jobbers and retailers of all varieties of Dry Goods and notions. They guarantee to fill wholesale orders at New York prices, and keep a full line of Silks, Satins, Velvets, and all descriptions of Dress Goods. Also Carpets, Rugs, Oil Cloths and Curtains—in fact, everything pertaining to a first-class Dry Goods establishment. (See page 188.)

John R. Turner.—Has been successfully engaged in the wholesale and retail Dry Goods and Notions business at his present store, No. 127 Sycamore Street, for the past ten years, during which period he has built up a large and profitable business and established himself in the confidence and respect of all with whom he has had dealings. He keeps a choice variety of all goods in his line, and his prices are very reasonable. (See page 188.)

WEARING APPAREL—BOOTS, SHOES, HATS, ETC.

Hall & Willcox.—Deal extensively in Boots, Shoes, Hats, Caps, Trunks, etc. Their goods are all excellent in quality and moderate in price. The business was established more than ten years ago, and has always held a prominent position. The senior partner, Mr. George W. Hall, holds a responsible office in the City Government—that of Commissioner of Revenue. (See page 189.)

C. B. Nunnally.—One of Petersburg's leading wholesale and retail dealers in Boots, Shoes, Leather and Shoe Findings. He is active and enterprising, but withal prudent and practical, and through his combined good qualities—and the good qualities of the commodities in which he deals—has succeeded in establishing a fine and increasing trade. (See page 189.)

Augustus Wright.—For enterprise, ability and integrity, this gentleman is without his superior in this or any other place, and is regarded as among the foremost of Petersburg's merchants. His wholesale business in Boots, Shoes, Trunks, Valises, Leather Findings, etc., is very extended, covering the central and western portions of Virginia, Tennessee, North and South Carolina, Georgia, and parts of several other States. About three years ago he opened a branch establishment at Roanoke for the accommodation of his many western customers. He owns and occupies the handsome and commodious three-story brick building on the corner of Sycamore and Franklin Streets, an engraving of which is shown on pages 94, and is undoubtedly one of the largest Boot and Shoe dealers in the South. He represents the Second Ward in the City Council. (See page 190.)

Munford and James.—This is a young firm, but both its members have acquired a thorough knowledge of their trade, and an excellent business training in the house last noticed—that of Mr. Augustus Wright. They keep a large and well-assorted stock of Boots, Shoes, Trunks, Valises etc., and are satisfied with a mere living profit on their sales. They enjoy an excellent reputation and have every reason for looking forward with confidence to an honorable and successful future. (See page 191.)

M. R. Saal.—Known—and justly known—as the "Reliable," for no one who has ever dealt with him has been heard to complain of a bad bargain. He is the only manufacturer in Petersburg of Shirts and Drawers, and in these articles he has discovered "perfection" as to make, material, fit and finish. He also deals in ready-made Clothing, Dry Goods, Hats, and Men's Furnishing Goods, and is one of the most pushing, industrious and honorable business men in the City. (See page 191.)

Thomas R. Moore. For nearly fifteen years this gentleman has been successfully engaged in the wholesale and retail Hat and Cap Trade, and owns one of the largest and best-stocked establishments of its kind in the South. Mr. Moore is universally respected as a conscientious and accommodating dealer, and his prices are uniformly low. His business relations in the wholesale department cover a large section of this State and North Carolina, while he also commands a large retail trade in the City and neighborhood. He makes a specialty of Ladies' and Misses' Cloaks, of which he keeps a large and select assortment in the latest styles. (See page 192.)

Harrison & Co.—This long-established and well-known firm keeps a full line of Ready-made Clothing of all qualities and prices, for men and boys. Also a complete assortment of Men's Furnishing Goods, Under Clothing, Neck-wear, Handkerchiefs, Collars, Cuffs, etc., and is generally considered one of the cheapest, best and most reliable houses in Virginia. Indeed "Harrison's on the Corner," enjoys a reputation far beyond the limits of this State. (See page 193.)

H. T. Miller & Co., Richmond, Va.—Proprietors of the famous "Dixie" Shirt and "Acme" Drawers Factory, on Main Street corner of Ninth. There is hardly a city, village or hamlet in Virginia or North Carolina in which these articles of "Miller's make" are not to be found, and they invariably give complete satisfaction. The firm employs none but experienced cutters, and their machinery, which is of the most approved kind, is operated by thoroughly skilled hands. (See page 194.)

A. Simon, Richmond, Va.—Successor to Solomonsky & Co. and a merchant Tailor of considerable skill. He has many customers in Petersburg whom he visits twice a month with a full line of samples. (See page 195.)

W. E. Butcher & Co.—The leading firm of Merchant Tailors in Petersburg. It is composed of Messrs William E. Butcher and James M. Quicke, both of whom are widely and favorably known in all the surrounding counties, and in North Carolina. Their fine store on Sycamore Street, near Washington, contains a splendid stock of cloth of all patterns, and their journeymen are kept busy all the year round making suits for city and country customers. (See page 195.)

Noah Walker & Co.—An agency of the well-known Baltimore house of Clothiers and Merchant Tailors of the same name. The Petersburg establishment is under the management of Messrs. Alex. F. Short and J. Geo. Wilkinson, Agents. (See page 195.)

FURNITURE.

W. M. Habliston & Co.—Carry an immense stock of Furniture of every description, equalling in quantity and variety that of any similar establishment in the South. They are thus enabled to offer superior inducements to customers, and it is admitted generally that they can duplicate any order, large or small, at as low prices as any other house in the country. The business was founded in 1878, and has grown and flourished since that date almost beyond precedent. (See page 196.)

Gary & Co.—Occupy a handsome three-story brick store on the corner of Sycamore and Bank Streets which is filled with a carefully-selected and valuable stock of Furniture, China, Glass Ware, Plated Ware, Lamps, and other varieties of House Furnishing Goods, which they offer at very low prices. (See page 197.)

L. Herring.—A substantial and highly respected merchant and manufacturer, whose stock comprises such articles as Wood ware, Buckets, Tubs, Crockery, Richmond Stone ware, Tin ware, Twine etc., of the very best quality, which are offered at most reasonable figures. Mr. Herring also manufactures Brooms, Brushes, Whisks and Tinware, all of Superior workmanship. (See page 197.)

King's Southside Dye Works.—Mr. King has been engaged in the business of Dyeing and Steam Cleaning since 1857, in which year the first-class premium and medal for "best work" were awarded to him by the Baltimore Mechanics' Institute. Since that distant period he has made great progress in his art, and guarantees everything he does to be first-class in every respect. (See page 197.)

James T. Morriss.—Established in 1858, and has therefore had twenty-seven years experience as a practical Undertaker. He keeps constantly on hand a fine selection of Metallic and Wooden Coffins and Caskets, plain, cloth-covered and ornamental, besides burial robes and other articles pertaining to his business. He gives prompt attention to all orders by letter or telegraph, and guarantees satisfaction to all his patrons. (See page 198.)

E. C. Leath.—A master of Photographic Art in all its branches and details. Owns two well-equipped galleries on Sycamore Street, and executes all kinds of Photographic work in the latest styles. Many of the best engravings shown on the foregoing pages were copied from photographs taken by him for this volume. (See page 199.)

BOOKS, STATIONERY, PIANOS ETC.

T. S. Beckwith & Co.—Of all the retail establishments of any kind, existing in Petersburg, the one now under review is perhaps by far the most important, as it exercises the most wide-spread influence for good in the community. It was founded nearly twenty years ago, and has been a successful business enterprise from its birth. The store was enlarged about two years ago by the addition of a large, lofty and well-lighted room, which is used as an Art Gallery and Music Hall. It also contains the 3,000 Books and Magazines of Beckwith's Circulating Library, which is an unspeakable boon to the City. The firm deals largely in Pianos and Organs from the most famous factories in the country, Book and Sheet Music, public and private School Books, Fancy Goods, Stationery and all other articles belonging to a first class Stationery Store, in great profusion and endless variety. Mr. T. S. Beckwith is also the head of the Book and Stationery house of Beckwith and Parham, in Richmond. (See page 200.)

Wm. L. Zimmer & Co.—This flourishing firm not only transacts a large and ever-growing business in all its many departments, but also sets a splendid example of spirited enterprise. It has also held a front place among dealers, and has within the last three years, branched out into an important industrial and manufacturing establishment. From a simple but first-class retail Book and Stationery Store, it has rapidly developed into into one of the most complete Printing and Book-binding, Engraving and Blank Book and Stationery Manufacturing houses in the South. The firm are also Jobbers and retail dealers in School and Miscellaneous Books, and are Agents for several of the best makes of Pianos and Organs in America. Their Wood Engraving Department stands alone in Virginia. It produced several of the Engravings shown in this volume. Blank Books are made to order on short notice and in best style, and the same may be said of their Book Binding, a sample of which is at this moment before the reader. They make specialties of Tobacco work, such as Machine-cut Tags, Strips and Labels. Their prices are very moderate and they guarantee everything they sell to be as represented, or they refund the money. (See page 201.)

Charles M. Stieff. Baltimore, Md.—The "Stieff" Pianos have earned a reputation as wide as the United States, and are everywhere endorsed by professors, teachers and musical connoisseurs, for their tone, workmanship and durability. At the Paris Exposition of 1878 they obtained the highest honors. Mr. Stieff is also wholesale agent for several leading Organs. He sells Pianos and Organs on easy instalments, takes Pianos in exchange, and keeps a large assortment of second-hand instruments on hand. (See pages 202 and 203.)

F. E. Pugh & Co.—Agents for all Periodicals at publishers' prices. Also Newsdealers, Stationers and dealers in Picture Frames and Fancy Goods, the best brands of Cigars, Tobacco, Snuff and Pipes. A most trustworthy house which has earned public confidence and esteem. (See page 204.)

Webster's Unabridged Dictionary.—It would seem presumptuous in a work like this to do more than mention with the utmost diffidence a book of such magnitude, influence and universal information as Webster's Dictionary. Suffice it, therefore, to say that no student or educated person can afford to be without it. It is handled exclusively by its publishers, Messrs. G. & C. Merriam & Co., Springfield, Mass., and their agents. (See page 204.)

J. H. Chataigne, Richmond, Va.—Not only as source of invaluable information to the merchant, manufacturer and even professional man, but also as unequalled advertising mediums, Chataigne's Directories are almost indispensable. He publishes separate Directories for the States of Virginia and North Carolina, and the cities of Richmond, Petersburg, Norfolk and Alexandria, and the line of the Chesapeake and Ohio railway. (See page 204.)

CARRIAGES, HARNESS, &C.

P. F. Johnson & Co.—The senior member and managing partner in this firm has had fifteen years' experience in practical harness making, the last ten of which have been passed in Petersburg. The house manufactures and deals in all kinds of Harness, Saddles, Bridles, and Horse Furnishing Goods, and guarantees satisfaction as to both quality and price. (See page 205.)

P. M. Steward.—In 1868 this gentleman succeeded his father, who had established the business twenty years previously. It is therefore one of the oldest, as it is also one of the most reliable and highly esteemed, business houses in Petersburg. Mr.

Steward deals extensively in Carriages, Phaetons, Rockaways, Buggies and other kinds of vehicles, which may be inspected at his commodious repository and show rooms, No. 13 Bollingbrook Street. His Harness Manufactory and axle rooms are at 52 Sycamore Street, where he manufactures all descriptions of Harness, Saddles, Bridles, &c., of different styles and qualities, and keeps a fine and selected stock of Robes, Blankets, Whips, Spurs and all other articles of a like nature. (See page 206.)

Wm. H. Harrison.—Manufactures all kinds of Harness and has secured a large town and country trade through his personal popularity and the fine quality of his goods. He is also a large dealer in Carriages, Buggies and Wagons. His extensive Harness factory and Carriage repository are at No. 9 Bank Street. (See page 207.)

BAGS AND BAGGING.

Carter R. Bishop & Co.—This industrious and enterprising firm was founded in 1882, and supplies a want long felt in this section. By importing direct, through the New York agents, they are enabled to purchase their burlaps at the most favorable figures, and to manufacture and deliver their Bags at any point in Virginia or the South at as low prices as are paid for the same goods in Philadelphia or Baltimore, thus saving to the consumer the cost of freight and handling. They make and print all kinds of Peanut, Grain, Flour and Fertilizer Bags, of all qualities and sizes, according to the purchaser's instructions. (See page 208.)

MISCELLANEOUS TRADES AND TRADESMEN.

Seward & Munt.—These gentlemen own and operate the "Eagle" Flour and Corn Mills, and the adjoining "Enterprise" Trunk Factory, at Campbell's Bridge, and are doing an extensive business in both branches of industry. Their specialties at the mill are Corn Meal and Pearl Hominy, which are of excellent quality and in great demand. At the factory they manufacture all kinds of Trunks, Valises, Satchels, Straps, &c., and have succeeded in establishing almost a monopoly for their goods throughout the sections lying to the South, East and West of Petersburg. The business was established in 1870 and is now a most prosperous concern. Mr. Simon Seward, the senior member of the firm, represents the Fourth Ward in the City Council. (See page 210.)

Charles M. Walsh.—Proprietor of the "Cockade Marble Works," which have been in successful operation since their establishment in 1865. Mr. Walsh manufactures Monuments, Headstones, Tablets, Crosses, Tombstones, &c., of every description, and is a complete master of his art. Hundreds of testimonials to his skill may be seen in Blandford Cemetery and in the rural graveyards for many miles around, as well as at his works on South Sycamore Street. That his work gives perfect satisfaction in design, workmanship and price is evidenced by the fact that he entirely monopolises this industry in Petersburg and challenges the world to compete with him. (See page 211.)

J. C. Wool.—In 1876 succeeded the firm of A. B. Demarest & Co. who established the "Old Dominion Planing Mill" five years previously. He manufactures and deals in all kinds of Doors, Sash, Blinds, Mouldings, Brackets. Newels, Ballusters, Stair Rails, Rough and Dressed Lumber and all kinds of Building Material and Builders' Hardware. Dressing, Kiln-Drying and Scroll Sawing promptly executed and all styles of Window Frames and Mantle Pieces made to order. He makes a specialty of Manufacturing Boxes and guarantees satisfaction to all his customers. Mr. Wool mostly uses the timber of native growth, believing it to be better adapted by nature to the peculiarities of the climate than that grown at a distant point and under different climatic influences could possibly be. This theory has been amply justified by experience, and has the great additional advantage of enabling Mr. Wool to patronise "home industry," while at the same time securing the most durable material and thus conferring additional benefit upon his customers. (See page 212.)

C. G. Taylor.—"The China Palace," of which Mr. Taylor is the proprietor, is one of the show-places of Petersburg. It is situated on Sycamore Street, a few doors above the Iron Front Building, and contains a profusion of the most elegant articles in China, Glass, Queensware, Silver Plated Ware, Table Cutlery, Tea Trays, Looking Glasses and other kindred articles of foreign and domestic manufacture ever gathered together under one roof in this city. The goods are undoubtedly first-class and the prices compete with the largest markets. Everybody should visit the "China Palace," and inspect its treasures. (See page 213.)

John A. Mallory.—An experienced and successful Florist, who began business fourteen years ago with only one small greenhouse. Industry, perseverance, integrity and skill in this case bore their legitimate fruit, and five years ago Mr. Mallory removed to his present premises on Bollingbrook, Fourth and Lombard streets, occupying a whole square now almost covered with glass, tastefully laid out, and altogether one of the most perfect and beautiful places of its kind in Virginia. Mr. Mallory deals in Cut Flowers, Bouquets and Funeral Designs, which can always be furnished at short notice. Also Greenhouse and Bedding Plants of the choicest kinds and at lowest prices. (See page 214.)

W. D. Poythress.—Florist; established in 1876. Has five well stocked greenhouses and will shortly build a new one—50x18 feet—to accomodate his increasing trade. Keeps every sort of Flower worth cultivating and deals in all varieties of Greenhouse and Bedding Plants. Executes all kinds of Cut Flower Work, Bouquets, Floral Designs for Decorations and Funerals, and supplies Flowers for parties and bouquets at short notice. Gives prompt attention to all orders by mail or telegraph, and guarantees satisfaction. (See page 215.)

J. M. Whitehurst.—The largest manufacturer of Mattresses—Hair, Shuck and Cotton Top—in the city. Also wholesale and retail dealer in Wall Paper, Window Shades, Oil Cloths, Mattings, Rugs, Door Mats, Lace Curtains, Upholsterers' Supplies, Cornices, Picture Frame Mouldings and other commodities of a like nature. He has been engaged in this line of business in Petersburg for nearly thirty-five years and has won the respect and confidence of all with whom he has had dealings. (See page 215.)

J. W. Young.—Succeeded J. T. Young & Bro., of which firm he was the junior member, in 1884, and now offers great bargains in Jewelry, Gold and Silver Watches, Diamonds, Clocks and Silver Ware. Makes Spectacles and Eye-Glasses a specialty. Repairs Watches and Jewelry in the best style, and executes all orders with guaranteed satisfaction. His stock is the largest and best selected in the city. (See page 216.)

A. D. Harding.—A practical and skillful Watchmaker and Jeweler, and dealer in Clocks, Watches, Gold and Silver Ware and all kinds of Jewelry. Gives special attention to Cleaning and Repairing, and makes Wedding and Gift Rings to order. He warrants all his work, charges very moderately and is thoroughly reliable in all respects. (See page 216.)

C. F. Lauterback.—Has been engaged in the Watchmaking and Jewelry business in Petersburg for the past fourteen years, the first five of which, from 1871 to 1876, were passed under the careful training of the late E. Richter. Deals in Watches, Clocks, Fine Jewelry and Silver Ware, and executes Repairs at short notice. (See page 217.)

D. Buchanan.—A practical Watchmaker and manufacturing Goldsmith and Jeweler, formerly of Glasgow, Scotland. He is about to remove to Richmond, where his address will be No. 111 Broad street. During the residue of his stay here he offers great bargains in all kinds of Jewelry, Watches, Clocks, Silver Ware, &c. (See page 217.)

James Smith & Son.—The Soap Factory of this firm on Pine Street was established more than forty years ago, and has a capacity of about 275,000 pounds a year. Their principal brands are "No. 1," "Family," "Olive," "Southside," "Palm," and "New." Their trade is principally local, though a good deal of their product is shipped to distant points through our merchants. The junior partner, Mr. Hugh R. Smith, represents the Fourth Ward in the City Council. (see page 217.)

J. B. Brady.—Gas and Steam Fitter and Mechanical Plumber, who has been established in business here for over a quarter of a century. His work gives universal satisfaction. Keeps a large stock of Pipes and other Fixtures with which to supply the trade. (See page 217.)

Stone & Friend.—Proprietors of one of the oldest and best arranged Sale, Livery and Hiring Stables in the city, having been established in 1867. Keep a fine assortment of Hacks, Buggies and Saddle Horses, and furnish excellent accommodation for drovers. (See page 217.)

Geo. A. Fittz.—For the past ten years engaged in the Livery business and keeps a first-class Livery, Sale and Exchange Stable at 18 Bank Street. Is prompt and reliable and has built up a good trade. (See page 217.)

J. D. Bowie.—Deals very extensively in Fish, Oysters, Game and Country Produce, and fills orders promptly and satisfactorily. (See page 218.)

A. J. Mann.—An energetic and trustworthy Practical Upholsterer and Paper-Hanger. Executes Plain or Decorative Work in good style at short notice. (See page 218.)

LUMBER, WOOD AND COAL.

Cooper & Spotswood.—Stand at the head of the Lumber Trade in Petersburg, and are numbered among the most useful, honorable and reliable of her representative business men. They own and operate extensive saw mills on the lines of the Norfolk and Western and the Seaboard railroads, and occupy the spacious yard on Washington

Street, opposite Watson & McGill's tobacco factory, in this city, as the receiving and distributing point for the enormous quantities of lumber they handle. Their transactions in this important product extend all over the country, and they have been largely instrumental in establishing Petersburg's commercial relations with distant markets. They make a specialty of Tobacco Box Lumber, which forms a very considerable item of consumption in Virginia and the Carolinas. (See page 218.)

Marks & Friend.—Among our largest dealers in Hay, Grain, Coal, Lime, Cement, Plaster and Lumber. As General Commission and Shipping Merchants they have established themselves firmly in public confidence during the past seventeen years, having been always found prompt and reliable. They cut Lumber Bills to order and manufacture Agricultural Lime in large quantities, thus contributing to the industrial as well as to the commercial prosperity of the city. (See page 219.)

J. W. Phillips.—Manufactures Bricks of the best quality and deals largely in Wood, Coal, Lumber, Railroad Ties, Hoop Poles. &c. Has recently enclosed spacious yards at the Canal Basin, head of High Street, supplied with every facility for transacting an immense business. Orders can be transmitted through telephone, or by mail, and will always receive prompt attention. (See page 219.)

Wm. J. Chappell.—An experienced and skillful Builder and Contractor, who guarantees satisfaction in all the work he undertakes. By industry, capacity and fidelity to the interests of his patrons, he has secured an excellent connection in the city and neighborhood. (See page 219.)

John L. Hobson.—Deals in all grades of Hard and Soft Coal and makes the famous Cumberland Coal a specialty. Orders for car loads or smaller quantities will be promptly filled at the lowest market prices. (See page 220.)

Wm. R. Nichols.—Is generally regarded as one of Petersburg's most energetic, honorable and trustworthy merchants, whose courtesy and excellent business qualifications have built up a flourishing trade in all kinds of Coal—Anthracite, Splint, Bright Hope and Steam Coal and Wood. He attends promptly to all orders, and guarantees the very lowest market prices. (See page 220.)

George V. Scott & Son.—General Commission and Shipping Merchants and dealers in Coal and Wood. They ship principally to the Northern markets, and are among the largest contributors to the shipping interests of the city. (See page 220.)

Harrison & Barksdale.—Deal in all kinds of Lumber, Laths, Posts, Wood and other similar commodities, and fill all orders at lowest figures. They are perfectly reliable and have secured an excellent trade. (See page 220.)

George J. Rogers.—Has been engaged for the past ten years as dealer in Wood and Railroad Ties, most of which he ships to Northern ports, where his business is steadily increasing by reason of the promptness and general satisfaction with which his orders are filled. (See page 220.)

CONFECTIONERY.

Charles C. Alley.—The large wholesale and retail Fruit and Confectionery establishment conducted by this enterprising gentleman was founded by his father a quarter of a century ago and has always been regarded as one of the most reliable and responsible business houses in the city. Mr. Alley manufactures all kinds of Candy and Cakes, deals by wholesale and retail in Foreign and Domestic Fruits, Confectionery, Tobacco, Cigars, Toys and Fancy Articles, and has earned an excellent reputation while building up a lucrative trade. He always carries a large and varied stock, and is kept busy the year round filling orders not only in Petersburg and its vicinity, but also in distant parts of Virginia, North Carolina and other States. (See page 221.)

S. H. Marks & Co.—The oldest, largest and most complete Confectionery house in the State of Virginia, if not in the Sunny South. It was established fifty-six years ago and has at all times carried on an enormous business in Fruits, Candies, Cakes, Canned Goods, Ice Cream, Smoking and Chewing Tobacco, Cigars, Cigarettes, Toys, Fireworks, and a thousand other articles, edible and otherwise, and is as widely known as any manufacturing establishment in this section of the United States. It carries a very large stock for the wholesale and retail trade, and the Candies, Cakes and Crackers of its own manufacture have become household words all over the Southern country. Every article dealt in is of excellent quality, and customers can therefore rely upon being perfectly satisfied with whatever they purchase from the venerable establishment of S. H. Marks & Co. (See page 221.)

INDEX.

⚏✻⚏

GENERAL SUBJECTS.

ILLUSTRATIONS.

CORRECTIONS.

In the List of the Mayors of Petersburg, on page 67, the name of "Edmund Pescud" occurs as incumbent in 1818-'19. This name should have been written Edward Pescud.

In the advertisement of J. H. Chataigne, on page 204, the price of the Alexandria Directory should have been stated as $3.00.

www.ingramcontent.com/pod-product-compliance
Lightning Source LLC
Chambersburg PA
CBHW030732280326
41926CB00086B/1177